DATE DUE

The Texas-Mexican Conjunto:
History of a Working-Class Music

Mexican American Monograph Number 9
The Center for Mexican American Studies
The University of Texas at Austin

The Texas-Mexican Conjunto:
HISTORY OF A WORKING-CLASS MUSIC

Manuel H. Peña

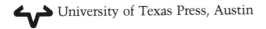 University of Texas Press, Austin

First Edition, 1985

Requests for permission to reproduce material
from this work should be sent to
Permissions, University of Texas Press,
Box 7819, Austin, Texas 78713.

Library of Congress Cataloging in Publication Data
Peña, Manuel H., 1942–
    The Texas-Mexican conjunto.

    (Mexican American monographs; no. 9)
    Bibliography: p.
    Discography: p.
    Includes index.
    1. Mexican Americans—Texas—Music—History and criticism.
    2. Music, Popular (Songs, etc.)—Texas—History and criticism.
    3. Music, Popular (Songs, etc.)—Mexico—History and criticism.
    I. Title. II. Series.
ML3481.P46 1985   781.7'268720764   84-27127
ISBN 0-292-78068-0
ISBN 0-292-78080-X (pbk.)

For don Américo and don Octavio,
and for my father—
cada uno a su manera una inspiración

Contents

Preface   *ix*

Acknowledgments   *xiii*

Introduction   *1*

Part I: Music and Musicians: A Descriptive History

1. Origins: Texas-Mexican Music Prior to 1930   *19*

2. Los Músicos de Ayer: The Formative Years   *46*

3. La Nueva Generación: Stylistic Consolidation
   (1948–1960)   *70*

4. Post–1960 Conjunto: The Limits of a Tradition   *100*

**Part II: The Evolution of a Style: Economic, Social, and
   Symbolic Dimensions**

5. La Gente Pobre: The Social Base of Conjunto Music   *113*

6. Social and Symbolic Dimensions of Conjunto:
   From Ascendancy to Decline   *134*

Appendices   *163*

References   *205*

Selected Discography   *213*

Index   *215*

Tables

1. Some Texas-Mexican Occupations Considered Contradictory
   and/or Middle Class   *124*

2. Persons of Mexican Nativity and Parentage in
   Texas, 1940   *126*

3. Occupational Distribution of Mexican American Males in
   the Southwest, 1930   *127*

4. Occupational Distribution of Texas-Mexican Males,
    1950   *128*

5. Occupational Distribution of Texas-Mexicans by Sex,
    1960   *129*

6. The Assimilation Variables   *165*

Illustrations

Photographs   *following page 110*

1. A Working-Class Orquesta

2. Orquesta Típica Laredo

3. Narciso Martínez and Santiago Almeida

4. Narciso Martínez

5. Ismael González, Santiago Jiménez, and Lorenzo Caballero

6. El Conjunto Cielito

7. Los Hermanos García Torres

8. Valerio Longoria and Valerio Longoria, Jr.

9. Rubén Vela and Eduardo Vela

10. Johnny Degollado

11. El Conjunto Bernal

12. Los Relámpagos del Norte

Figures

1. Origins of Mexican Colony   *27*

2. Differences in *Bajo Sexto* Style   *96*

3. Common Rhythmic Patterns Used in Polkas
   and *Corridas*   *96*

4. The Relationship of Contradictory Class Locations to the
   Basic Class Forces in Capitalistic Society   *121*

5. Distribution of Texas-Mexican Classes and Contradictory
   Locations   *123*

6. Estimated Boundaries of Texas-Mexican Classes, 1960   *132*

Preface

The emergence of a highly popular type of accordion music, commonly known as *conjunto,** among Texas-Mexicans (*tejanos*) beginning
around 1930 poses some timely questions for the student of music.
Particularly noteworthy, for example, is conjunto's rapid crystallization into a standardized mode of performance by the late 1950s. But
these questions hold significance for social scientists as well because,
as the ethnomusicologist John Blacking has proposed (1974), the interpretation of musical activity can serve as a key to understanding other
aspects of a group's culture and social organization. This interpretation can be especially useful when we link theoretically musical
culture to its social base. It is in this spirit that the research for this
study on conjunto music was conducted.

In undertaking the task of an interpretive history of conjunto music,
I have tried to adhere as closely and explicitly as possible to certain
ideas, in the nature of hypotheses, that I had developed on the basis of
extended observation of key aspects of the music, especially its close
association with a specific segment of tejano society: the working
class. These hypotheses, in turn, were informed by my own interpretation of a large body of literature on culture generally, on ethnic
cultures specifically, as well as an equally extensive literature on
class, ideology, and cultural hegemony.** Added to this was, of
course, my reading and understanding of the literature on folklore and
ethnomusicology. In short, utilizing a set of theoretical principles, I
set out to attempt an interpretation of the crucial connection between
conjunto music and the society within which it found expression.

The methods I used were those that I felt would most adequately
clarify that connection given the research resources I had at my

---

*The Spanish terms *conjunto, orquesta,* and *tejano* will be italicized only the first
time they appear.
**As I use them, the terms "class," "ideology," and "hegemony" all have specific
meanings. See Appendix A.

disposition. I settled primarily on the ethnographic interview, which always aimed at obtaining as complete an oral history as possible from each person interviewed. Most of these were performers, though less extensive interviews were held with nonperformers, including three disc jockeys, four recording company owners, two dance promoters, and an unspecified number of common people, lovers of conjunto music. In the case of the musicians, the information gathered included personal data, which were then integrated with the person's musical career, his relationship to other musicians and to his audiences, and his understanding of the music's history and its development. Lastly, I spent many hours as a participant observer at dances, which have been the principal context for the enactment of the music since the accordion first made its appearance in Texas-Mexican society.

In the course of my research I came to the realization that the relationship between a field worker and the people he or she studies is always a delicate one. Of particular concern to me was the problem of what, for lack of a better expression, I will call ethnographic justice. It is essentially an ethical problem: as researchers we are inescapably accountable for the reports we write. Consequently, we bear an exacting responsibility, first, in presenting fair and accurate accounts of the information our collaborators so graciously consent to share with us and, second, in analyzing and interpreting the words and actions of those collaborators with a minimum amount of error or distortion on our part.

I must confess that I was many times confronted with serious doubts about my ability to transpose the richness of conjunto music, as revealed through the accounts of the musicians and others and as I myself had long witnessed it while growing up in Texas, into a coherent, impartial, yet sympathetic report. The musicians were fully aware that they were entrusting me with the task of "telling our story," as one of them put it. I did not take the responsibility lightly; I have tried to present as balanced an account as I could, given the constraints I faced of time, resources, and, of course, my own personal limitations.

Not all the musicians, nor others vitally connected with the music, have received their due attention (least of all the innumerable supporters who have given the music life and transformed it into a dynamic cultural symbol). That would have been an impossible undertaking in a study such as this. Nonetheless, I trust that the present work has achieved at least the most fundamental goals that I had set for myself: to present a constructive account of the emergence of this important cultural expression among the tejano working class and to provide an analytic interpretation that would violate neither my informants' testimonies nor the canons of social science inquiry.

I trust that a satisfactory balance has been achieved. If errors of omission (or commission) are to be found, they are entirely of my own doing and should not reflect on the men and women who willingly shared with me their most intimate knowledge and sentiments about Texas-Mexican people and their music. Here I can only assure them that I did my best to reconcile my interests, born at least partly out of academic commitments, with their own. Lastly, I want to express my heartfelt gratitude to all those people who collaborated with me, and I especially thank them for their patience in the face of my persistent questions. If this work contributes toward an understanding of and an advocacy for working-class tejanos and their culture, that patience will have paid off.

Acknowledgments

In working my way through the initial research and the ultimate completion of this work, I was fortunate to have received the helpful advice of several people, including Richard Bauman, Archie Green, Doug Foley, Gerard Béhague, and José Limón. I am especially grateful to Américo Paredes, to whom I owe an incalculable debt for all he has taught me. I wish to express my deepest gratitude to him for his generous comments and criticism as well as his patient encouragement. Of course, the descriptions and interpretations contained here are my own, and neither don Américo nor the others mentioned share any responsibility for errors or distortions.

I also wish to thank the Music and Chicano Studies Departments at the University of California at Berkeley, and more specifically Bonnie Wade and Alex Saragoza, for their support during my tenure as Chancellor's Post-Doctoral Fellow, which enabled me to complete revisions of an earlier draft of the manuscript.

I would also like to thank Elizabeth Yeager and Tina Plaza of the publications staff of the Center for Mexican American Studies at the University of Texas at Austin, and, especially, Ricardo Romo for coordinating this publication and José Flores for his fine editorial work.

Lastly, I want to thank my wife María, whose unwavering faith in what I was doing helped carry me through many a doubtful moment.

The Texas-Mexican Conjunto:
History of a Working-Class Music

Introduction

Social and Musical Developments in Texas-Mexican Society

This study aims not so much at a comprehensive history of Texas-Mexican conjunto music as an interpretive one. Consequently, while the historical scope is broad—covering the period from about 1860 to the present—the main focus is on the period from 1935 to 1960, especially the decade or so after World War II. This is the historical moment when conjunto emerged as an ensemble with a highly organized style and a strong base of social support that turned it into a powerful symbol among the Texas-Mexican working class.[1] Within the interpretive framework, my intention is, briefly, two-fold: to describe conjunto's stylistic evolution and to analyze the link between this evolution and the fundamental changes Texas-Mexican society entered into as a result of World War II.

Underlying my analysis and interpretation is the assumption that musical style, "like many other human things," to quote Alan Lomax, "is a pattern of learned behavior common to the people of a culture" (1968:3). As such, the methods I have employed emphasize the symbolic aspects of musical style, or, in the fashion of Clifford Geertz, attempt to lift style to the status of a cultural system. In this respect an important point needs to be raised: This study considers musical style only—to the exclusion of the linguistic content nowadays associated with conjunto music. It is undeniable that the musico-linguistic whole forms a special symbolic structure, but I believe that for analytical purposes musical style can be treated as a system in its own right, just as myth is sometimes considered separately from ritual. Or, to take a case closer to our objective here, folklorists have long studied the literary aspects of ballads as if they had an existence separable from their musical content. In any case, we should keep in mind that conjunto originated as instrumental music and, but for few exceptions, lyrics were not added until World War II—one significant accretion out of several that will be examined later.

Conceived as a discrete cultural system, musical style may be defined as a regularly occurring combination of sounds produced by vocal, instrumental, and/or other means, arranged into recognizable patterns and situated within specific social contexts, wherein the style will acquire varying degrees of symbolic significance. The last point is especially critical for a culture-sensitive conception of style, because only when we recognize the symbolic dimension can we account for normative rules of composition and performance as well as evaluative criteria. As these rules accrue upon a given style, they gain a determinative role in the acceptance or rejection of modifications that innovative artists may introduce. Moreover, within its social context a musical style can associate with and reinforce other "crucial behavior patterns upon which the continuity of a culture hangs" (Lomax, 1968:8). The notion of constancy is implied in this conception. As Schapiro noted: "By style is meant the constant form—and sometimes the constant elements, qualities and expression—in the art of an individual or group" (1953:287).

The elements of style coalesced around the accordion ensemble that Texas-Mexicans forged between 1928 and 1960 and that came to be known as *norteño* music generally,[2] or conjunto music to the Texas-Mexicans. Tentative and emergent at first—especially before 1935—the ensemble and its musical style rapidly acquired a recognizable form after the war. By the 1950s, to borrow a phrase from Schapiro, a system of musical sounds had emerged with a "quality and a meaningful expression through which the personality of the artists and the broad outlook of the group [were] visible" (1953:287).

As we trace the development of modern conjunto music from its inception in embryonic form with the appearance of Narciso Martínez's first commercial recording in 1935 to its full-blown stylization in the hands of such artists as El Conjunto Bernal in the late 1950s, two specific questions challenge us. The first is, formally, a musicological one: How did conjunto evolve stylistically—that is, how can we describe musically both the stable and changing elements that gave shape to the style? Linked to this question, but involving the interplay between music and society, is the second one: Given that the accordion and at least one other instrument that lends a recognizable form to conjunto music have been extant on both sides of the Texas-Mexican border for the better part of a century, why did this distinctive, durable, and highly cherished style of music not reach fruition until the post–World War II years? Or, to state the question in a different manner, what social and cultural variables were present during the years surrounding the war that made it possible for conjunto music to establish itself as a culturally sanctioned artistic expression?

As I briefly indicated earlier, then, it is a two-fold purpose that serves as the organizing principle for this study on the emergence of conjunto music. On the one hand, even a cursory listening of commercial recordings produced during the period from 1928 to 1960 reveals marked changes between 1928 and 1948—and even more drastic ones thereafter. The technical articulation of the main instrument, the accordion, had changed decidedly by the early 1950s. Additionally, beginning with the two staple instruments from early on—the accordion and *bajo sexto*—the ensemble's makeup was eventually transformed, first by the inclusion of the contrabass, or *tololoche*, and afterward by the adoption of the standard dance-band drum set in the early 1950s. Still another alteration was wrought in the mid-1950s, when the *tololoche* was replaced by the electric bass. To document the evolution that took place, I propose to examine selected samples of the most popular recorded music as it developed, especially between 1935 and 1960, into a well-defined style that has since remained virtually unchanged.

On the other hand, the analysis proposed above, formal as it is in its intent, serves but a corollary aim in this study. It will be undertaken only to illustrate how a musical style was evolving during the period in question. More compelling for the purposes I have outlined is an interpretation of the relationship that ought to exist, if our theories are valid, between the developments at the level of musical discourse and those at the level of social discourse, as Mantle Hood (1971) has advocated. Clearly, as this study will hopefully demonstrate, the rapid crystallization of conjunto music did not take place by mere chance, or in a socioesthetic "art-for-art's-sake" vacuum. On the contrary, profound and well-documented changes were taking place simultaneously within Texas-Mexican society of the post–World War II years.

And, as we shall see, these changes coincided and interacted with the musical innovations I will describe, just as they coincided with shifts in language usage, folklore, dress, and such social diacritics as educational and occupational mobility. All of these contributed to a deepening intraethnic conflict that had been set in motion by disparate rates of urbanization, social mobility, and cultural assimilation at the different socioeconomic levels of tejano society. But this is merely to say that in the case of conjunto music stylistic developments went hand in hand with the complex movements taking place at the infrastructural base of Texas-Mexican society. Or, to paraphrase Hymes's statement on language and social life (1972), conjunto music and musicians were expressing the multiple relations that exist between musical means and social meaning.

In fact, a basic assumption that guided the initial research was my early impression (since my days as an *orquesta* musician, actually) that, at one level at least, the musical preferences espoused by conjunto and orquesta musicians—orquesta, or *orquesta tejana*, being conjunto music's rival style among tejanos—betrayed a certain esthetic cleavage attributable to the social status of their respective clientele. To put it in the simple words of Narciso Martínez, an early and famous exponent of conjunto music, "Conjunto era pa' la gente pobre, la gente de rancho; la orquesta era pa' high society" ("Conjunto was for poor people, rural people; orquesta was for high society"). In such succinct language can the socially defined functions of conjunto and orquesta be summed up. In such clear language also may be discerned the tension between conjunto's proletarian, Mexicanized, and originally rural folk base on the one hand and orquesta's urban, middle-class, and necessarily more Americanized base on the other. It was, in short, a tension born of incipient class differences.

Nonetheless, the cleavage was not quite that clear cut. Orquesta and conjunto were actually symbolic expressions (with distinct esthetic horizons, to be sure) that were forged amidst an intimate, now hostile, now cooperative relationship that existed between two increasingly divergent classes in tejano society, classes not so readily distinguishable until the postwar period, when socioeconomic differences began to materialize more fully. These classes were the traditional proletarians (at first mainly agricultural, later unskilled or semiskilled and urban) vis-à-vis an expanding middle class that included white-collar workers, mid- and low-level managers, petit bourgeoisie, and professionals.

But emerging class differences among tejanos were complicated by a powerful ethnic boundary that had long stood between Mexicans and Anglo-Americans throughout the Southwest. Originally the two groups had been in competition for the same ecological niche, but in time the Anglos had gained the ascendancy, and thereafter ethnic relations based on "complementary differentiation" (Bateson 1972)—of Anglo domination/Chicano subordination—had obtained. Within this state of affairs Anglos controlled the means of production generally, while tejanos were relegated almost exclusively to a dependent economic status as proletarian workers (Montejano 1979; Barrera 1979; M. García 1981). Under this arrangement it is not surprising that economic inequality should so closely parallel the ethnic cleavage between the two groups. When Chicanos began to experience some upward socioeconomic movement during and after World War II, ethnic inequality intervened, excluding them from any but the most minimal "structural" assimilation of the "primary-contact" type, into American society (see Appendix A; cf. Gordon 1964). It was into this milieu of persistent ethnic segregation but increasing intraethnic class differentiation that conjunto and orquesta were cast.

What I am proposing is that the years surrounding World War II—roughly from the post-Depression economic recovery to the Korean War—marked an important turning point in the history of tejanos. At this time a wholesale shift occurred from rural to urban patterns of residency, from agricultural to nonagricultural occupations, and from a relatively homogeneous, preindustrial folk group to a community with increasingly divergent class interests. In Chapter 5, I will present a more detailed profile of the changes I am introducing here—changes that I contend were crucial for the development of conjunto music (as well as orquesta). For the moment I want only to note that the period I am discussing, particularly the postwar decade, marked a threshold in the lives of tejanos that changed their society in irrevocable ways.

Kenneth Boulding has described "thresholds" where certain social conditions can "profoundly change the subsequent parameters of a social system" (Schermerhorn 1974:3). These conditions may be slow in building ("continuous processes"), or they may burst forth suddenly ("discontinuous processes" or "one-shot" events), but the summary effect of these processes is to precipitate turning points that present a society with new alternatives. In many ways the period I am discussing here constituted such a threshold for Texas-Mexicans. The years during and immediately after the war, in particular, opened up many new and heretofore largely inaccessible opportunities for participation in American economic activity. Of course, tejanos moved quickly to take advantage, so that this participation did contribute measurably to their occupational upgrading (and, hence, to class differentiation; see Chapter 5). However, by moving into new socioeconomic fields they exposed themselves to new sets of social relations that inescapably shut off time-tested cultural strategies. Unforeseen social tensions resulted due to cultural dislocation: The transition from rural to urban modes of life, from Mexican to American cultural environments, and lastly, from proletarian to middle-class status was not easy.

To what degree these changes affected artistic expression is of course a major concern of this study, and I shall devote much space to such a discussion. At this point we can tentatively propose, however, that changes at the infrastructural base had their repercussions at the symbolic, expressive level and, more specifically, at the level of musical activity. In this respect we may borrow a phrase from Ackerman on style formation: If the creative impulse from which new styles spring may be thought of as a "class of related solutions to a problem—or responses to a problem," e.g., as a "protection against chaos" (Ackerman 1962:228), we may suggest that the kind of challenge posed by the events surrounding World War II demanded solutions to a number of unprecedented problems. In fact, it was not until this time that intensified participation in American life—fraught, as it was, with new kinds of social and economic promises and uncertainties—precipitated a cultural crisis for tejanos, one which they attempted to solve in various ways. Symbolic expression offered one solution, and, as we shall see, stylistic developments in conjunto music (as well as orquesta) suggest themselves as a specific example.

Actually, some stylistic elaboration did characterize at least some of the music of the pre–World War II era, particularly in vocal, folk song performance. By the 1920s (and probably much earlier, we may suspect) a distinctive style of duet singing was common, as evidenced by the recordings of the time. As was true with much Texas-Mexican music, this style was no doubt derived from Mexico, where duet singing, in *primera y segunda* (first and second voices, usually in parallel thirds), was an old tradition. In any case, by the early 1930s the duet style had become by far the most prevalent, at least in the semi-commercial market that existed among tejanos. Among the most popular were those of Gaytán y Cantú and Rocha y Martínez (see Folklyric Records, *Texas-Mexican Border Music*, vol. 6). Duets such as these had large followings throughout the Southwest. Stylistically, a nasal, strongly quavering voice quality was the norm, with background accompaniment normally provided by guitars, although sometimes other instruments were enlisted—for example, mandolins, *bajos sextos*, and even a violin or two.

In the late 1930s female duets appeared, among which the first and most popular was Las Hermanas Padilla.[3] No doubt their appearance was hastened by the existence at that time of similar "sister" duets in the United States. Las Hermanas Padilla, in particular, were especially influenced by such developments. And, since companies that recorded American popular music were the same ones that recorded Mexican music, the introduction of such duets into Mexican music found ready acceptance—if not initial impetus—among recording interests. Female duets became a permanent part of Mexican popular music both in the United States and Mexico, successfully competing with their male counterparts for public acclaim. Like American versions, most Mexican female performers (save, perhaps, for more traditional folk singers like Carmen Moreno and the legendary Lydia Mendoza) leaned toward a "cleaner," more polished style of singing, as opposed to the male duets, which were by and large more nasal and raspy. The lead part usually featured a mezzo-soprano range, with clear vibrato tones. Lastly, a few male-female duets made their appearance in the 1930s, but these seemed not to have had the success of their unisex counterparts. Included among these were Chicho y Margarita, the latter none other than one of the Padilla sisters.

Toward the late 1930s a mariachi-like ensemble, probably originating from the Jalisco area, began to gain some currency among tejanos, providing the musical backdrop for a number of duet recordings. Particularly active was a group known as Los Costeños, which accompanied many of the singers on the various labels, including Decca, Bluebird, Okeh, Vocalion, and others that were then exploiting what must have been an increasingly lucrative ethnic market.[4] None of the duets or other types of ensembles featured the accordion, at that time scarcely beginning to make its impact on commercial recordings.

In addition to the singing duets there had existed in Texas, since the nineteenth century, at least, an assortment of instrumental ensembles that apparently were utilized primarily to provide music for dancing occasions. I shall discuss these more fully in Chapter 1, but they consisted for the most part of ad hoc instrumentations, improvised for the occasion and at various times featuring exclusively string instruments (violins, guitars, mandolins, etc.), wind instruments (clarinets, trumpets, etc.), and sometimes even combinations of the two types. A special type of string orquesta (apparently not used for dancing), which had its origin in Mexico in the late nineteenth century, was to be found in Texas by the 1920s. This was the so-called *orquesta típica*, whose name was indicative of the obvious attempt on the part of Mexicans on both sides of the border to revitalize in a romantic spirit what was believed to be "typical," or folk Mexican music, including *huapangos*, *aires nacionales* (national airs), *canciones rancheras* (ranch songs), and the like.[5] In their efforts to capture the "essence" of "typical" Mexican music, *orquestas típicas* even adopted *charro*-style costumes for added authenticity.

Yet, despite the proliferation of ensembles, the accordion alone survived all of the earlier and sundry musical groups. These succumbed apparently to unavoidable changes wrought chiefly by World War II.[6] Indeed, there is good reason to advance the hypothesis at this time that conjunto music's supersedure over these earlier groups, as well as its rapid movement toward a common stylistic expression and its concurrent entrenchment in the Texas-Mexican working-class consciousness, is tied precisely to (1) that group's response to the challenge posed against traditional Mexican culture by a growing and increasingly influential class of upwardly mobile people who espoused the American ideology of assimilation (cf. McLemore 1980); and (2) the former's tacit recognition not only of its ethnic isolation, but its existence as an economic class "for itself." This recognition carried with it an incipient understanding on the part of the proletarian workers of their position vis-á-vis not only the Americans (who were all perceived as *ricos*), but the more affluent tejanos as well. Conjunto music was thus part of a wider response; it was a cultural solution to a social problem.[7]

Providing added tension for the working class's sense of threat to its traditional values were the inexorable changes set in motion by the process of urbanization. This urbanization, which accelerated greatly between 1930 and 1950, begot a host of conflicts. Some of these were related to the emergence of the new middle class, which made little effort to conceal its disdain for the lifestyles of the more traditional working class. But the conflict was augmented by the equally inexorable process of cultural assimilation, a phenomenon that, as Richard García has pointed out, "could be delayed, even modified, but not aborted" (1978:41). We may propose, then, that these interrelated developments—urbanization, class differentiation, and cultural assimilation—were the three crucial variables in the polarization of Texas-Mexican society and in the emergence of conjunto music. Socioeconomic differentiation and the ideology of cultural assimilation, in particular, formed the contrastive elements in tejano society that set off conjunto music from more middle-class and more Americanized symbolic expressions such as orquesta music.

Moreover, all the above factors, when linked to the always precarious existence of the tejano working class, deepened the latent divisions already found in Texas-Mexican society even before its wholesale contact with American society in the twentieth century. These divisions and their attendant intraethnic conflict had ramifications at various levels of symbolic expression—for example, in the verbal art forms of *agringado* joking so lucidly analyzed by José Limón (1978). The conflict was further aggravated by the working class's sense that *agringado* segments of tejano society were at one and the same time betraying their ethnic heritage while becoming snobbishly "high class."[8] In this jockeying for strategic cultural position conjunto functioned as a kind of banner for the folk-tradition orientation of the proletarians. Hence, the music's immense popularity and strong association with that group and its subsequent label, "la música de la gente pobre" (the music of the poor people).

Meanwhile, modern orquesta, which had its predecessors in the ad hoc wind ensembles of the pre-1930s period, began in the 1930s to acquire its own distinctive character. In the hands of such noted leaders as Beto Villa and Balde González, orquesta came of age among tejanos beginning in the 1940s. Furthermore, aspiring to be more "sophisticated," it turned to both the instrumentation and the repertory of American dance bands of the Glenn Miller-Tommy Dorsey type, not failing, however, to keep abreast of developments in greater Mexican orquesta music. The latter orquestas were influenced, too, by currents in American dance band music; however, they generally maintained closer ties to Afro-Hispanic music, particularly through their steadfast adherence to the Mexican version of the bolero and the *danzón*.[9] At the same time, *orquesta tejana* began to be increasingly associated with an upwardly mobile segment of Texas-Mexican society—at least in the decade or so after the war. And, while it maintained an intricate relationship with conjunto, it nevertheless was considered, as Narciso Martínez put it, "música pa' high society" (music for high society). In short, I would propose another hypothesis at this point: If conjunto music represented a proletarian response to social change, orquesta represented a similar response on the part of a growing middle class.

Thus, in its style *orquesta tejana* was a creation of and for the new "high society." It attempted to satisfy the esthetic preferences of this emergent group. However, the correspondence between orquesta and the middle class was never as strong as that between conjunto and the more traditional working class. It is true that upwardly mobile tejanos were highly conscious of their self-ascribed class difference—their status as *gente de roce social* (people of genteel breeding), as opposed to *la gente raspa* (the lowest people; scum). Yet in many instances their objective position within the American political economy as workers rather than the true middle class (see Chapter 4), as well as their inability to break down the ethnic barrier, held them hostage within the broader social network of a generalized, ethnic tejano culture. Hence, the reason for orquesta's uneasy relationship with conjunto.

Neither an American dance band nor quite a Mexican orquesta of the various types that existed then (e.g., those of Luis Arcaraz and Carlos Campos), *orquesta tejana* from the early days of Beto Villa tended always to look over its shoulder, as it were, to see what conjunto music was about. It is true, as I have pointed out, that orquesta music has traditionally been viewed by tejanos as music of a higher, more modern, or "sophisticated" order than conjunto. It has also been considered—accurately, as a cursory listening will reveal—more Americanized. As Carlos González, a veteran orquesta musician explained, "la música de orquesta siempre ha sido más sophisticated . . . El conjunto yo lo considero como música vernácula" ("Orquesta music has always been more sophisticated . . . I consider conjunto a vernacular [i.e., native, folk] music") (personal interview, May 8, 1980).

In reality, however, most orquestas have, in varying degrees, attempted to negotiate a middle ground between a Mexican/tejano and an American mode of performance, both in style and in repertory. Beto Villa, the acknowledged "father" of modern *orquesta tejana*, perhaps better than anyone else in the early days successfully mediated between American and Mexican dance band and conjunto styles. One has only to compare an early recording of "Rosita Vals," which, interestingly enough, he recorded with Narciso Martínez, with a later one of "Adiós Muchachos" (a tango converted into a fox-trot!) to realize the dramatic shifts in Villa's music. "Beto Villa traía de todo," said one music promoter; "lo que le ayudaba era que podía tocar ranchero y 'high class' " ("Beto Villa had everything; what helped him was that he could play both ranchero and 'high class' ").

The concept of *lo ranchero*, as it exists in the consciousness of the Texas-Mexicans, merits a few comments. To understand the significance of the concept we must first be aware that it is a component of a larger ideology of romantic nationalism that is rooted in Mexican thought on both sides of the border. This ideology has been nurtured for a very long time (see Lafaye 1976), but its most recent manifestations can be traced to the Mexican Revolution of 1910 and the intense nationalism it spawned (Franco 1970:84). Romantic nationalism in Mexico has exerted a unifying influence by appealing to the glory of the nation's "unique" heritage. As components of this nationalism, the concept of *lo ranchero* and the symbols that cluster around it—of which *música ranchera* is one—have contributed to the ideology by ennobling the existence of hacienda and rural life in general, portraying this existence as idyllic. Since the 1930s the principal vehicles for this portrayal have been film and music, often used in combination. In sum, among Mexicans *lo ranchero* evokes the ideal combination of qualities that Mexicans ascribe to themselves, qualities that are embodied in the twin symbols of the charro and the campesino. These are: manliness, self-sufficiency, candor, simplicity, sincerity, and patriotism, or *mexicanismo*.

Among tejanos this *mexicanismo* is fundamentally conveyed by *música ranchera*. The music is, in fact, a powerful symbol for the concept of *lo ranchero*. I would go so far as to classify *música ranchera* as a "summarizing" symbol (Ortner 1973) of the kind that "speak primarily to attitudes, to a crystallization of commitment . . ." by way of its "drawing-together, intensifying, catalyzing impact upon the respondent" (Ortner 1973:1342). Thus, in its interstylistic dimensions the music condenses a wide range of moods, attitudes, and values into one musical moment. People respond, instinctively, to a ranchero sound, whether it be interpreted for them by a conjunto, an orquesta, or a mariachi. And inevitably, by virtue of its symbolic association, it gives rise to vaguely articulated feelings of *mexicanismo*—momentary recreations of a simpler and romanticized folk heritage, tempered nonetheless by the realization that it is an ineffable existence, lost forever like the elusive lover of most ranchera song lyrics.

Attached to this deeply entrenched, affect-laden concept in the Texas-Mexican musical consciousness—even among the upwardly mobile urbanites—the ranchero sound has always been striven for by all but the most Americanized orquestas. In the words of one orquesta musician: "I think it has to do with our heritage . . . It [*lo ranchero*] goes back to our ancestors and the type of music they liked and we listened to when we were little." It is hardly necessary to add that among tejanos conjunto music, the unrivaled symbol of *lo ranchero*, captures the contact with "our ancestors" as no other music can. That fact was, of course, never lost on profit-conscious orquestas.

Yet, as Turner observed about "root metaphors" (a concept equivalent to "summarizing" symbol), they can be misleading (Turner 1974:27). In the case of *lo ranchero*, its sentimental value has long evoked a negative opposite. For if it awakens, even to this day, illusions of an unspoiled existence shorn of the complications of modern life, these illusions are quickly dispelled by the tejano's struggle for social and economic acceptance in modern American life. Thus, the attitude toward *el rancho* can easily shift from nostalgia to disdain: Today, as in the past, an *arrancherado* individual (usually a *campesino*, not the dashing *charro*) is someone without *roce social*; he is low-class, coarse, backward, and too Mexicanized to fit in with the more culturally assimilated tejano's notion of progress and adaptability to the demands of American society. The feeling of despair and rejection of the clumsiness of *el mexicano arrancherado* in the face of American cultural and technological demands is captured in the well-worn expression, "Mexico, recoge a tu gente." An appeal is made in the refrain for Mexico to come and reclaim its wayward children, who are making fools of themselves (and us!) by their inappropriate responses to the more sophisticated American cultural and social atmosphere.

That fact was not lost on orquestas, either. Thus, for many orquestas—even those of the 1960s "second generation," brought up not on Glenn Miller but on Bill Haley and Fats Domino—"*mexicano* wasn't in," as one informant admitted. "Todos nosotros," he continued, "including the Royal Jesters [from San Antonio], cantábamos puras piezas americanas . . . hasta que Manny Guerra se metió con los Sunglows, y [entonces ya] tocábamos inglés y español" ("All of us, including the Royal Jesters, sang only American songs . . . until Manny Guerra got in with the Sunglows, and [then] we played English and Spanish"). In the 1940s and 1950s, too, *lo mexicano* was strongly rivalled by American music. (Recall also that many Mexican songs of the time were absorbed into American popular music, e.g., "Bésame Mucho"). One of the most outstanding examples of what we might call musical code-switching was the popular Balde González, singer and leader of an orquesta that played as much American as Mexican music. Even the latter he often Americanized by fitting the Spanish lyrics to fox-trot rhythms. In this respect González was not at all atypical.[10]

Nonetheless, orquesta was never able to extricate itself from its links with conjunto. Always straddling the boundary between an urbanized, American dance band music and the Texas-Mexican conjunto folk tradition, orquesta constantly equivocated. In fact, the ambivalence of orquesta and its partisans—their condescending yet sensitive attitude toward developments in the field of conjunto music—clearly reflected the ambiguous stance of the middle class from which the music originally sprang. Like their music, the upwardly mobile tejanos of the postwar period never quite succeeded in dissociating themselves from their ethnic, if not their working class roots.

Thus, perhaps, the reason for the eventual "rancheroization" (and proletarianization) of orquesta—its drift, beginning in the late 1950s

(in the person of the orquesta musician Isidro López), toward an unmistakable convergence with conjunto music. Leaning ever toward
a ranchero sound more aligned symbolically and stylistically with
conjunto music, all but the most Americanized orquestas were in
due time appropriated by elements of tejano society closer in
outlook to the less culturally assimilated, more hard-core partisans
of conjunto music.

A full and adequate treatment of orquesta music deserves its own
study. Since that style of music will play but a contrapuntal part in
the analysis and interpretation of conjunto, perhaps its relation to
the latter can be summed up at this early juncture by quoting the
words of Delia Gutiérrez, a veteran orquesta musician:

> . . . they [*orquestas tejanas*] did play some of the ar-
> rangements of the big orchestras (like) Les Brown, Glenn
> Miller, Duke Ellington. A lot of people used el tema de (the
> theme of) Glenn Miller. But también tenían como los con-
> juntos (they also had like conjunto) and all that. You had to
> give people a little bit of both to keep them happy. If you
> would play pura pieza americana (only American pieces) and
> all that, then something was missing. That's why you had to
> come up with polkas and boleros (personal interview, July 7,
> 1979).

In this way, then, orquestas could negotiate the contradiction between upward mobility and cultural assimilation on the one hand
and ethnic allegiance on the other: American music satisfied the
demands of the former, *las polkas* the latter, with the bolero capturing both the Mexicanness and the sophistication of orquesta music's
clientele.[11]

I mentioned earlier that cultural assimilation was inevitable for
Mexicans in Texas. That is true, but this assimilation did not take
place without a good deal of reinterpretation and syncretism.[12] That
is, we must understand that in facing the reality of their economic
absorption and social domination in American life the Mexicans in
Texas have been under considerable pressure to adapt—economically, culturally, and psychologically—to the conditions that life imposes on them. These conditions, often uncompromising, have forced
Texas-Mexicans to yield to the stronger power, but not without
resistance, not without a determined effort to counter American
cultural hegemony by striving to maintain some of their antecedent
symbols—or creating new ones as they reinterpreted newly introduced American cultural elements into more familiar symbolic

structures.   As a countercultural symbol forged by proletarian artists, conjunto falls under the former category; as a symbol of the
middle class's doubly contradictory position vis-à-vis the working
class and a formidable ethnic boundary, orquesta falls under the latter category.

Notes

1. For the purposes of this study the terms "working class," "proletarian,"
"workers," and "proletariat" are all used as equivalents and are to be distinguished
from the term "middle class."   See Appendix A for further discussion.

2. Due to various problems that would make the study of the conjunto much more
intractable—notably the increasingly different politico-economic realities that faced
norteño Mexicans and Texas-Mexicans after 1930—I have excluded Mexican *norteño*
music from consideration, except for a brief discussion in Chapter 4.   In agreement
with conjunto musicians' own perceptions, I have chosen to distinguish between the
norteño and the Texas-Mexican conjunto.   Although historically the two musics
undeniably overlap, with Narciso Martínez's commercial debut in 1935, the two
types of ensemble began to diverge sharply, with the Mexican groups retaining more
of the characteristics of the rudimentary pre–1930s style that had been universal on
both sides of the border.   After World War II tejano conjuntos developed in a totally
new direction, leaving their Mexican counterparts far behind.   It was not until the
1960s that the latter began to narrow the gap.

3. These were not the first female recordings, of course.   Lydia Mendoza had by this
time developed her own distinctive style.   Accompanied by her family, she made her
first recording in 1928 (R. Spottswood, personal communication).

4. A number of recordings featuring duets with *Los Costeños*, as well as many
others with duets and sundry accompaniment groups, are to be found in the Mexican-
American Library Project record collection at the University of Texas at Austin.

5. To cite an example of how enthusiastically the Mexicans received the news of
the spread of *orquesta típica* in Texas, I refer to the full-page spread that appeared in
Excelsior, Mexico City's largest newspaper, on the founding of a "Nueva Típica Mexicana en Houston" (March 6, 1930).

6. Some of the reasons for the accordion's ascendancy over other popular instruments (e.g., the violin) are discussed in Chapter 1.

7. This awareness on the part of the proletarian class of its subordinate position
manifested itself in direct social action, too.   Witness the strikes and other disruptive
activities by tejano workers in the 1930s (García 1978; Nelson-Cisneros 1975).
Similarly, as I argue elsewhere (Peña 1982), the symbolic import of *corridos* began to
shift decidedly in the 1930s with the appearance of more direct calls for group
resistance to social and economic exploitation.

8. The problem of class, ethnicity, and cultural assimilation has drawn the increasing attention of scholars.   Compare, for example, Limón's cited work (1978) and
McLemore (1980).

9. The influence worked both ways, however.   In the 1940s American bands turned

increasingly to "Latin" music and musicians for inspiration, integrating many Afro-Hispanic genres and their styles into their repertories. Xavier Cugat's popularity in the United States is a good example of this influence.

10. Of course, even in Mexico City, which had for some time been under the influence of commercial interests from the United States (notably RCA), composers were also trying their hand at fox-trots with Spanish lyrics (Garrido 1974).

11. In this respect the comments of the manager of orquesta leader Sunny Ozuna are revealing. "Sunny," he said, "tries to cater more to the middle-class people than Little Joe does" (personal interview). We may compare this statement with that of Tony Guerrero, leader of the Tortilla Factory orquesta and a lead trumpeter with Little Joe's orquesta for a number of years. In an obviously humorous characterization he said, "I call Little Joe the country mouse; Sunny is the city mouse" (personal interview). A few local orquestas still cater almost exclusively to the tejano middle class.

12. Cf. Baron (1977:213): "Syncretisms are by nature ambiguous and exhibit palpably how the complex effects of acculturative contact shape the emergent qualities of cultural forms."

Part I
Music and Musicians: A Descriptive History

1. Origins: Texas-Mexican Music Prior to 1930

A vexing aspect of the study of folk music in its historical context is the incomplete or at times nonexistent record of a people's early music. This has been especially true of "primitive" groups, but it applies equally to the folk music of modern societies, where musical traditions—performance practices, stylistic features, vocal or instrumental combinations, and even melodic structures—were rarely preserved on paper, but learned either wholly or largely by oral and aural means. The scarcity of sources becomes particularly critical for those periods that precede the introduction of mechanical and electrical recording equipment, when at least some of the music of these societies began to be documented. This was the situation with Texas-Mexican music prior to 1900; it did not improve appreciably until the 1920s.

It is true that there are scattered written reports of festive tejano celebrations involving music here and there. Perhaps more detailed accounts remain to be discovered in forgotten diaries, newspapers, archives, or other repositories. Indeed, some aspects of musical activity have been rather fully re-created—for instance, in Paredes's study (1976) of early folk song in the lower Texas border area and in Dinger's accounts (1972) of the nineteenth century celebrations of tejanos along the lower border.

Despite these accounts, the special problem of describing the musical style or styles of pre–twentieth century music in Texas-Mexican society remains untouched. For example, we simply do not know with any degree of certainty what combinations of instruments were most common among the tejano folk, nor when or how such combinations came into existence. To cite one unknown: What kind of instrumental ensembles were prevalent in the nineteenth century among tejanos? For that matter, was there a "typical" accordion ensemble prior to the 1920s, and, if so, what instruments did it normally include? Or, as evidence indicates, were tejano folk music ensembles of the nineteenth and early twentieth centuries nothing more than makeshift combinations improvised depending on the availability of instruments and musicians? Lastly, in light of the scanty information we have on musical groups and styles, is it possible to identify at least some of the immediate predecessors of modern Texas-Mexican music?

We now have enough secondary information for preliminary answers to these questions on the nature and origin of Texas-Mexican music. Naturally, since this study concentrates on a more recent history of the music, only an incomplete sketch and some tentative propositions are possible here, but they can shed some light on the beginnings of conjunto and other types of Texas-Mexican music.

The Monterrey Link

Recent research points toward a stronger contact than hitherto realized between Monterrey, the northern industrial capital of Mexico, and Mexican Texas during the nineteenth and early part of the twentieth centuries.[1] This contact needs to be considered in assessing musical developments in Texas-Mexican society, because, as we shall see, Monterrey was an important source of both material goods and culture for Mexicans living in Texas. Particularly significant for the development of a Texas-Mexican music is the era of the Porfiriato—or actually from about 1860 on, when Monterrey reached its pinnacle as a commercial center first and then afterward as an industrial capital. Both developments contributed heavily to the city's cultural influence.

Under Maximilian and Porfirio Díaz, Mexico looked abroad for cultural guidance, just as it did for economic assistance. At this time in Mexican history, as historians Meyer and Sherman wrote, "the true measure of aristocratic success was to see how French one could become in taste and manners" (1979:473). Of course, this desire on the part of the Mexicans for Europeanization was not new. As a dependent colony of Spain, cast often in the role of stepchild, Mexico (as well as the rest of Latin America) had long deferred to Europe for cultural affirmation.[2] With specific reference to music, Mexico maintained strong links with Spain throughout the colonial period (Mendoza 1953; Stevenson 1971). However, in time Spanish music had become "Mexicanized"—folklorized, in many instances—in the process of diffusion throughout the different strata of Mexican society.[3] This was the fate, for example, of the *villan-*

cico brought from Spain to the New World in the sixteenth century. But the nineteenth century, particularly during the Maximilian and Porfirian eras, witnessed a significant shift in the context of Mexican music.

Ever since the "overrun of Mexican life by Italian opera" (Mayer-Serra 1941:62; translation mine), Mexico had fallen captive to the latest vogues originating from Europe. With the revolution of 1810 the fetters of an overbearing Catholic Church were lifted, and, along with independence, Mexico seemed to have experienced a musical liberation of sorts.[4] New musical ideas, particularly romanticism, were quickly embraced. As Mayer-Serra has indicated, opera maintained an especially strong influence throughout the century ("the Operatic Nineteenth Century" Stevenson called it [1971]). While earlier Spanish musical forms, such as *el romance* and the religious *alabado*, retained their currency in Mexican musical life, it was the opera that engaged the attention of first the bourgeoisie and then later, in a degraded and fragmentary form, the rest of Mexican society. Mayer-Serra summed up the situation when he wrote of the effects that the diffusion of operatic music had on Mexican musical production:

> . . . two types of production emerged: one of high status, esoteric, and, in principle, accessible only to the elites; the other of inferior quality, cheap, mass-produced and aimed at the lower classes, who were hungry for participation in the advances of civilization (Mayer-Serra 1941:70; translation mine).

In this manner, according to Mayer-Serra, the bourgeois elite would attend the opera house to hear and acclaim the great Caruso in the role of Rigoleto, while "the daughter of a petty bourgeoisie family should be satisfied with a potpourri of tunes from the same opera" (Mayer-Serra, 1941:70).

But other musical fashions were invading Mexico from Europe besides the opera. I refer, of course, to the salon music and dances that swept Mexico in the second half of the nineteenth century (Galindo 1933:522). This music and dance included such favorites as the polka, redowa, schottische, waltz, minuet, cuadrille, and others. And although older and more deeply rooted forms such as the *danza habanera* were also in vogue, "not because of this," as Galindo wrote, "did the [European] dances become scarce—no, they abounded, to a colossal degree . . ." (1933:518; translation mine). Ultimately, due to the pressures for Europeanization, the polka and the schottische prevailed everywhere in Mexico, from the "urban salons to the village house" (Galindo 1933:552). We may sum up the influence of all of these dances by citing Galindo again. He wrote that after 1850

> the older dances of Spanish origin were fading out gradually from the aristocratic repertory, with the habanera . . . the waltz, schottische and polka remaining as the new and unyielding repertorial core. Meanwhile, with each passing day society divided itself into groups: the erudite, lovers of opera and concert music, the semi-erudite and sports-about-town, lovers of the imported salon dance . . . the mestizo adherents to the dances derived from a mixture of rhythms (1933:552-553; translation mine).

The influence of salon music was felt throughout Mexican society. Moreover, in a generalized fashion the musical tastes of the operatic aristocracy descended to the next level, that of the salon music of the petty bourgeoisie, and then finally to the popular or folk strata, a process described as well for Argentina by Carlos Vega (1944:77). It was the operatic influence also that "gave birth to the Mexican *canción*" (Mendoza 1956:93) that was to so thoroughly dominate the popular music of twentieth century Mexico. To cite Mendoza further, the oft-performed operas of Bellini, Donizetti, Rossini, and countless others were the exemplars that "developed a taste for *bel canto* among the inhabitants of Mexico's cities" (Mendoza 1956:93; translation mine). "Very quickly," he continues, "this preference descended to the rural classes" (Mendoza 1956:93; translation mine).

While this neo-Europeanization of Mexico was under way, Monterrey was emerging as the northern outpost of Mexican and, by extension, European artistic culture by virtue of its undisputed position as the *sultana del norte*, as someone christened it. At the time salon music reached its apogee in Mexico, during the Porfiriato,[5] Monterrey became the "Pittsburgh of Mexico" (Meyer and Sherman 1979:449). "By 1910," wrote Meyer and Sherman, "Monterrey was without question the industrial capital of Mexico" (1979:450). With industry came economic and cultural influence.

Monterrey assumed its role as a regional commercial center early, as an industrial capital later. Several events contributed to this development. Among the most important were the city's location with respect to adequate water supplies and its geographic relation to the border and the interior of Mexico; the American Civil War, which converted Monterrey into a crucial link between Confederate cotton and European buyers; and the Mexican government's creation of a tariff-free, forty-mile-wide zone along the border with the United States, which engendered an enormously profitable contraband of goods that had ramifications for the economy of not only Monterrey but the whole *norteño* area (Vizcaya Canales 1971:17, 71-72). I cannot discuss all of these factors here, but an example will perhaps illustrate Monterrey's commercial advantage.

By the 1850s, as a result of the lucrative trade with the United States that the tariff-free zone and its contraband trade fostered, Monterrey had become the chief distributor for European goods, as well as Mexican products, for the entire north (Vizcaya Canales 1971:xiii). This meant that those duty-free, European imports that were destined for the United States by way of the ports of entry of Reynosa, Laredo, Matamoros, Camargo, and Ciudad Mier were controlled by Monterrey-based commercial interests. In fact, the border cities of Reynosa, Matamoros, Laredo, and the others (including Piedras Negras) operated, in effect, as commercial satellites of Monterrey (Vizcaya Canales, 1971:xiii).[6] Additionally, the border city of Matamoros served as the *regiomontano* capital's most important port for duty-free trade with Europe. As a result, throughout this period—at least up until 1900—Matamoros and Monterrey maintained a close, symbiotic tie. In a sense, the former aspired to be a "little Monterrey," functioning as the most important outpost of *regiomontano* economy and very likely culture as well. Vizcaya Canales has described the relationship thus:

> The bond that existed between Monterrey and Matamoros for so many years should be emphasized, as well as the influence that each city exercised over the development of the other (1971:viii; translation mine).

But Monterrey's influence almost certainly did not stop at the border. For example, from early on, San Antonio apparently maintained a special relationship with the *regiomontano* city. As early as 1863 a direct, regularly scheduled stagecoach route had been established between the two cities. Operated by a certain August Santleben, the stagecoach run was routed from San Antonio to Piedras Negras, then to Lampazos, Nuevo León, and finally to Monterrey. The stagecoach left Monterrey for San Antonio on the fourteenth of the month and started the return 524-mile trek on the first of each month (Vizcaya Canales 1971:7). An indicator of the active interaction between the two cities is Santleben's recollection that on one occasion the eighteen-passenger coach "arrived at Lampazos with 23 persons aboard" (Vizcaya Canales, 1971:7)—despite the fact that at one point the stagecoach must cover non-stop a 90-mile stretch, no simple matter in those days.

At the height of Monterrey's commercial dominance in the early 1880s—before this activity declined in favor of heavy industrial production—it was the main supplier for a wide area on both sides of the border of such goods as soap, wax, liquors, clothing, tile, brick, and a score of other items, including two for which it was renowned—hats and leather goods. In addition, Monterrey served as a clearinghouse for European goods.   With the opening of the railroad to Laredo in 1882 Monterrey merchants opened branch offices there and in other nearby communities, thereby improving their economic position in the border area.   The commercial influence of Monterrey on the border is summed up by Vizcaya Canales.   In addition to Monterrey products,

> the merchandise [brought to the border] consisted generally of European goods, since at that time available American goods were of low quality, and residents on the American side of the border would come and make their purchases in the duty-free centers [i.e., Laredo, Reynosa, etc.] (1971:28; translation mine).

If Monterrey exerted such commercial influence over the north —and we should include at least South Texas here—we may surmise that its cultural influence did not lag far behind, although this aspect of the interaction between Monterrey and its neighbors to the north is not as well documented.   In any case, we do know from Madsen's findings that in the late nineteenth century among South-Texas Mexicans "prestige came from south of the border" (1964:5). Moreover, according to Madsen, at least among the upper-class Mexicans,

> families did not consider their daughters properly married
> unless the wedding ceremony was performed in Mexico with
> all the splendor of the Catholic Church . . . Expectant
> mothers also crossed the Rio Grande to give birth in the more
> civilized surroundings of a Mexican town where trained doctors and midwives were available . . . Members of the old
> families take pride in the fact that they were born and married south of the border because these rites establish their ties

with the older and more sophisticated culture of Mexico
(1964:5).

On the basis of our knowledge of Monterrey's economic and
cultural domination over the entire north, we may suggest that the
prestige Madsen refers to ultimately emanated from Monterrey,
since it alone could claim the title of "Sultan of the North."

To turn to music specifically, except for Matamoros, only Monterrey had the kind of socioeconomic organization to maintain well-
organized orchestras and military bands. Moreover, only Monterrey
could boast such art centers as El Teatro Juárez, El Teatro Progreso,
and of course the famous Casino Monterrey, where the most elite
groups congregated for social occasions of all types. And, as an example of the general musical life of the city, we may mention La
Plaza Saragoza, the traditional *regiomontano* center for public
celebration. Here in the late nineteenth century public concerts
were conducted three or four times weekly featuring the "excellent
military bands" that the city possessed. According to Vizcaya
Canales, the usual programs consisted of "pasodobles, marches,
polkas, schottisches, fantasias, overtures, cuadrilles, contradances,
mazurkas, redowas, and the like" (1971:47).

But artistic cultural expression in Monterrey ran the gamut from
circuses to puppet shows to public concerts and, lastly, to exclusive
events where only the elite participated. Included in the latter was
"what was always considered a major event: the arrival of an opera
company" (Vizcaya Canales 1971:54). Numerous and regular appearances were made by the most famous of European and Mexican
companies, including an eighteen-day run in the winter of 1883 by
the famous Angela Peralta's company (Vizcaya Canales 1971:55).[7]
In sum, Monterrey's position as cultural arts leader was somewhat
defensively proclaimed by one of the newspapers of the time:
"Poetry, sculpture, painting, and music have their altar right next to
that golden calf which, it is said, is so worshiped around these
parts" (Vizcaya Canales 1971:119).

To what extent was Monterrey culture in general, and music in
particular, diffused throughout Mexican Texas? As mentioned, we
do not have the kind of extensive evidence that exists for the
economic influence; however, as Madsen pointed out, there was the
unquestionable prestige attached to the culture from south of the
border. Moreover, on the basis of economic activity and the movement of people between the two areas, we may infer a considerable
degree of social and cultural interpenetration. Quite likely, as the

early stagecoach runs to San Antonio indicate, migration to and from was probably constant. Here another bit of evidence may serve our purpose. According to John Peavey, an immigration official, prior to 1917 every rancho on the Texas side of the Rio Grande kept a rowboat, probably to ferry people and goods across the border. And still another significant piece of evidence comes from the Hidalgo County Lands Record, which indicates that most of the nonresident purchasers of land in 1920 were from the Mexican states of Tamaulipas, Nuevo León, and San Luis Potosí respectively. Among these purchasers, the following occupations were listed: farmers (75), laborers (293), merchants (181), doctors (2), and teachers (2).[8]

What all this points to is that, beginning in the latter part of the nineteenth century, there was a steady movement of norteños into Texas (and vice versa). According to Saragoza, the prosperity of Monterrey attracted, on the one hand, the attention of American businessmen (300 Houston businessmen visited the city in 1910 to promote commerce between the two cities); but, on the other hand, despite prosperity, oppressive working conditions for workers in Monterrey, as well as the uncertainties of the revolution, caused a considerable exodus toward Texas. This exodus was further encouraged by the intensified economic activity in Texas after 1910 in agriculture, mining, railroads, and industry (Saragoza 1978:164). However, we do not know the magnitude of Mexican immigration into Texas during much of this period, because records of immigration were nonexistent prior to 1893 (Grebler et al. 1970:63) and not very reliable after that. We do know, as I indicated above, that the Mexican revolution "spurred the first substantial and permanent immigration to the United States" (Grebler et al. 1970:63). And, as Figure 1 reveals, the preponderant majority of those immigrating to Texas were from the northeastern states of Nuevo León, Coahuila, and Tamaulipas.

It is thus evident that both economic and cultural ties were maintained between northern Mexico and Mexican Texas during both the nineteenth and twentieth centuries. Furthermore, since Monterrey was the undisputed economic and cultural center of this area, we may conclude that its prestige was a significant factor in such ties. And lastly, the increased immigration of Mexicans into Texas after the turn of the century ensured that norteño culture was constantly reinforced in an already Mexicanized tejano society.

The immigration to Texas was undoubtedly facilitated when travel accommodations improved immensely with the arrival of the railroads that linked Monterrey with the border cities. The last of

Figure 1: Origins of Mexican colony.
A. Winter Garden District, south Texas, 1884–1928.
B. Corpus Christi Consular District, Texas, 1928–1929.

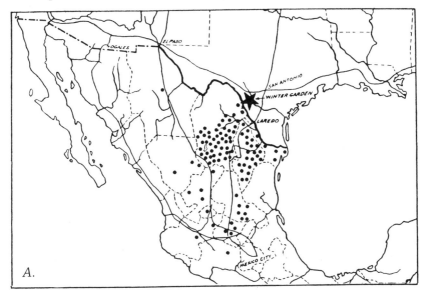

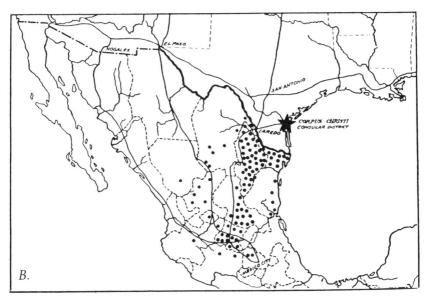

One dot = 1 percent. Source: Taylor, 1968, p. 42.

these, to Matamoros, was completed in 1905. After that time, and particularly during the Mexican Revolution, newcomers (and probably some old ones) from Mexico must have arrived daily. It is certain that among the rush of immigrants of this period many musicians were included. By the 1920s, as my older informants verified, there was no shortage of *maestros de música* (music teachers) from Monterrey. These same informants remembered a number of highly respected *profesores* who hailed from that city—another indication, surely, of the mystique that surrounded all that came from *la sultana del norte*.[9]

Here a couple of examples can be cited. First, there is the case of the orquesta leader, Beto Villa, whose father had been a musician in Monterrey before he immigrated to the United States. Villa's first music teacher was also from the Monterrey area. Like the elder Villa, he too had migrated to Texas in search of better opportunities to practice his profession.[10] Another bit of evidence on Monterrey's prestige comes from Octavio García, my father-in-law. He has in his possession a photograph, taken circa 1940, of Pedro Peña's orquesta from Mercedes, Texas. Peña's orquesta plaved locally in the Rio Grande Valley, and his musicians, including Octavio García, were all natives to the area, except two, who were from Monterrey. Pointing out the two in the photograph, don Octavio remarked that "esos eran musicazos" ("those were real musicians"), and he went on to explain that this was to be expected, since in those days the finest musicians came from Monterrey. In the case of the two gentlemen in question Peña had met and enticed them to play for him while they were appearing in nearby Matamoros with an orquesta from Monterrey.

Other cases can be cited—for example, that of Vicente Cerda, a *señor maestro* from Monterrey who, according to don Reymundo Treviño, "enseñó casi todos los musiquitos que han resultado de aquí de Alice" ("taught most of the musicians that have resulted from Alice") (personal interview, March 14, 1980). But the point of all this, of course, is that even as late as 1940 Monterrey still commanded considerable respect among Mexicans in Texas, at least with regard to its musical resources, as the statements of Octavio García and others attest.

To sum up the discussion so far, I would suggest that, as far as Texas-Mexican society was concerned, in the late nineteenth and early twentieth centuries Monterrey functioned as an economic and cultural metropolis, with Texas forming part of its hinterland. Notwithstanding the fact that after 1900 cotton agribusiness and other American capitalist activity began to absorb (if slowly at first) Mexican laborers into its web of social relations (cf. Taylor 1934:105ff.), Monterrey's influence continued to radiate outward as far as the Texas cities of Laredo, San Antonio, and Corpus Christi. This influence did not begin to diminish until the 1920s, at the earliest, when American economic expansion into deep South Texas finally closed off the border and effectively eclipsed, first, Monterrey's economic dominance and then, afterward, its social and cultural dominance as well.

Early Instrumental and Vocal Music

On the basis of the foregoing discussion we may propose that whatever music was extant in Monterrey, or at least some of its elements, was eventually diffused northward to Mexican Texas. Following the general pattern for Mexico, this diffusion was probably effected in two ways. First, the music and styles popular in bourgeoisie salons and social clubs of Monterrey may have been carried over more or less intact to similar salons in Laredo, San Antonio, and other Texas cities with a sufficiently cohesive bourgeoisie. We must assume in this respect that musicians trained in Monterrey migrated regularly to Texas to provide the music for social occasions and the training for aspiring Texas-Mexican music students. As noted, the migration of Mexican musicians increased during the revolutionary period, but it is not unreasonable to assume that even in the nineteenth century the movement of musicians was common enough, in particular those who might find the competition in Monterrey too demanding. Lastly, the prestige attached to formally trained musicians meant that they would be engaged only by people of financial means, who could afford their services.

This process of diffusion undoubtedly went hand in hand with another, whereby the styles of music of the elite became part of a *gesunkenes kulturgut*, as they were absorbed into the traditions of the proletarian masses. This "sinking of the good culture" could take place both locally or regionally. That is, the music of the Salón Tivolí, Club Alemán, and others (Vizcaya Canales 1971:108) may have filtered down to the masses in Monterrey first, then diffused as laborers moved northward in search of jobs. Then, again, some of the music could have undergone proletarianization after diffusion in its genteel form to a city like Laredo, for example. In its new locale the music or style of playing (e.g., a particular instrumental combination) would first gain currency among the upper class and then eventually be absorbed by the working class, though in a simplified fashion, in the form of makeshift ensembles.

Finally, yet another more generalized manner in which the music from Mexico found its way to Texas was through the musical and entertainment touring groups of the time. Various assortments of *maromas* and other tent shows, all of which included sundry musical acts, were touring Texas by the turn of the century. Additionally, musical groups from Mexico toured the United States as early as 1884, when La Orquesta Típica Mexicana was invited to appear in New Orleans (Baqueiro Foster 1964:546). On another occasion the "Spanish Orchestra Company, Typic [sic] Mexican," to quote the *San Antonio Express* (April 4, 1890), spent a week performing at the opera house of that city. According to Octavio García, even as renowned an *orquesta típica* as that of Juan Torre Blanca made an appearance in the small town of Harlingen, on the lower border, in 1920.

In sum, whatever means of diffusion prevailed—though a combination seems most plausible—by the early twentieth century all of the salon music that had been popular in Mexico during the Porfiriato (as well as Spanish forms introduced much earlier, of course; see Paredes 1976) was present and equally popular among tejanos, as confirmed by the early recordings (see Folklyric Records, *Texas-Mexican Border Music*, vols. 4, 5, 6) and by comments of musicians like Pedro Ayala. But equally important for the topic being explored here is the stylistic nature of that music as it was found in Texas until the 1920s. In short, the question to be answered is this: What types of ensembles existed in Texas-Mexican music prior to that time, and what was the state of their stylistic development? Evidence from the newspapers and other sources indicates that, in addition to a rudimentary accordion ensemble, at least two other modes of public musical performance were common: some type of wind and/or string ensemble, and solo or duet (mainly male) singing with guitar accompaniment. I shall now discuss the last two modes of performance, with an eye toward discovering the stylistic development that might be expected from each. The accordion is discussed below.

First, the string ensembles—or *orquestas típicas*, as some of these were called. To begin with, sundry string groups existed in Mexico throughout the colonial and post-independence periods. In fact, full-fledged orchestras for the performance of religious music were in evidence almost from the time of the conquest (Stevenson 1971:52ff.). In the nineteenth century small string ensembles with violin as the melody instrument were popular and widespread.

Sometime in the middle of the nineteenth century the Mexican writer Ignacio Altamirano, travelling in a rural area of Mexico, witnessed a "small popular orchestra" featuring a psaltery, violin, *bajo,* contrabass, clarinet, cornet, and a flute (Mayer-Serra 1941:116). This sounds like the ad hoc ensembles found among tejanos until the 1930s, but a more common ensemble, perhaps the most "typical" *orquesta típica,* was that which consisted of violins, psaltery, guitar(s), mandolins, and contrabass (Baqueiro Foster 1964:532). The use of these instruments apparently originated earlier in the various bourgeois productions of *zarzuelas, tonadillas escénicas, follas,* and even operettas. From here, according to Baqueiro Foster, they found their way into the *pulquerías, plazas,* and fiestas where the proletarian masses celebrated; and these groups in turn evolved into the *estudiantinas* and *orquestas típicas* of the latter nineteenth century (Baqueiro Foster 1964:532).

As we can see from Baqueiro Foster's statements, it appears that, as with so many aspects of Mexican social life, orquestas—or, better yet, orquesta-like ensembles—originally were in use as adjuncts to upper-class social occasions and then filtered down, as a kind of *gesunkenes kulturgut,* to the proletarian masses. Some changes took place, however, in the organization of instruments, for example, and the harmonies, too, may have become simplified. One suspects that the lower-class orquestas resembled the groups described by Altamirano more than the latter, so-named *orquestas típicas.* In fact, in the organization of the latter something like the opposite of *gesunkenes kulturgut* seems to have taken place. That is, the first actually designated *orquestas típicas*—for example, the Orquesta Típica Mexicana, founded in 1884 at the Conservatorio Nacional de Música (1974:59)—were distinctly middle-class groups that out of a spirit of nationalism or *costumbrismo* adopted certain elements of the *pulquería* groups described by Baqueiro Foster (1941:533).

In Texas, string orquestas and their *típica* variety—the latter obviously an imitation of the Mexican *típicas*—were to be readily found by the early twentieth century. We may expect, however, that makeshift ensembles—the genuine, folk, typical ensembles of the kind observed by Altamirano—must have been in currency long before. These continued to exist until the 1930s, when better-organized wind orquestas, patterned after the American swing bands and featuring saxophones, trumpets, and piano began to appear with increasing frequency. Incidentally, like their string counterparts, the wind ensembles—and even combinations of the two—must have been present throughout much of the nineteenth century, but they too were probably improvisational for the most part. *Orquestas típicas*, meanwhile, were present in various combinations. Lastly, based on information available from newspaper accounts and older informants, it is apparent that a few of the better-paid orquestas did attain a measure of stability and continuity.

Still, permanent, well-organized orquestas, whether wind, string, or a combination of these, were probably few in number—particularly the larger ones, which required both formal training, instruments (not so readily attainable in those days), and adequate remuneration. For this reason only those musical groups attached to the patronage of "society" families could be expected to maintain a permanent organization. Perhaps representative of these was La Orquesta Fronteriza, a group from El Paso in the 1920s and 1930s. Even by modern standards its sound was reasonably sophisticated. Strachwitz has described this orquesta as "typical of the larger string bands that played at society parties and balls for the wealthier families" (n.d.).[11]

In sum, then, by the early twentieth century a few fully outfitted orquestas did operate in Texas. Indeed, in the city of Matamoros, directly across the river from Brownsville, a sort of "pops" concert orchestra existed by the 1910s. Eugenio Gutiérrez, who many years later was to lead a modern orquesta tejana (in which I played), was performing violin solos in public concerts with the Matamoros "symphony" in 1918 (Delia Gutiérrez Pineda, personal interview, July 7, 1979). However, despite the presence of such orquestas, a majority of musical groups that depended on the working class for employment—whether these be dance orquestas, típicas, or other types of ensembles, such as those that relied on wind instruments—were still groups without permanent design, assembled on an ad hoc basis.

To cite two examples, Octavio García, who started his musical career in the early 1920s, for a number of years played saxophone in groups which featured as few as three and as many as seven musicians, depending on the occasion and the availability of musicians. And according to the father-in-law of poet José Flores Peregrino, on the ranchos in the Laredo area, music for *bailes* (dances) in the early days was provided by makeshift groups—ensembles featuring, but not limited to, violins, *bajo sexto*, guitar, and *pitos* (horns), with the number and combinations of instruments dependent on the occasion. The variability of the ensembles cited is explainable by the fact that tejanos of the early twentieth century were overwhelmingly poor and to some extent isolated. Thus, a socioeconomic organization broad enough and stable enough to support large or permanent musical groups was simply nonexistant, with the exception of small pockets of petty bourgeois groups in cities like Laredo Brownsville, San Antonio, El Paso, Houston, and perhaps Corpus Christi.

At this point I will advance the suggestion that in early Texas-Mexican music well-established ensembles of any kind, large or small, were the exception, and that stylistic development—at least of the kind obtainable through stable relationships among permanently combined instruments—was, as a result, in a state of atrophy. That is, the development of enduring ensembles, with their own characteristic styles, was inhibited by two factors: the lack of economic support and the difficulty of obtaining instruments and instruction (though the latter seems to have improved after the Mexican Revolution). The lack of these would be expected to have an adverse effect on ensemble development and style formation.[12] It is in this sense that we can speak of tejano musicians of the nineteenth and early twentieth centuries as *bricoleurs*—music makers who enlisted a "heterogeneous repertoire" of instruments, to borrow a phrase from Levi-Strauss (1966:17). The Texas-Mexican musician played with "whatever is at hand" (Levi-Strauss 1966:17). Under such circumstances some stylistic patterns would emerge, but they would be limited, because the variability of the instrumentation would preclude any stylistic breakthrough. One important prerequisite of ensemble style—fixed relationships among regularly employed instruments, as in the classical string quartet—was missing.

If the development of traditional ensemble style was hindered by lack of musical organization, style development in solo performance—in both vocal and instrumental music—was not. One reason for this is the fact that some of the problems to be solved for the emergence of ensemble style do not apply (or apply less so) to solo performance. These problems have to do with the number and type of instruments to be combined, the solution of which determines, first, the resultant sonority and overall volume of the ensemble. They include, too, the juxtapositions between melody, harmony, and rhythm instruments as well as matters related to tempo, phrasing, articulation, range of genres, times and places of performance—in short, all those things upon which any performance tradition hangs. It is true that some of these—for example, phrasing and articulation—are stylistic problems that need to be solved at both solo and ensemble levels; but the complexity of those problems increases in direct proportion to the size of the musical group.

On the basis of these observations on stylistic development and its problems we may propose that, given the social and musical climate in early Texas-Mexican society, solo or, at most, trio performance practices prevailed and that these probably crystallized from early on into basic stylistic patterns. Thus, solo and duet singing, in most cases with guitar accompaniment, were undoubtedly an established tradition by the turn of the twentieth century. It was this tradition and its style that was taken over by the major recording companies and propelled into the first Chicano mass-market commodity. Meanwhile, in instrumental music solo musicians, mainly on accordion and violin, were the rule, though duo combinations of guitar (or *bajo sexto*) and violin as well as *tambora de rancho* and accordion were not uncommon. As mentioned, larger ensembles were the exclusive property of elites.

We know little about singing styles in Texas-Mexican society prior to 1900, but two general modes of delivery may be suggested. The first, probably more prevalent among the elites, was very likely derived from the bel canto style popularized in Mexico after the introduction of Italian opera (Mendoza 1956:93). As was the case with the introduction of instrumental music, we may presume that this style of singing was originally imported from Monterrey. In Mexico itself the style was closely connected with upper-class music, specifically with the popularized *canciones románticas*, which were surely linked to the lieder of European romantic music.[13] These *canciones*, according to Mendoza, were related to the popularization of Italian opera music in the 1820s. Mendoza writes:

> The bel canto gripped the tastes of the society and the musi-
> cians in our provincial capitals; but it flourished as a new
> genre in the Bajío region, in the form of the romantic and sen-
> timental *canción* . . . and in this manner it suffused the soul
> of our mestizos, and during the length of the nineteenth cen-
> tury saturated every corner of our land   (Mendoza 1956:14;
> translation mine).

Later, Mendoza states that "all the formal elements of opera were assimilated not only by the aristocracy, but by the Mexican populace: idiom, versification, orchestra, singers, style—in short, all of the techniques" (Mendoza 1956:93).

Unlike the situation described by Mendoza in Mexico, and judging from later stylistic development in twentieth-century music, in Texas the bel canto style was never as prominent among the Mexican masses, though it may have been cultivated in the more elite circles, and particular features may well have been in general evidence. For example, an open, full-voiced quality, considerably different from the pinched, nasal style of later tejano folk singers (e.g. Rocha y Martínez) may have had some currency. Perhaps it was that full-voiced style of singing that Paredes had in mind when he wrote that "El Corrido de Gregorio Cortez" should be sung with "head thrown back and mouth wide open" (1958:34). Of course, he may simply have been referring to volume rather than voice quality, since he adds, "Fill your lungs [it was said], so they can hear you at the pasture's farthest end" (Paredes 1958:34).

In any case, after the advent of recorded music in the 1920s the quavering, pinched, and nasalized style of such folksingers as Gaytán y Cantú and Rocha y Martínez soon overshadowed all others. Moreover, these singers had undoubtedly inherited the style from an earlier period. In the absence of training facilities that a properly delivered bel canto requires, more traditional and far less polished styles prevailed, as Rocha y Martínez demonstrate. To round out the description of these early tejano folksingers' style, we need only add that the ubiquitous guitar's accompaniment was more or less standard by this time.

Early Accordion Music

The introduction of the accordion into Texas-Mexican music took place sometime after 1850, though the 1860s seem more likely. As is the case with other aspects of musical culture, Monterrey and northern Mexico are the logical source. During the Porfiriato (and even earlier) the city certainly had its share of immigrants from Europe, where the instrument had been invented a bit earlier (the 1820s). These immigrants may well have been responsible for the appearance of the accordion in the area. For example, by 1860 Germans had begun to establish themselves in the north and assume Mexican citizenship. Prominent examples were Eduardo Bremer, who had settled in Matamoros in 1860, and his son-in-law, Juan Reichman, described by Saragoza as "a leading member of the prosperous German colony in Monterrey" (1978:69). By 1910, "nearly seventy percent of all foreigners in Nuevo León lived in Monterrey" (Saragoza 1978:69). Included in these were many German workers, among whom the accordion is said to have been popular. Of these, 113 were living in Monterrey by 1895, many of whom were employed as brewmasters in the city's brewing industry (Saragoza 1978:154).

There is, of course, the possibility, advanced by Strachwitz and others, that Polish, German, and/or Czech immigrants settling in areas around San Antonio during the 1840s may also have served as donors. However, despite such suggestions of an American-Mexican interchange, the evidence indicates otherwise. My comments, of course, are not intended as proof of the accordion's provenience; that may never be known. What I want to suggest is that a Mexican introduction seems more plausible because, despite the contact between Anglos and Texas-Mexicans, we must remember that this contact was violent and that cultural interchange between tejanos and Anglo-Americans was minimal throughout the nineteenth century, sporadic in the early twentieth. It was not until the 1920s, when American economic development began to encroach deeply into Mexican Texas, that an American musical repertory presented itself as an alternative.[14]

On the other hand, there was the unquestionable link with Monterrey and *el norte* generally. Before the 1920s Mexicans in Texas quite simply owed most, if not all, of their artistic activities to currents emanating from Monterrey and northern Mexico—indeed, from greater Mexico in general. By way of example, it is worth noting that men like Eugenio Abrego of Los Alegres de Terán and Pedro Ayala, who were both born in Nuevo León, had fathers who had played the accordion. Such a fact attests to the instrument's popularity in northern Mexico by the late nineteenth century; its introduction there by way of the United States seems less likely. For these reasons, then, the theory of Mexican provenience seems more acceptable at this time.

Since everywhere in Mexico instrumental music was very often an adjunct to dance and since the accordion required little or no accompaniment, it is not surprising that by the 1890s it had become associated in Mexican Texas with celebrations that usually included dancing. These for the most part consisted of weddings and other fiestas, or *funciones*, as they were called. Thus, we have the description in the *San Antonio Express* of the accordion musician "wending his way" through one of these celebrations,[15] as well as my own father's recollections of weddings and other festive occasions in South Texas at the turn of the century (he was born in 1895). And Pedro Ayala, Santiago Jiménez, and Eugenio Ábrego all had fathers who had played the accordion for these types of occasions. In combination with the *tambora de rancho* it was apparently an indispensable instrument in the musical activities of the folk in both northern Mexico and Texas.

In the early years of the twentieth century weddings were elaborately celebrated events, lasting all day and all night and

sometimes even longer. The musicians were expected to play virtually without intermissions. *Funciones* were celebrated on an even
larger scale, lasting three or four days and including a variety of activities ranging from cockfights to *bailes de regalos*. They were
often attached to special calendar dates, such as the sixteenth of
September, *el cinco de mayo*, or some religious holiday, though
lesser occasions may have served just as well (Dinger 1972:31).

An integral part of the *función* was the *baile de regalos*, which
was already popular in the nineteenth century (Dinger 1972).[16] Narciso Martínez and Pedro Ayala relate that in the 1920s *funciones*
and their *bailes de regalos* were still frequently held in South Texas.
Dinger, Martínez, and Pedro Ayala all agree that the *baile de
regalos* acquired its name from the customary practice of requiring
young men to offer their female partners gifts of candy, sweet bread,
peanuts, or other condiments for the privilege of dancing with them.
These delicacies were bought from vendors who set up "crude but
decorated stalls" (Dinger 1972:37) around the dance area, usually a
platform of rough boards nailed together or more simply a patch of
hard-beaten ground.[17] At chosen intervals the musicians would in-
terrupt the dance piece they were playing and strike up "La Canción del Panadero" ("Baker's Song"), whereupon the young men
were required to escort their partners around to the stall of their
choice and purchase for them a bag of peanuts, cookies, and so on.
Dinger describes the finale:

> By that time [the end of the dance] the pockets of the male
> dancers were empty, the sacks of the mothers of popular
> daughters were bulging with several days' supply of
> sweets . . . and exhausted families were ready to start the
> homeward journey after a long festive evening" (1972:37).

Both the *función* and the *baile de regalos* as Texas-Mexican traditions ceased to exist by 1930.

Unfortunately, Dinger does not indicate what types of instruments
were used for these dances. She does, however, mention that in announcing celebrations "a feature of local custom . . . was the calling
together of the populace by the beating of a tom tom" (Dinger
1972:38). Almost certainly this was the *tambora de rancho* mentioned
by Narciso Martínez and Pedro Ayala. We may thus infer that the accordion, often accompanied by a *tambora de rancho*, occasionally by
a guitar or *bajo sexto*, was present at some if not most dances by the
last quarter of the nineteenth century. However, wind and/or string
ensembles (again, of the *bricoleur* type) were by no means displaced.

Moreover, it is likely that in more urban areas and among the wealthier groups a greater variety of these ensembles, particularly string bands, were utilized. To cite two examples: During the *fiestas patrias* celebrations in September of 1886 in San Antonio, we have a description of "two string bands and two rooms of dancers . . . going at once" (*San Antonio Express*, September 16, 1886); and in San Angelo for the *fiestas patrias* of 1910, "the delightful music of a local Mexican string band" was featured (de Leon 1978:7; quoted from the *San Angelo Standard*, September 15, 1910).

In sum, then, sometime around the turn of the twentieth century the accordion established itself as the preferred instrument for the musical activities of the tejano folk. Why this happened may be explainable in terms of its ready availability and inexpensiveness, especially the popular one-row button models imported from Germany and Italy and cheaply obtainable at the duty-free ports of entry like Reynosa. Additionally, the cost of hiring one musician (or, at the most, two, if a *tamborero* was included) was well within the means of the working-class tejano. Lastly, as the accordion gained in popularity it gained also in symbolic value: Culturally it was becoming appropriated by the tejano working class, even as the latter was being absorbed into the American economic system. Thus, coupled with the salon-derived dances of the polka, schottische, mazurka, and redowa (this last known as *vals bajito*) as well as the older and more traditional *huapango*, the accordion and its dance repertory began to take on the earmarks of a tradition. To repeat, while it was often played singly, an incipient ensemble had emerged, combining the accordion with the *tambora de rancho* or perhaps some string instrument such as the *bajo sexto*.[18]

The *tambora de rancho*, incidentally, was apparently of purely folk origins; that is, it was never commercially produced, though the body may have been fashioned from old, second-hand parade drums. In any case, as improvised by tejano musicians, it consisted of native materials for the most part, including the goatskin heads, wire rims, mallets, and the henequen that was used as a fastener. It was strapped to the waist somewhat like a parade drum and played with a pair of mallets whose tips were wrapped with cotton and covered with goatskin. According to don Pedro Ayala, on a still night the sound of the *tambora* could be heard for miles, serving as a primitive sort of advertisement that somewhere in the vicinity a dance celebration was under way. However, like the *baile de regalo*, the *tambora de rancho* did not survive beyond the early 1930s.

One reason for the demise of the *tambora* may well have been the increasing popularity of the *bajo sexto*. By the 1920s this instrument and the accordion had become paired favorites—a prototypical ensemble of the modern conjunto. Exactly when these two instruments, so basic to the later conjunto, were first combined remains a mystery. For that matter, the origins of the *bajo sexto* itself are difficult to pinpoint. None of the musicians I spoke to knew where this double-coursed, twelve-string bass guitar had originated. Most suggested Mexico as the likely source, and they are probably correct if the statements of one informant have any validity. This man, a *bajo sexto* maker originally from Guanajuato, Mexico, said he had learned to make the instrument in his native village and had continued to ply his trade when he moved to San Antonio in the 1930s. Since, in fact, Guanajuato, Michoacán, and Jalisco are famous for their manufacture of guitars, *vihuelas*, and other similar instruments, it is not unreasonable to suppose that this may have been an early home for the *bajo*.

At any rate, by the late 1920s the accordion and the *bajo sexto* were firmly wedded in the fledgling conjunto ensemble, with the *tambora*, which had served so well in the past, rapidly losing favor among the musicians. The reason for this, at least according to Pedro Ayala, was simple. The bajo complemented the accordion far better than the *tambora*. Played, as it was, with a plectrum, a good percussive effect was added to the fundamental bass-and-strum technique, all of which rendered it a more suitable accompaniment than the "noisy" *tambora*. It was this latter quality, in fact, that spelled the final demise; in the words of Pedro Ayala: "La tambora era la mas vieja de los instrumentos . . . Se usaba, y luego la dejamos por ruidosa—tapaba a la acordión y al bajo" ("The *tambora* was the oldest of the instruments . . . It was used, and then we dropped it because it was noisy—it covered up the accordion and the *bajo*").

In this manner, without fanfare, the *tambora de rancho* disappeared forever from the emergent conjunto ensemble, a victim of the changes that had begun to take place by 1930.

The 1920s—Watershed Years

The 1920s marked a watershed in the development of Texas-Mexican music. It was during these years that large American recording companies such as Vocalion, Okeh (a subsidiary of Columbia), Decca, and Bluebird (RCA) launched a major effort to record native Chicano musicians and singers. These companies had begun earlier to exploit commercially black folk music (the so-called "race" records), and, having been successful, they set their sights on the possibilities that a

Chicano market might offer. They moved in with vigor. Since such a move was not without its consequences, some of which were long-lasting, at least a brief discussion of early recording activity among tejanos seems necessary.

Among Mexicans in the United States the honor for the first commercial recording evidently belongs to Los Hermanos Bañuelos, a duet with guitar accompaniment, who recorded the *corrido* "El Lavaplatos" in Los Angeles on May 11, 1926. This was with Victor (Spottswood, personal communication, November 10, 1980). The brothers Bañuelos were reportedly from Mexico originally (Strachwitz 1975a:32). With their recording of "El Lavaplatos" they not only ushered in what Strachwitz called the "Golden Age" of the recorded corrido, but an era also in which every type of traditional Mexican music in the Southwest found its way to the wax disc. Other diverse groups quickly followed, including Pedro Rocha and Lupe Martínez, vocal duet with guitar (1928), La Orquesta Típica Fronteriza (1928), El Cuarteto Carta Blanca (1928),[19] and many others. The year 1928 also witnessed the first accordion recording; the accordionist was Bruno Villarreal (Spottswood, personal communication).

According to the recollections of such early musicans as Narciso Martínez and Santiago Jiménez (cf. Strachwitz 1975a), the major companies would place advertisements in local newspapers, announcing auditions for musicians and singers. Often, local Chicano entrepreneurs—men like Señor Acuña, "who had a furniture store on West Commerce" (in San Antonio)—acted as go-betweens for musicians and company agents (Santiago Jiménez, personal interview, April 5, 1979). The artists who were acceptable would then be brought to the city where the recording team had set up temporary studios (usually in hotels in San Antonio, Dallas, or Los Angeles), depending on the area targeted for the "discovery" of talent. Strachwitz gives us an idea of what a typical recording day was like:

> Looking over the ledger sheets of some of these sessions, perhaps one from a week in April of 1934, gives you an idea as to the different kinds of music recorded: Octavio Mas Montes and his guitar, Los Hermanos Chavarría, Gaytán y Cantú, Trío Texano, Cuarteto Monterrey, Pedro Rocha y Lupe Martínez, accordionist Bruno Villarreal, Los Hermanos San Miguel, W. Lee O'Daniel and His Light Crust Dough Boys, Rafael Rodriguez and his guitar, and finally blues singer Texas Alexander (1975a:30).

To take a more specific example, Santiago Jiménez related how recording sessions permitted little rehearsal—undoubtedly because of the heavy scheduling. Thus, the finished product was expected within the first or second "take." Of his first recording (in 1936) Jiménez recalled: "No practicamos casi nada porque los músicos que él [Sr. Acuña] nos presentó ya habían grabado antes con otros grupos de violín . . . y la polquita que yo llevaba no era muy difícil . . . Luego, luego se acoplaron" ("We practiced almost none at all, because the musicians that he [Mr. Acuña] introduced to us had already recorded with other violin groups . . . and the *polquita* that I had was not too difficult . . . They fit in right away") (personal interview, April 5, 1979). An interesting sidelight of Jiménez's comments is the fact that even at such an early date a corps of studio sidemen was already in evidence among tejano musicians.

No study has ever documented either the financial success of the major recording companies or their effect on Texas-Mexican musical culture. I shall defer a discussion on the second point until the next chapter. With respect to the first point raised, the major labels' continued activity up until World War II would indicate that the venture was lucrative enough to encourage continued investment. Considering the following points, we may safely conclude that the major labels accurately foresaw the commercial possibilities that a Chicano market held.

First, already by the 1920s there was obviously an active pool of musical talent among *mexicanos* throughout the Southwest and northern Mexico that attested to a well-established musical tradition among this population. Once the companies gained contact with Chicano talent brokers, merchants like the Acostas in San Antonio and Enrique Valentín from Brownsville, who knew the performers well, it became relatively easy for these companies to pick the best from the field.[20] Secondly, it is obvious that to most Chicano musicians the lure of a recording date was both a novelty and a matter of enormous prestige—the latter an accomplishment that cannot be underestimated. Many would have done it for nothing simply to achieve whatever small degree of immortality this might bestow upon them. Consequently, it was with the utmost ease and with the most minimal expense that recording companies signed one performer after another. Lastly, the Chicano populace by the late 1920s was sufficiently acculturated to the electronic age to be receptive to the commercialization of their traditional music. With the advent of Spanish-language broadcasting, radios and phonographs were coming into demand (see Gutiérrez and Schement 1979:5ff.).

By modern standards, which include contractual rights, royalties, and so forth, the early "contracts" (nothing more than verbal agreements) were wholly advantageous to the recording companies. Narciso Martínez and Santiago Jiménez were paid a flat fee—anywhere from $15 to $20 per record. Admittedly, to the musicians this was a handsome earning, but considering that records sold for 35¢ even in those days, it did not take the sale of too many records to recoup artists' fees. There were, of course, other expenses, but all in all the recording of Chicano artists should be considered a low-investment, high-yield enterprise.

No one knows how many Chicano records marketed in the 1920s and 1930s were sold. It may be true, as Narciso Martínez said, that at this time not many people owned phonographs;[21] yet Lydia Mendoza, who was also paid a flat fee per recording, once told Paredes about a notice she had received from the Internal Revenue Service for overdue taxes on earnings of several thousand dollars from her recordings—this despite the fact she received absolutely no royalties. Someone, it would seem, had informed the IRS otherwise. In any case, on the basis of the phenomenal popularity of Narciso Martínez, Santiago Jiménez, duets like Gaytán y Cantú and a host of other performers, we can be certain that the Chicano recording market was, indeed, a profitable one for the major labels.

Summary

We may now summarize this necessarily brief sketch of early Texas-Mexican music by listing the factors that spurred the rise of a musical tradition (in its broad sense) that in the 1930s gave birth to modern conjunto music:

1. With the evidence we now have at hand it is possible to advance the thesis that a strong commercial link existed between Monterrey and Mexican Texas in the latter part of the nineteenth and early twentieth centuries, up until the 1920s. This thesis supports the following points:

2. A cultural exchange obtained between Monterrey and *el norte*, including Mexican Texas, such that new musical forms and their combinations sweeping through Mexico were diffused via the *regiomontano* region northward to Texas. In the ensemble category these forms included orquestas—both string and wind (originally of the *banda militar* variety)—and their ad hoc derivatives as well as

their representative genres: polka, redowa, schottische, etc. (The *huapango* was not of *regiomontano* but *huasteca* origin.) In the solo category the most important feature diffused was the bel canto style. As for the accordion, it too was probably introduced by way of Monterrey, or at least the *regiomontano* region; however, from the moment of its arrival in Texas, it seems to have become a working-class instrument.

3. Because of class cleavages that existed even in the period under discussion, cleavages that affected the diffusion of music in Mexico generally, musical styles diffused from the upper to the lower classes underwent some alteration, largely as a result of the latter's inaccessibility to the necessary instruments and musical training.

4. As a result of the above, style formation among the proletarian folk, insofar as ensemble organization was concerned, tended to remain static and of a diffuse nature, though solo and duet performance did experience considerable stylization.

5. Within the limitations of solo music and dual-instrument combinations the accordion, with or without accompaniment, emerged early as a preferred instrument, with its own style, among the proletarian folk.

6. With the advent of recorded music, existing musical combinations and their styles and representative genres proliferated in the 1920s and 1930s. These included both folk-based and genteel musics. Among the former would be included vocal duets with guitar/mandolin accompaniment, accordion with *tambora* and/or guitar-*bajo sexto*, and occasionally other combinations, such as violin and guitar. Genteel recordings consisted mainly of orquesta music, sometimes of the *típica* variety. The accordion, which was soon to eclipse all other instrumental groupings, was introduced in 1928 by Bruno Villarreal.

7. Lastly, the commercialization of the various types of music then extant among Texas-Mexicans had the effect of narrowing, at least temporarily, the range of stylistic variation. Further stylistic reduction took place during and after World War II, when the modern conjunto eclipsed other groups and emerged as a full-fledged ensemble with its own unique musical style. The one major exception to this reduction was the modern *orquesta tejana*, which, together with conjunto, succeeded in amalgamating at least some of the features

of the ensembles competing with the accordion in earlier years (e.g., vocal styles and genres like the *canción*).

Notes

1. The best work on Monterrey's commercial and industrial development is Vizcaya Canales's (1971). I have drawn extensively from it. No comprehensive work linking Monterrey with Texas exists. Alex Saragoza is currently investigating social, economic, and cultural aspects of Monterrey during the Porfiriato (see Saragoza 1978). His comments on the link between Monterrey and Mexican Texas have been extremely helpful.

2. Mexico's imputed lack of self-affirmation, its "inferiority complex," has been the subject of a number of works. See, especially, Ramos (1962), Paz (1961), Lafaye (1976), and Echánove Trujillo (1973).

3. See Galindo (1933:514): "Spanish *sones* and popular melodies were preserved intact in the small communities of Spain . . . and . . . in Mexico both Spanish and mestizo [were preserved]" (translation mine).

4. According to Béhague, in the colonial period the church "supported the only truly well-organized musical life . . . " (1979:59). Any and every type of secular musical activity could be the subject of investigation by the Inquisition (cf. Stevenson 1971:183 ff., for a denouncement of the *pan de jarabe*).

5. According to Stevenson, "The amount of salon music published in Mexico between 1870 and 1900 was enormous" (1971:205).

6. On the balance of trade between Mexico and the United States, Colonel J. L. Haynes, customs inspector on the Rio Grande, commented, "Our imports from Mexico are much greater than our exports." He cited the contraband entering through the duty-free Mexican ports of entry as a major cause (*San Antonio Express*, September 15, 1882). Quite simply, Texans could obtain whatever they desired through Laredo or Matamoros at prices that U.S. merchants could not compete with. Customs inspection was, needless to say, totally ineffectual in those days.

7. According to Américo Paredes, Ángela Peralta, the "Mexican Nightingale," also made an appearance around this time in Matamoros, a fact that attests to the demand even in such remote regions for such forms of "high" art (personal communication).

8. Unfortunately, the source for this information cannot be cited because it comes from a manuscript sent by a journal to Alex Saragoza for blind review. It was written in 1981.

9. I personally recall with what pride my own father used to refer to an uncle of my mother, who, as a result of his musical ability, had gained a position as an orchestra director in Monterrey. The man had originally been from Ciudad Mier, on the Texas-Mexican border.

10. I owe this information to Linda Fregoso, who interviewed Villa in 1980.

11. A recording of this group may be found in the Folklyric Records *Texas-Mexican Border Music* series (vol. 5: "The String Bands"). In the jacket notes the editor, Chris Strachwitz, does not add the label típica to La Orquesta Fronteriza; however, Dick Spottswood, who has been working on an extensive discography of ethnic music,

specifically mentions that La Orquesta Típica Fronteriza first recorded in El Paso for Victor in 1928 (personal communication, November 10, 1980). What is more likely is that many of the musicians who participated in dance-type string orquestas also donned their charro costumes and played for *orquestas típicas* when the occasion required it. Thus, it is very possible that La Orquesta Fronteriza used such a designation when playing for dances and added the *típica* label for nationalistic festivals or for recordings.

12. The objection could be raised that some primitive societies, far worse off, technologically speaking, than the Texas-Mexicans, still managed to develop powerful musical ensembles and styles. That is true, but in primitive societies music was traditionally an adjunct to religious rituals deeply imbedded within the group's social organization. This powerful impulse was absent among the tejanos, where a socially compartmentalized Catholic Church made its own music. Furthermore, if we accept the semicolonized status of Chicanos and the social and cultural suppression that such status imposed, then we may begin to understand why, in this state of persistent marginalization that Chicanos found themselves, any sort of organization was difficult. That a cultural foundation survived and, indeed, underwent revitalization is the more remarkable, though perhaps inevitable, as colonized groups have often demonstrated (cf. Fanon, 1965).

13. On this point we may quote Mayer-Serra: "What the [Mexican musicians] inherited and adopted as the objects of their creative impulse were, in addition to Italian opera, the second-hand scraps of European Romanticism, in the form of salon music . . . " (1941:76; translation mine). Chopin, Schubert, and Liszt are offered as models.

14. Octavio García and Eugenio Gutiérrez, two early orquesta musicians, began to incorporate American tunes into their repertories in the 1920s (personal communication).

15. This information was provided by Dan Dickey. I have not been able to determine the exact date of the newspaper entry.

16. Dinger does not call the celebrations she describes *funciones*, though they coincide with those described by Martínez—the horseracing, *baile de regalos, lotería*, etc. The bulk of Dinger's information comes from a diary kept by a woman in Hidalgo County between the years 1850 and 1904.

17. In an interview Narciso Martínez recalled the impressions the dust gathering around the dance area made on him, inspiring him to title one of his compositions, a polka, "La Polvadera" (sic), i.e., "The Dustcloud."

18. For an early recorded example of an accordion/*tambora/bajo sexto* combination from the 1920s see *Texas Mexican Border Music*, vol. 4.

19. According to Spottswood, this was the legendary Lydia Mendoza's first recording (personal communication).

20. This information was pieced together from personal interviews with Armando Marroquín (January 11, 1980), Santiago Jiménez (April 5, 1979), and Narciso Martínez (August 3, 1978).

21. See, however, Gamio, 1971. In this monograph, originally published in 1930, Gamio reported that in the survey of returning Mexican immigrants both records and phonographs were favorite acquisitions: "The musical and artistic tendencies of the immigrants are indicated by the figure as to phonographs, which is 21.82, and as to records, which is 118.00 [per every 100 immigrants surveyed]" (1971:70).

2. Los Músicos de Ayer: The Formative Years

When we trace the development of conjunto music as it was molded into a dynamic musical expression at the hands of a group of musicians who spanned a period of some thirty years, we need to keep in mind that this was, in every sense of the concept, a folk development. Beginning with Narciso Martínez, I shall shortly present profiles of some of the most important contributors to the style, and we shall see that the vast majority of these artists had two characteristics in common: They were for the most part either partly or totally illiterate and they were members of a proletarian class, whether rural or urban. They were, in fact, folk musicians, who learned and transmitted their music exclusively through aural means, "agarrando ideas aquí y ahí" ("picking up ideas here and there"), as someone once put it. Not surprisingly, from the very start Martínez and his contemporaries, who were the founders of modern conjunto music, forged and popularized a style that in its most characteristic form came to epitomize a Texas-Mexican folk, proletarian musical esthetic.

In the beginning, of course, no one could have foreseen the impact of conjunto music on tejano society. Before they were lured by American recording companies into the commercialization of their music, accordionists Bruno Villarreal, José Rodríguez, Narciso Martínez, Santiago Jiménez, Lolo Cavazos, and others probably never imagined themselves or their music to be anything more than representatives of one very common tradition among traditions. The accordion certainly had plenty of competition. There were, for example, the orquestas, in their various forms, a variety of vocal duets, and a host of sundry other groups, all of which were drawn into the commercial market at the same historical moment. And all were vying for the first time commercially for a virgin public's attention. This variety of groups had been flourishing locally for some time; and while the accordion ensemble was immensely popular, so were the other types of groups. Especially favored were the vocal duets with guitar accompaniment, and these certainly offered the most solid competition in the recording market.

One fortuitous circumstance, however, moderated the competition between singing duets and accordion, namely the fact that the accordion ensemble and the vocal duet each had been assigned by social convention its appropriate time and place for performance. Quite simply, except for informal, spontaneous gatherings, the accordion as a rule was designated as most appropriate for providing instrumental music for dancing, where, at the same time, vocal music was discouraged. This, incidentally, was true of all instrumental, dance-type ensembles. On the other hand, vocal music, mostly in the form of *canciones* and *corridos* (Paredes 1976), was for listening, to be enjoyed on occasions devoid of dancing. Besides the cantina, these might include informal gatherings of friends, a *mañanita* or other serenade, and even an *aficionado* contest. On some of these occasions the accordion might be present, but it was understood that for the moment it had become divorced from its more normal dance context. After 1930, however, increasing opportunities were available in the home for people to gather round a radio or phonograph and listen to *both* instrumental and vocal music.[1]

But why was vocal music discouraged at dances? Both Narciso Martínez and Pedro Ayala feel that the more or less general taboo on singing at early Texas-Mexican dances was linked to (1) the association of the song-dance combination with the atmosphere of a cantina and (2) the rules of propriety attached to the presence of women, specifically *mujeres decentes* (decent women). To expand this point: In a cantina, where dancing with *mujeres de la calle* (street women) was thought to be customary, it was not unusual for singers to intersperse their songs with the instrumental dance music common even in such places. These songs inevitably elicited a round of *gritos* and (or so it was claimed) other boisterous and gross behavior. Now this kind of behavior, so closely linked in the public mind with the licentiousness of a cantina, could hardly be tolerated in a *baile decente*—a wedding dance, for example. Thus, by way of ensuring the proper behavior on the part of the men—and no doubt to distinguish a "decent" dance from a cantina—only instrumental music was permitted. This practice finally ended after World War II, a result of many factors, one of which was the likely influence of the radio and phonograph, where vocal and instrumental music possessed no inherent social distinctions.

Considering that in the postwar period the *canción* soon replaced purely instrumental music for dancing, the earlier ban on singing at dances may seem odd, but given the prevailing social conventions, the explanations of Ayala and Martínez do make sense. However, there appears to have been yet another element that entered into the instrumental–vocal music dichotomy and its relation to the dance. I refer to the notorious if euphemistically labeled *baile de negocio*, a taxi dance of sorts that had been a part of the scene for some time—perhaps as early as the 1870s, to judge from an article in the *San Antonio Express* on "fandango houses" in that city (April 19, 1874). Moreover, despite their dubious reputation, these "business dances" were probably the first public for-pay dances, antedating the popular ballroom dances of the postwar period by at least fifty years. However, unlike these latter-day dances and the *bailes decentes* of the time (weddings, *bailes de regalo*, anniversaries, and the like), *bailes de negocio* were obviously held in low esteem by those who considered themselves morally upright, regardless of socioeconomic status.

It thus seems reasonable to assume that every effort would be made to separate symbolically the function of a *baile de negocio* and a *baile decente*. The injunction against singing at the latter seems to have played just such a symbolic role.

Interestingly, Narciso Martínez defended the *baile de negocio* as at least in some instances a perfectly legitimate and, indeed, welcome source of income for needy families, especially during the Depression. According to Martínez a man could bring one, two, or more of his daughters to such a dance, each of whom could earn two dollars or more per night. The method by which the women (as well as musicians and empresarios) earned their money was as follows: A man or woman who could afford to build a *plataforma* (usually made of wooden boards) and hire an accordionist could then organize a *baile de negocio*. Women in attendance who received an invitation from a man to dance collected from him a chip that he had bought at the door for, say, fifteen cents. Each woman collected all the chips given to her and turned them in before she left the dance, receiving five cents for each chip she had accumulated. The remainder was the empresario's profit, out of which he recovered the salary paid the musician(s).

It is difficult to assess positively Martínez's assertions, in light of his own statements that the dances lasted from sundown to sunup and that "Ya pa' estas horas llegaban las primeras bailadoras—pos, con la idea de hacer un nicle. Y luego llegaba un borrachín o dos" ("By this time the first women dancers would arrive—well, with the idea of making a nickel. And then a drunkard or two would show up"). Under such circumstances it seems hardly likely that a protective father would bring his daughters to such an event. In fact, Pedro Ayala, Reymundo Treviño, and my own father have assured me that the *bailes de negocio* were places of ill repute that were frequented by *mujeres de la calle,—* "loose" women of no financial means who were often engaged in acts of prostitution as part of their participation in these affairs. Furthermore, according to my father, it was not uncommon for these *bailes* to be operated in connection with cantinas. He recalled one such place in Santa Rosa, run by a certain doña Isabel, where the *plataforma* had been built adjacent to the cantina. "Allí tocaba el mismo Chicho Martínez, El Huracán del Valle," he said. "Y luego llegaba una pandilla de viejas que traían de por allá del area de Brownsville" ("The same Chicho Martínez, El Huracán del Valle, played there, and usually following him was a bunch of floozies that they brought over from the Brownsville area") (personal communication).

But perhaps it was Pedro Ayala who made the most realistic assessment of the *bailes de negocio* and the women who were involved in them: "Venían a trabajar," he said. "Era trabajo . . . mujeres solas, solteras que no tenían hombre, no tenían nada. Se iban a bailar, y así sacaban su vida" ("They came to work, it was work . . . single women who had no man, who had nothing. They came to dance and made their living that way"). But often, as Ayala said, in order to keep working they had to resort to prostitution. With prostitution—or even with their mere presence at such places—came stigmatization. Not surprisingly, while the women and the *baile de negocio* itself might be condemned, the musicians and the men who patronized them were not.

Obviously the explanation for the differential treatment between men and women lies in the nature of tejano society: It was and is male-dominated, as are, for that matter, both Mexican and American societies. Thus, the men's behavior was considered, if not "natural," then at least predictable. For their part, the musicians were exonerated: they were simply plying their trade. For that reason they could hardly be banned from playing at *bailes decentes,* since their association with the *bailes de negocio* in no way reflected on their character as men. To be sure, they were in fact heirs to a kind of stigma, but this stigma was attached not to their characters as men, but as *musicians.* I am speaking here of the kind of stereotyping that Alicia González described in relation to the Mexican *panadero* (baker), wherein the unorthodox nature of the occupation surrounds him with an aura of danger and pollution (González 1981). In both the case of the musician and the *panadero* their special talents, irregular working hours, and, above all, the "ludic" character of their artwork invest them with a "liminoid" quality (cf. Turner 1974), which is a function of their relation to the rest of society. Rightly or wrongly, they are perceived by others as existing at the margins of conventional society, as being "outsiders" (cf. Becker 1963:

chapters 5 and 6)—hence their threat as potential deviants and pollutors.

It is no doubt true that among tejano musicians, as among those studied by Becker, "the feeling of being a different kind of person" (1963:86), "an artist who possesses a mysterious gift" (1963:85), served to reinforce the general society's beliefs about them. Thus, though many of my informants were at great pains to deny it of themselves, among tejanos musicians were and are considered licentious, inveterate womanizers, drunkards and/or drug addicts (particularly marijuana), and generally a collection of loafers who disdain any kind of work outside their music making. In spite of these negative perceptions—or more likely because of them (i.e., the layman's perception of the musician as a strange, "mysteriously" endowed creature)—Martínez, Ayala, and the other musicians were highly regarded by their constituents, at least with respect to their talent. They never were at a loss for a place to perform.

There was one group of people, however, who regarded conjunto music and musicians, as well as any bailes they played for, as vulgar. I refer, of course, not only to the upwardly mobile, "respectable" class of Texas-Mexicans who, especially during and after World War II, became more influential, but also to the more traditional tejanos who for one reason or another—wealth, ideology, and/or social status—dissociated themselves from the activities of the proletarian masses.   To those people especially, the baile de negocio was representative of all that was wrong with "low-class" Mexicans: their profligacy, their thriftlessness, and their hopeless degeneracy. "Nomás consiguen un peso," it was said, "y van y lo gastan en la cantina ("As soon as they get a buck they go spend it in a cantina"). In this, however, they were merely adopting the stereotypic attitudes that had long been current among Anglo-Texans.

The following account from the San Antonio Express gives us an idea of some of the views that pervaded Anglo-Texan society vis-à-vis Texas Mexicans and their dances.   It is not, incidentally, an isolated observation (cf. Paredes 1958:17; Foley 1977:46). Reporting on the "prime joy" of Mexicans in Cameron County in South Texas, a news item adds:

> The fandango is their prime joy. For days and nights they
> beat their drums and whirl in the dance. These fandangos are
> becoming so frequent they are a great curse to the country.
> The respectable class of Mexicans do not attend them
> (August 20, 1881).

But, as we shall see, despite such condemnations, both on the part of the Anglo and the "respectable" Mexican, conjunto music and its dances thrived, eventually eclipsing its chief competitors and rising to become a powerful symbolic expression of the Texas-Mexican working class.

Meanwhile, as the phonograph, the radio, and Spanish-language broadcasting became more widespread among Mexicans (both in Mexico and the United States (c.f. Gamio 1971:70; Gutiérrez and Schement, 1979), the major American record companies increased their efforts to capitalize on the diversity of talents and styles available—from accordion-*tambora-bajo sexto* combinations to vocal duets to soloists like violinist El Ciego Melquiades (see *Texas-Mexican Border Music*, vol. 11) and, finally, to more genteel groups like La Orquesta Fronteriza. Most of these groups found acceptance, since they formed part of already well-established traditions. Yet no one could have predicted in those heady days of the first recording activity what the course of tejano music would be. More specifically, no one could have known then that the commercialization of tejano music through records would sound the death knell for most styles, with only a chosen few destined to survival. That was an unforeseen cultural legacy left by the American recording industry's intervention in Texas-Mexican music.

Now, in retrospect, we can see that the dominance of the accordion, incipient in the days before commercialization, was merely hastened by that same commercialization. It was perhaps inevitable, though as I suggest below, not simply because of its commercialization: competition abounded. Yet, only vocal music, duet singing in particular, was able to hold its own—and even that was eventually appropriated by the modern conjunto. Thus, of all the early ensembles only that of the accordion, then groping for its own unique stylistic expression, was the sole survivor. An explanation for this phenomenon is a major task of this study; however, I shall approach that issue more extensively in Chapter 6. At this time I wish only to suggest that commercialization cannot adequately account for either conjunto music's push toward a standardized style or its overwhelming appeal to tejano proletarian workers. Now I will trace the beginnings of the then-fledgling style, concentrating on the most important exponents of the music.

Forerunners

Narciso Martínez has aptly been called the "father" of conjunto music (Strachwitz 1975b), but he is the last to make such claims for himself. In point of fact there were others who were popular commercially, on the radio, before and during his time. It is true that Martínez's style departed from that of his predecessors and that it laid the stylistic basis for the emergent ensemble, but at least two other accordionists, Bruno Villarreal and José Rodríguez, had recorded commercially and were well known before Martínez's debut. Martínez himself admits that he had "competitors," if not predecessors, though he is quick to point out that "no se vendieron" ("they did not sell"), at least not in comparison to his own music.

Narciso Martínez recalled for me the kind of competition that existed between early accordionists, particularly between himself and José Rodríguez. "Estaba tocando José Rodríguez cuando yo llegué, " he said ("José Rodríguez was playing when I arrived"). Rodríguez was playing at a *baile de negocio* when Martínez came up to listen in. "Al rato José me divisó" ("After a while José saw me"). " 'Ah,' dijo, 'ya me frego. Ya me robó cuatro o cinco piezas' " (" 'Oh,' he said, 'Chicho's got me now; he must have stolen four or five songs by now' ") (personal interview, August 3, 1978).

"He was right," continued Chicho. "I had snatched them from him. I was recording by then. He was recording, too, but he had not sold."

In such less than amicable ways, then, did the early musicians apparently jockey for position in the initial phase of conjunto music's development, amidst the heightened atmosphere of competition the American recording industry had evidently engendered. Friendships and rivalries coexisted. Speaking of another accordionist, Pedro Ayala, Martínez said, "Se hizo amigo mío—bueno, en aquel tiempo no me miraba bien, que digamos, porque asina es la vida" ("He eventually became my friend—well, at that time he wasn't very fond of me, shall we say, because that's the way life is"). On the other hand, Ayala himself recalled that a *compadre* of his, reportedly an excellent accordionist who had been offered an opportunity to record by an American company, recommended Ayala instead. Furthermore, he even gave Ayala one of his polkas to record as Ayala's own. Unfortunately, the talent scout sent by the company did not like Ayala's playing and he had to wait another ten years before his opportunity came.

In sum, both cooperation and jealousy—no doubt coupled with excitement—attended the efforts of Narciso Martínez and his contemporaries as they attempted to project their fledgling style, to launch it on its commercial way, as it were. Martínez "stole" musical material from others, but they in turn exploited his. Indeed, after

1935, when Martínez's style became the standard-bearer, the others began to turn more and more to him for stylistic direction, if not for repertory. Pedro Ayala, for one, acknowledged Martínez's leadership: "Que podía yo tocar? Tocaba nomás a como tocaba Narciso Martínez" ("What could I play? I merely played like Narciso Martínez did").

But, as I have pointed out, Narciso Martínez was not the first on the new musical scene. Bruno Villarreal arrived first. "Bruno Villarreal, *El Azote del Valle* (The Scourge from the Valley)," wrote Strachwitz, "is today remembered by people as far north as Amarillo, Texas, playing with a tin cup attached to his piano accordion . . ." (Strachwitz 1975b). He was virtually blind. But it appears that among accordionists the first recording honor—at least with the large American companies—belongs to him. That was in 1928 (Richard Spottswood, personal communication). According to Narciso Martínez, Villarreal was born in La Grulla, a village in South Texas near the Mexican border. He played a two-row button accordion originally, but at some point in his career he switched to the piano accordion. My father remembers him in the 1930s, living on a *ranchito* three miles from Santa Rosa, at the north end of the Rio Grande Valley, and walking every day into town—half blind as he was—to play his accordion for whatever money was offered. At times he also hired out to play at *bailes de negocio* or other kinds of celebrations. According to my father, he was never as popular as "Chicho" Martínez (personal interview).

José Rodríguez and Jesús Casiano, the latter known as *El Gallito* (The Little Rooster), were also early contenders. The former began recording sometime in the early 1930s, while the latter made his debut about the same time as Narciso Martínez. Both Rodríguez and Casiano, as well as Bruno Villarreal, hark back to an earlier period in their style. While showing some affinities to the style of Martínez, their heavy use of the left-hand, bass-and-chord elements on the accordion sets them apart from the latter, who began almost immediately to deemphasize that side of the accordion in favor of more marked and better articulated melody lines at the treble end.[2]

Again it is necessary, in order to delineate the various stages that conjunto music underwent, to point out that Villarreal, Casiano, and Rodríguez—and others probably, though I have no additional samples—besides employing the different technique from Martínez just described, also made extensive use of the *tambora de rancho*, even after 1930. Additionally, even the *bajo sexto* technique, with its lack of the heavily emphasized, well-defined strum of later *bajo* players, contributed to this difference. In its totality the mode of performance of these forerunners of modern conjunto music may thus be considered a kind of "pre-conjunto" style.

The "Father" of Conjunto Music

Unquestionably, of all the early names that of Narciso Martínez is the best remembered in conjunto music. He was certainly the most prolific and most popular accordionist after 1935. More importantly from our viewpoint, Martínez, in collaboration with *bajo sexto* player Santiago Almeida, was probably responsible for establishing the accordion and the *bajo sexto* as the most basic constituents in the then-embryonic conjunto style. As indicated, Martínez's technique differed considerably from that of his chief competitors. This difference was demonstrated in several ways. First, Martínez's articulation was definitely more marcato, generally, than that of Rodríguez, Villarreal, and Casiano. It had what some people have referred to as a "snappier" quality. The difference was further accentuated by Martínez's increasing disregard for the bass-chord accompaniment elements on the accordion, whose presence in the technique of Rodríguez and the others created a drone-like effect. Instead, Martínez let the very capable Almeida provide the needed accompaniment on the *bajo sexto*, a practice that allowed the latter complete freedom to display the unique qualities of that instrument. The *bajo* was not new to the accordion ensemble, of course, but in the past it had had to compete with the bass-chord elements on the accordion itself, an arrangement that masked the *bajo's* peculiar sonority.[3]

Narciso Martínez was born on October 29, 1911, in Reynosa, Tamaulipas, Mexico, across the border from McAllen, Texas, on the lower Rio Grande.[4] He was brought to the United States that same year and has lived in Texas since then. Interestingly, when I asked if he had ever become a naturalized American citizen, Martínez, like so many of his compatriots, revealed that he had not. "No me he hecho ciudadano porque no he querido," he said ("I have not become a naturalized citizen because I have chosen not to"). Shortly afterward, however, he said he considered himself a *mexico-americano*, though stressing his Mexican descent: "No puedo ser *americano*, porque mi papá y mamá eran mexicanos" ("I cannot consider myself American [i.e., unhyphenated], because my father and mother were Mexicans"). A distinctive allegiance to his Mexican heritage, then, forms part of Martínez's conception of his identity, even though for all practical purposes, as he pointed out, he is an American citizen.

Martínez's ethnic allegiance was not unusual; it was shared by all of the conjunto musicians I had contact with, even those who were native American citizens.

Like many conjunto musicians before and after him, Narciso Martínez was raised in a rural, proletarian setting. (There were exceptions; e.g., Santiago Jiménez was raised in San Antonio.) As a youngster his family moved about, working in the fields around the Corpus Christi area, in tiny settlements like Bishop, Chapman Ranch, and Rivera. Martínez received almost no schooling, because the kinds of conditions he and his contemporaries experienced were not conducive to the formal education of children, and he was no exception. In point of fact, there is no longer any doubt that these conditions of poverty, transience, and illiteracy were abetted by the Anglo-Texan majority. Ample literature exists to verify this state of affairs (cf. Taylor 1934; Montejano 1979; Reisler 1976); Weinberg's statements succinctly summarize the situation:

> By 1920 a pattern had emerged for Texas as a whole: separate schooling in greatly inferior facilities for Mexican-American students; deliberate refusal to make educational use of the child's cultural heritage, especially the Spanish language; and a shorter school year (1977:145).

The attitudes of the Anglos are graphically illustrated by the statements of a superintendent interviewed by Herschel T. Manuel in the 1930s:

> Most of our Mexicans are of the lower class. They transplant onions, harvest them, etc. The less they know about everything else, the better contented they are. You have doubtless heard that ignorance is bliss; it seems that it is so when one has to transplant onions . . . If a man has very much sense or education either, he is not going to stick to this kind of work. So you see, it is up to the white population to keep the Mexican on his knees in an onion patch . . . This does not mix well with education (Weinberg 1977:146).

Narciso Martínez displayed no bitterness about his lack of education. "Tuve muy poca educación, casi no tuve escuela," he said simply ("I had very little schooling; I had almost no education"). "En aquellos tiempos no había la oportunidad que hay horita," he added ("In those times there wasn't the opportunity that there is now"). And, in an ironic twist he commented, "Conozco las escuelas porque he tocado en ellas" ("I'm familiar with schools because I have played for them").

Having received no formal education to speak of, Martínez says he reads and writes very little, and he speaks almost no English. At least partly as a result of this (outright exclusion of Mexicans is another reason), his opportunities in the American labor market have been severely restricted. On his work history Martínez said, "He sido troquero, he trabajado en la labor con la pala, he manejado tractor" ("I have driven trucks, worked in the fields with a shovel, driven tractors"). All of these are the kinds of labor that traditionally have been available, sometimes exclusively, to the men of don Narciso's race and class. Possibly his most rewarding work experience (other than his music) was his stint with the Gladys Porter Zoo in Brownsville, where he fed the animals. Now retired from that, he proudly emphasizes, "Claro que quedé bien con ellos. Trabajé tres años siete meses" ("Of course I left a good impression. I worked for them for three years and seven months").

And of course there has been, since 1927, his other career, his music. Here is how he recalled his initiation:

Yo empecé a tocar la acordeón como el 1927, '28 . . . a tocar acordeones muy malas, porque no podía uno comprar acordeones buenas—puras mugritas de una linea, y luego de dos, pero—bueno, puro mugrero. El único que tocaba acordeón primero que yo era mi hermano Santos, el hermano mío, tocaba poquito la acordeón.[5] No era gran cosa, pero tocaba. Y allí comencé yo con ellos a instruirme; ya para'l 1928 ya empecé a tocar—en bailecitos con acordeón doble, pero puro mugrero, como te digo. Mi primer acordeón nueva la vine comprando como el 1930, en Kinisvil [Kingsville]. Era Hohner.

(I started playing the accordion around 1927, '28 . . . playing on very bad accordions, because one couldn't buy good accordions—nothing but little pieces of junk, with one row, and then two, but—well, nothing but junk. The only one who played accordion before me was my brother, Santos, my brother—he played the accordion a bit. He was no great thing, but he played. And that's where I started to instruct myself, with them; by 1928 I already began to play—in little dances with a double accordion, but nothing but junk, as I told you. I didn't get to buy my first new accordion until about 1930, in Kingsville. It was a Hohner.)

By 1935 Martínez had completely abandoned the antiquated one-row model and had mastered the considerably more flexible two-row button accordion. It was at this time that he and *bajo sexto* player Santiago Almeida began their highly fruitful collaboration. The pair's talents soon became known to the agents of Bluebird (through the efforts of Brownsville furniture dealer Enrique Valentín), who in that same year brought them to San Antonio for a trial recording session. The results were impressive: the original recording, a polka with the title of "La Chicharronera" (flipside: "El Troncanal," a schottische), became an immediate success, and thereafter Bluebird had him in for what became regular, multiple-recording sessions. For example, in one such session, on October 21, 1936, Martínez and Almeida recorded twenty titles (Richard Spottswood, personal communication), surely an unheard-of feat by today's recording standards, where musicians and technicians spend endless hours fastidiously adding and deleting material from a single number on multitrack tapes that can cover up any technical errors.

Martínez recorded prolifically for Bluebird between the years 1935 and 1940. Besides polkas like "La Chicharronera" other popular favorites covered the gamut of musical genres popular in those days: redowas (*vals bajitos*), schottisches, waltzes (*valses altos*), *huapangos*, and even a few mazurkas. The majority of these tunes were Martínez's own compositions, to which we may add a few that he pirated from other musicians (as he admitted). They were, consequently, new materials, though wrought upon traditional forms. The tunes bore titles that strongly evoke the folk ambience from which they sprang. There were *huapangos* with titles like "El Relámpago" ("The Lightning") and "El Tecolote" ("The Owl"); redowas such as "El Zurco" ("The Row") and "El Barrilito" ("The Little Barrel"); and schottisches like "El Troncanal" ("The Tree Stumps"), "El Senderito" ("The Little Trail"), and "El Arbolito" ("The Little Tree"). But by far the most popular of Martínez's compositions were the polkas, at that time rapidly becoming the hallmark of the unfolding conjunto style of music. These, likewise, carried titles strongly suggestive of Martínez's cultural background: "La Parrita" ("The Little Grapevine"), "La Polvadera" ("The Dustcloud"), "Los Coyotes," and many others.

By Martínez's own estimates, over 90 percent of his recordings of this period were instrumental music, as opposed to the vocal music recordings popularized by duos like Gaytán y Cantú. This was so because Martínez considered himself an accordionist above all, and more specifically a dance music performer. Besides, as I mentioned earlier, dance music, especially at the *bailes buenos* (as Pedro Ayala once called them) that "decent" people attended, was, in accordance with public dictate, restricted to instrumental pieces. Thus, although Martínez's music became extremely popular as a result of its commercial distribution, he nonetheless continued to compose instrumental music almost exclusively. Moreover, as he admitted, it was much easier for him to compose music for his accordion. Fitting lyrics to his tunes involved twice the effort—hardly worth his time, since they were destined for dance performances anyway.

Meanwhile, with the success of "La Chicharronera" and other subsequent recordings, Martínez's popularity began to soar. He became a household word, according to most people whose memories extend to that period. He was given the epithet of "El Huracán del Valle" by a record promoter, a name that was almost synonymous with accordion music and a recognition on the part of the people that he was, indeed, a pathfinder. (The epithet practice had, of course, been established by Bruno Villarreal, "El Azote del Valle.") With popularity came demand. Martínez played at hundreds of weddings "de sol a sol" ("from sundown to sunup"), as he recalled, as well as other domestic celebrations. He also played for *fiestas patrias* and other kinds of public celebrations, not the least of which was the notorious *baile de negocio.*

It almost seems contradictory that a performer of Narciso Martínez's stature would be compelled to play for such low-status affairs as the *baile de negocio.* This can be explained on several grounds. First, it is undeniable that while major recording companies must have gained at least adequate returns on their investment in Chicano musical talent, the musicians themselves were totally excluded from any financial share (except for the token recording fee). Thus, their economic livelihood depended on whatever performances they could garner, regardless of working conditions. This was particularly true in the 1930s. Bruno Villarreal, for example, besides being almost totally blind, was quite destitute, often playing on street corners to eke out a living. Martínez's fate was hardly better, and neither was that of Lolo Cavazos, Santiago Jiménez, or any of their contemporaries.

Secondly, the early conjunto musicians' constituency was certainly in no position to enrich its artists, especially during the Depression. They might buy their recordings, but, as mentioned, this was of no benefit to the performers. In short, the musicians played and earned just enough to satisfy a few—not all—of their economic needs. There simply were not enough dances during a week for full-time employment: Saturday and Sunday were practically the only days for celebrating. That is why most of the early musicians resorted to other kinds of work—in the fields, for the most part.

Lastly, conjunto musicians' stature, even that of outstanding ones like Martínez, was a very relative thing in those days. Regardless of his fame, a conjunto musician was never accorded "stardom" privileges of the kind mass-market American and Mexican performers were and are accustomed to. Rather, while conjunto musicians were respected and admired for their special talent, they were considered mere entertainers who were there to fulfill a social function. The musician played his music, the dancers danced: no applause, no adulation. If his music was considered good, they would come back to dance to it another time. If not, someone else was brought in. It is true that in later years, notably after 1960, highly popular groups like El Conjunto Bernal and Ramón Ayala (one of the few to attain near-idol status) commanded handsome fees for their music, but in the first days of commercial conjunto music, at least in the tejano circuit, the entertainment industry was neither commercialized nor glamorized enough to offer its practitioners financial security or privileged status.

Narciso Martínez may have made little money, but he earned many followers. He remained popular in the 1940s, and he was well known even in the 1950s. In fact, he was one of the first conjunto musicians to begin touring beyond the state of Texas—to New Mexico, Arizona, and California. This was in 1952. Meanwhile, during the war Martínez did not record commercially, though his music's popularity did not diminish. Here it is worth mentioning that unlike mass-market music, whose individual productions enjoy short-lived popularity, many conjunto tunes are absorbed into an expanding corpus that is tapped repeatedly by many musicians over the years. They become, in short, part of a folk tradition. This was the case with many of Martínez's compositions.

Shortly after the war, when Armando Marroquín and Paco Betancourt founded Ideal Records, Martínez was immediately hired to record his music, but at this time he also became a house accordionist of sorts, providing the background music for many of the singers that the young company signed up in the ensuing years.[6] Martínez continued to record for Ideal for several years, very much in the same style of his prewar years. But by that time modern conjunto music, which he had been so instrumental in founding, was about to launch a new phase.

Santiago Jiménez: El Flaco de San Antonio

Of all Narciso Martínez's contemporaries perhaps only Santiago Jiménez, "El Flaco" ("The Skinny One"), as he was nicknamed, approached the former's reputation. Jiménez was born and raised in San Antonio, in a barrio known as "La Piedrera" (from *pedrera*—a quarry).[7] He began his recording activities in the same city in 1936. His first recording featured two polkas, "Dices Pescao" [sic] ("Says You, Fish") and "Dispensa el Arrempujón" ("Excuse the Shove") (See Appendix B, no. 4). He is best remembered, however, for his polkas "La Piedrera" and "Viva Seguín."

Like most accordionists of his time, Jiménez was undoubtedly influenced to some extent by Narciso Martínez. His first polkas, for example, exhibit the stylistic features of the earlier accordionists, with their emphasis on the bass end of the accordion. Yet by 1942, when he recorded "Viva Seguín," he too had virtually abandoned that style of playing. Nonetheless, Jiménez retained what we may describe as a "softer," more legato mode of articulation than Martínez's decidedly marcato style. Moreover, he was never the rapid-fire technician that Martínez was, opting instead for compositions with fewer sixteenth-note patterns. As he himself said, "Narciso tenía mucho más dedos para executar la acordeón; executaba muy a prisa" ("Narciso had a lot faster fingers to execute on the accordion; he executed very rapidly"). Additionally, to this day Jiménez prefers to play without a drummer, and he has remained loyal to the two-row accordion that his early contemporaries used.

Jiménez does hold one notable distinction: He was the first to incorporate the contrabass, or *tololoche*, as tejanos called it, into the conjunto. This he did on his very first recording. Given the tenuous organization of the accordion ensemble at that time, this was no trivial accomplishment, since it anticipated the trends of a more mature conjunto style by at least ten years. However, Jiménez's innovation had no impact on other conjuntos at the time. As indicated, the *tololoche* did not become a standard feature of conjunto music until the late 1940s. It was, however, a short-lived member of the conjunto: By the late 1950s it had for the most part been replaced by the electric bass.

It is worthwhile at this point to compare the life and career of Santiago Jiménez with that of Narciso Martínez, because the two provide interesting parallels and divergences. The first parallel lies, of course, in their socioeconomic background. They were both raised in the essential poverty of the tejano worker, though Jiménez did acquire a minimal education, advancing as far as the fifth grade. "Llegué nomás al cinco grado," he said, "porque en ese tiempo mi padre vivía enfermo, mistiaba yo mucha escuela, y ya no pudimos hacerla, nomás de ponerme a trabajar. Yo comencé a trabajar muy chico" ("I made it only to the fifth grade, because my father was always sick, and I used to miss a lot of school; we weren't able to make it any more, so nothing to do but to start working. I started to work when I was very young"].

There was, however, one occupational difference between Jiménez and Martínez, due presumably to their different upbringing—the one rural, the other urban. Unlike Martínez, who worked almost exclusively in agriculture, Jiménez, as he put it, "siempre le tiré a los trabajos de las escuelas, de janitor, porque era muy seguro" ("I always tried for jobs in the schools, as janitor, because that was very secure"). Fully aware of his shortcomings, Jiménez continued:

> Yo no podía la mera verdad desempeñar un trabajo más alto, pero hice mi vivir muy bién así, antes de comenzar a tocar. Después empecé la música y le revolvía el trabajo con la música, y así es como empezamos a vivir un poco más desahogados. (In all truth, I couldn't perform at a higher job, but I managed to live very well that way, before beginning to play. Later I started in the music and I mixed the job with the music, and that is how we began to live a little more comfortably.)

Then, in a manner both poignant and succinct, Jiménez summarized his feelings about the poverty that surrounded the Mexicans in his youth:

> Todos eramos muy pobres . . . En ese tiempo no había mucho—los americanos la mera verdad siempre han visto poco mal al mexicano. No le daban chanza de aprender algunas cosas. Les daban nomás hasta cierto tiempo de escuela. Cuando miraban ellos que iba uno aumentado más pa' arriba, no faltaba quien hablara mal, y lo aplacaban a uno, y uno como no sabía muy bien defenderse, pos, este—Es lo que le hecho yo la culpa, que no le daban a uno chanza de aprender más. Ellos tenían sus buenas escuelas, y el mexicano siempre iba a las escuelas mas pobres . . . Hasta que no empezaron los mexicanos a comprender que—a defenderse, verdad . . .
> (We were all very poor . . . At that time there weren't many—to be honest with you, the Americans have always looked down on the Mexican. They wouldn't give him a chance to learn certain things. They allowed him only so much education. When they saw that we were making gains upward, there was always someone to badmouth you, and then they would shove you back down again. And, since we didn't really know how to defend ourselves, well—that's

where I put the blame, in that they wouldn't give us a chance
to learn more. They had their nice schools, and the Mexican
always went to the poorest school . . . until the Mexicans
began to realize that—to defend themselves, you see . . .)

In this way, nearly fifty years later and from a Mexican's viewpoint,
don Santiago Jiménez corroborated what the school superintendent
had once told Herschel T. Manuel about the Anglo-Texan's intention to keep the Mexican illiterate and "on his knees in an onion
patch."

An interesting difference between Jiménez and Martínez and the
environments they represented may also be discerned in the
former's ignorance of the *baile de regalo* and *funciones*. This does
not mean these did not exist in San Antonio, perhaps at an earlier
time, but, according to Jiménez, the *baile de regalo* was not common in San Antonio when he began playing, though the *baile de
negocio* was. Additionally, evidently from early on a more commercial approach to dancing prevailed in the city; according to
Jiménez, by the late 1930s twenty cents to a quarter was charged
men for admission to public dances. At least in South Texas, this
practice seems not to have taken hold until the war years or after.
Lastly, one more difference seems to have distinguished San Antonio music from that of South Texas: Apparently true to its
designation, *la tambora de rancho* was not to be seen in urban San
Antonio by the time Jiménez became musically active. At least he
is not familiar with it.

Oddly enough, while Martínez and Pedro Ayala were familiar
with and even played American music (e.g., "Nix Blues"), Jiménez's
comments were that "en ese tiempo la gente de mi camada no ponía
mucha atención a las piezas americanas" ("at that time the people
my age didn't pay much attention to American pieces"). I do not
know why this was so. Since San Antonio was a thoroughly urbanized American city in the 1930s, we would expect Jiménez and
his colleagues to be at least as "acculturated" musically as Martínez
and Ayala, who were much farther removed from mainstream
American life and music. I would suggest, however, that Jiménez's
contact with American society—at much closer range than that of
someone from the border area—was unrewarding enough (witness
his comments above) to foster an even stronger attitude of cultural
resistance. This should not surprise us, since, as Landolt observed,
"Until World War II, San Antonio's Mexican Americans were
treated as second-class citizens . . . restricted to the West Side
because of restricted [housing] covenants" (1976:349). In any case,

generally speaking conjuntos have never subscribed appreciably to American music—a fact that attests to the ethnic character of the music and musicians.

Jiménez began to play accordion when he was eight years old. His father, a native of Eagle Pass, Texas, was an accordionist who played on a one-row model. When he saw little Santiago begin to show some promise on the instrument, he bought him a two-row accordion. The young Jiménez began playing for local dances in the early 1930s. Somewhat in the manner of Martínez, don Santiago at first claimed that he had created his own unique style, without the benefit of previous models, save perhaps that of his father. This is perhaps understandable and even at least partly true, but, as he acknowledged later, when it came to basic style his was very much like that of all the early musicians, as opposed to that of the next generation. As he put it, "Al final casi todo viene a la misma cosa . . . al estilo ranchero" ("In the end it all comes to the same thing . . . the ranchero style").

When Jiménez produced his first record in 1936, it was for the Decca label, for which he recorded a total of three. The following year he switched to the Mexican Victor, because, as he stated, the fee they offered per recording increased from the twenty-one dollars he received from Decca to, for him, an astronomical seventy-five dollars. He recorded twelve records for Victor, most of which were well received. Some, like "Viva Seguín," became extremely popular. At this time, in the late 1930s, Jiménez also became a regular performer on a Spanish-language radio program in San Antonio which aired under the evocative title of "La Hora Anáhuac." After the war don Santiago recorded for a California label, Imperial, and then shortly afterward for Globe, a local company.

In the late 1960s Jiménez moved from San Antonio to Dallas and lived there for several years, during which time he was for the most part inactive as a musician. He was working full time as a school janitor. He moved back to San Antonio in 1977 and recently began to play regularly once more, mostly in restaurant bars where older people, especially, come to listen to his music. Thus, like Martínez he remains active in the 1980s, but unlike Martínez, who once toured widely throughout the Southwest (and still does, occasionally, though mainly as an ethnic attraction in American folk festivals), Jiménez, as he always has, confines his playing to San Antonio. And lastly, in a more fundamental way than Martínez, Jiménez has remained faithful to the style of playing that made him popular: To this day he continues to use the two-row button accordion, accompanied only by a *bajo sexto* and bass (a *tololoche*, if he can find one, though these days he has had to resort increasingly to the electric bass, since *tololoche* players are rapidly disappearing).

Lolo Cavazos, Pedro Ayala, and Others

Despite the enormous popularity of Narciso Martínez and, to a lesser extent, Santiago Jiménez, Jesús Casiano, and others, conjunto music as developed on both sides of the border in its early days was a collective folk phenomenon. A consensus was continously being worked out between performers and the public that sustained them. All, performers and audience alike, were working-class folk who shared a strong sense of ethnic and, to a certain extent, class consciousness.[8] The musical consensus was negotiated through the intervention of "tradition"—that is, a body of musical ideas shared by performers and audience. These ideas extended into the past, antedating the commercialization of the music, and were perceived as constituting the framework for present and future innovations. In recognizing the collective and consensual nature of conjunto music, we should be aware of the fact that many anonymous musicians surely contributed to the propagation of the emergent style. It is, however, simply impossible for me to account for all the contributions that these nameless artists undoubtedly made.

Thus, while Martínez and Jiménez justifiably point to their successful innovations, it is well to recall Jiménez's caveat: "In the end everything comes down to the same thing," i.e., everyone was engaged in a common artistic endeavor. Others borrowed from Martínez, but he drew from the creativity of others as well (recall his run-in with José Rodríguez). Pedro Ayala was perhaps the most candid in acknowledging the contributions of his fellow accordionists, particularly those who are not generally remembered. While he at first attributed his stylistic development to his own initiative (as did Martínez and Jiménez), in later interviews he freely admitted the impact of other musicians—both in a general way and on his own style. "Hubo muchos músicos," ("There were many musicians"), he said. There were performers like Fidencio Alaniz, Manuel Rodríguez, Juan López, and Enrique Vela, the latter two "buenos músicos," as Narciso Martínez himself admitted. And there was Arnulfo Olivo, "buen gallo para tocar" ("a 'class' musician"), as Pedro Ayala put it, as well as Chon Alaniz, who, according to Ayala, "tocaba tan bonito que se me quedó todo le que él tocaba" ("played so well that everything he played stayed with me"). Finally, of Juan López, Martínez said, "Juan era la gran cosa"

("Juan was the real thing"), but just as important, "todos tocábamos en el mismo estilo"—they all shared the same basic style.

It was in this manner, through a collective effort on the part of the musicians—with their public probably approving some changes and rejecting others—that the style began to gain acceptance at the same time that it was changing. Among those musicians who distinguished themselves must be included the unheralded Lolo Cavazos. Although none of the musicians I had contact with attributed any special signficance to the man, the few recordings that were available impressed me for their generally clean execution and inventiveness. In a retrospective analysis of the then-embryonic style he surely deserves recognition. While clearly in the model of Narciso Martínez, the technique in some of his recordings nevertheless adumbrates the style of the next generation of musicians.

Cavazos was born on January 5, 1906 (Strachwitz 1975b). Now deceased, he came from El Capote, a village near Reynosa, according to Narciso Martínez. He was apparently extremely poor. Martínez remembers him as a "good friend" who could not even afford to buy his own accordion. "Yo le facilitaba acordeones a él pa' que tocara," said Martínez, "porque afortunadamente yo tenía, y el no tenía" ("I used to let him have accordions so that he could play, because fortunately I had them, and he didn't"). Sometime during his youth Cavazos moved to San Diego, Texas, where he launched his recording career. In the 1930s he recorded for Okeh Records (Columbia), and, while I do not know the course of his career during the 1940s, Armando Marroquín of Ideal Records told me that in the 1950s he had worked for his company.

An adequate discussion of the first generation of modern conjunto musicians ought to include the name of Pedro Ayala, "El Monarca del Acordeón." Although, as I have indicated, his recording debut came about rather late, in 1947, Ayala rightfully belongs to the first generation of musicians, if for no other reason than his age. While he arrived late on the commercial scene, he had been involved musically since the late 1920s, when Martínez, Casiano, and the others of that generation launched their careers. But perhaps more importantly, by 1947 Ayala's style, more than anyone else's from his generation, clearly presaged the changes that were about to propel conjunto music into its final stage. Ayala may therefore be considered a transitional artist who shared much with his older contemporaries but who also pointed toward new stylistic trends crystallizing in the late 1940s.

Ayala was born in 1911 in General Terán, Nuevo León, some one hundred miles southwest of Reynosa (personal interviews,

September 5, 1978; November 11, 1978). He was brought to the United States when he was eight years old. Like Narciso Martínez, Ayala is an uneducated farm laborer. Despite their poverty the Ayalas were a musical family who apparently always had in their possession an assortment of instruments. For example, Ayala's father kept a clarinet and an accordion, both of which he played professionally (for pay), according to Ayala. An older sister played the violin, one brother played accordion, and another the guitar. In this environment it is perhaps not surprising that from an early age Ayala himself was drawn toward music. He tried his hand at all of the available instruments, apparently becoming rather adept at all of them, though, of course, without benefit of formal instruction. Ayala even learned how to play the *tambora*, which he recalls was the first instrument he played publicly—as accompaniment for his father's clarinet at a *baile de regalo*. He was then ten years old.

By the time he was fourteen, Ayala had begun to play the two-row button accordion, an instrument he admits he was especially fond of. At this time he was also playing guitar (Ayala never played the *bajo sexto*) with one of his favorite accordionists, the aforementioned Chon Alaniz. For a short time in the early 1930s he also played guitar with an orquesta, but it was then that his musical career was interrupted by the untimely death of a brother—just as he was beginning to feel competent enough to try his hand professionally on the accordion. However, after his brother's death his aggrieved mother decreed that there would no more music in the house. It was not until three or four years later, at the age of twenty-four, that Ayala began to play again. This time he concentrated on the accordion.

Don Pedro actually had an opportunity to record in the 1930s, when a talent scout from one of the American record companies came around to hear him play. The company representative had actually intended to enlist accordionist Arnulfo Olivo, a *compadre* of Ayala's, but he demurred and recommended the latter instead. But, as Ayala said, "Yo, pos, apenas estaba comenzando" ("I was barely beginning"), and, unfortunately for him, the agent insisted on Olivo. Neither man got the opportunity. It was thus not until 1947 that Ayala was given his first chance to record, though he continued to play locally throughout the intervening years, mostly in *bailes de negocio*. In 1947 he recorded his first polkas, "La Burrita" and "La Pajarera," as well as several others with Mira, a newly established record company in McAllen, Texas. Owned by a young entrepreneur by the name of Arnaldo Ramírez, the company was soon renamed Falcón, under which label it eventually became the largest and most successful Chicano recording company ever.

As mentioned, Ayala's style of playing evinced many of the characteristics of his younger successors, some of whom were then mere novices, like Valerio Longoria and Tony de la Rosa. Like Martínez's style, Ayala's may be described as "snappy," his polkas featuring fast sixteenth-note fingerings, but there is in Ayala's first recordings an even more marcato technique than that of Martínez's, closer in style to that of the men who followed. Additionally, Ayala was the first accordionist since Santiago Jiménez to add the contrabass in his recordings. As I mentioned, the latter was the first to attempt that, but no one else had followed his example. Now, with Pedro Ayala's reintroduction, it rapidly took hold, and after 1948 most of the recordings began to feature a three-instrument ensemble: accordion, *bajo sexto* (sometimes guitar), and *tololoche* (see Appendix C, no. 5).[9]

Both Ayala and Narciso Martínez, in cooperation with orquesta leaders Eugenio Gutiérrez and Beto Villa respectively, were responsible for another innovation in conjunto music, although, while eminently popular, this innovation did not produce any lasting results. Sometime in 1948 Ayala and saxophonist Eugenio Gutiérrez, both of whom worked for Falcón, joined their talents to record a polka, "El Naranjal," with guitar and *tololoche* accompaniment. Whether it was the novel combination, the catchy tune, or both is hard to determine, but the recording was an instant success. I recall that it was constantly requested on radio programs, and it soon became part of the standard repertory of most dance groups—conjunto and orquestas. However, for unexplainable reasons, Ayala and Gutiérrez never went back for a repeat performance, though we may suspect that the reason for this involved matters of musical territoriality: Gutiérrez's orquesta was coming into its own at that time, and modern orquestas like Gutiérrez's were now making conscious attempts to establish their own audience. (This audience in fact existed and was, moreover, decidedly more Americanized and less proletarian, at least in ideology, than that of conjunto music.)

Meanwhile, Falcón's rival, Ideal Records, countered with their own alto saxophone-accordion combination in the persons of none other than Narciso Martínez and Beto Villa, who more than anyone else was responsible for the resurgence of orquesta music after World War II, though in a much more modern guise than its prewar counterparts. In 1948, under the prodding of Ideal co-owner Armando Marroquín, Martínez and Villa joined forces to record "Rosita Vals," an extraordinarily popular piece that probably set a sales record for the time. According to Marroquín the record sold some 60,000 copies, a feat he admits they were never able to duplicate (personal interview, January 31, 1980). Unlike Ayala and Gutiérrez, Martínez and Villa teamed up for a number of recordings. Most of these were in the polka-*vals* tradition, but there were a few that were nothing short of amazing—for example, "San Antonio Rose," which featured a highly sophisticated clarinet solo by a young Henry Cuesta (later of Lawrence Welk fame), juxtaposed against don Narciso's game but awkward attempts at improvisation. Perhaps nowhere else was Marroquín's claim that "Villa traía de todo—'high class' y ranchero" ("Villa had everything— 'high class' and ranchero") better demonstrated than in these recordings with Narciso Martínez.

The addition of Narciso Martínez's accordion to Beto Villa's orquesta, as, for example, in "San Antonio Rose," requires some comment, as do their more conjunto-oriented efforts such as "Rosita Vals." This comment applies also to the Ayala-Gutiérrez combination. First, as I suggested in the introduction, while orquesta and conjunto shared a common ethnic ambience, the two ensembles nevertheless represented two distinct socioesthetic horizons. To a significant extent each had its own audience. Thus, the incorporation of the alto saxophone into the conjunto or of the accordion into the orquesta did not signal a change whereby the two ensembles would merge into one. Of course, such experimentations were not without significance either, as I shall shortly explain. But while the alto saxophone-conjunto and accordion-orquesta experiments proved, de facto, the presence of a musico-cultural overlap (as witnessed in the overwhelming popularity of "Rosita Vals" and "El Naranjal"), these experiments did not lead to any permanent changes.

The point is that with or without the alto saxophone, conjunto remained conjunto, and although the saxophone did add a new dimension, except for sporadic use, it never became an integral part of the ensemble.[10] In the case of orquesta the same thing happened. While the addition of Martínez's accordion expanded the musical horizon of orquesta in the direction of its sister style, it did not alter the fact that it was still Beto Villa's orquesta that people were listening to. Nonetheless—and this is the second point I wish to make—the mere attempt to unite the two ensembles at this early juncture represents an important symbolic gesture that served, in effect, to publicize the common ethnic, if not socioeconomic, provenience of the two musics. The only surprising outcome of this early union is the lack of follow-through: For nearly twenty years, despite persistent stylistic cross-borrowing, the two musics maintained a more or less rigid separation.

Meanwhile, within conjunto music's domain Pedro Ayala's record-ings of the late 1940s bring the curtain down on the first scene of conjunto's stylistic development. It was at this time that a new generation of musicians began their careers—artists such as Tony de la Rosa, Los Tres Reyes, and Valerio Longoria, to name but a few. Originally taking their cue from the older musicians, particularly Martínez and Ayala, the younger performers soon began to forge their own conception of what conjunto should strive for musically. Not surprisingly, this conception was more attuned to the social and cultural developments then taking place in Texas-Mexican society. In the next chapter I shall describe the musical changes that took place and sketch the careers of some of the musicians responsible for those changes.

Notes

1. According to Gutiérrez and Schement, the first Spanish-language broadcast took place in San Antonio in 1928. After that, "Spanish-language radio continued to grow in the Southwest, and by the late 1930s a number of stations were airing Spanish pro-grams" (1979:7).

2. See Appendix C, nos. 1 and 2, for transcribed examples of the music of Villarreal and Rodríguez, respectively.

3. See Appendix C, no. 3, for transcribed examples of Narciso Martínez's 1930s recordings that illustrate the new relationship between *bajo* and accordion.

4. Biographical information on Martínez, as well as all quotes attributed to him, are from personal interviews I had with him on August 3, 1978, August 7, 1978, November 4, 1978, and February 2, 1979.

5. Here don Narciso was obviously "forgetting" that Bruno Villarreal and José Rodríguez had begun to record before him.

6. The rise of tejano recording companies is discussed more fully in Chapter 3.

7. Biographical information on Jiménez, as well as all quotes attributed to him, are from personal interviews I had with him on April 5, 1979, and April 30, 1979.

8. Thus, it is my conviction that, despite conjunto music's commercialization, the music and its interpreters remained "organically" linked to the tejano working class, not merely as consumable commodities but as vital links in a cultural consensus that amounted to an act of resistance to American cultural hegemony. I shall expand on this point in Chapter 6.

9. See Folklyric Records, v. 24 ("The Texas-Mexican Conjunto"), for recordings of Ayala and other accordionists mentioned in this book.

10. This is not true of Mexican *norteño* groups, among whom the saxophone gained much wider acceptance, as typified by Los Gorriones del Topo Chico, a group quite popular on this side of the border as well. However, a constant flow of *norteño* workers to Texas no doubt helped in establishing the popularity of such groups on this side of the border.

3. La Nueva Generación: Stylistic Consolidation (1948-1960)

Commercial Recording after World War II

The World War II years witnessed a sharp drop in the commercial recording of Texas-Mexican music. This was due, at least in part, to the scarcity of raw materials. The most important result of this curtailed activity was the major labels' decision to discontinue permanently their operations in the Texas-Mexican music field (as well as that of Mexican music in the United States generally). Why American companies decided to withdraw is unclear, but two reasons can be suggested. First, the explosion of American popular music after the war may have provided a powerful incentive for companies like RCA and Decca to concentrate on mainstream American music to the exclusion of more marginal markets such as that of the Mexican community in the United States.[1]

Secondly, it is apparent that by the early 1940s RCA and the other major labels had begun to realize that a much more lucrative Hispanic music market lay ready for exploitation in Mexico. Actually, according to Alex Saragoza (personal communication), since 1929 RCA had been sending engineers with equipment into Mexico to record musicians there, but it was not until 1935 that the company finally established a permanent studio in Mexico City (Garrido 1974:74). Apparently, when the Mexican market finally began to bear fruit during World War II, RCA and the other major labels decided to eliminate their regional operations in the United States and turn their attention exclusively to the greater Mexican music industry.

The strategy of the American companies was evidently to concentrate on the increasingly lucrative Mexican music market, and then to promote that music throughout Latin America, as well as the United States. The strategy worked to perfection. Teaming up with

Mexican entrepreneurs like Emilio Azcárraga, RCA and Columbia, in particular, took advantage of a highly successful genre of Mexican film, the *comedia ranchera* (Saragoza 1983a). This type of film, which was the Mexican version of the American musical, had been growing in popularity since the spectacular debut of *Allá en el Rancho Grande* in 1936. By 1940 a number of *ranchera* film stars had achieved phenomenal success as recording artists as well (Saragoza 1983b). Included among these were Tito Guizar, Jorge Negrete, Pedro Vargas, and the idol of the Mexican masses, Pedro Infante. But most importantly, since Mexican movies exercised a monopoly in Mexican-movie theatres in the United States, all of these stars—and many others—were equally idolized on this side of the border, thanks to both screen and radio exposure.

Thus, as a result of major-label domination, Mexican music came to pervade Hispanic broadcasting in the United States, one result of which was to stymie the production and distribution of home-grown Chicano music, especially outside Texas. As Martín Rosales, a veteran disc jockey with experience in Texas, California, and New Mexico, told me in an interview, by executive orders Mexican music reigned supreme in radio stations everywhere in the Southwest except Texas, where on many stations conjunto music was simply too much in demand to cede its territory. It is not surprising, then, that it was in Texas where the most successful Chicano recording companies established themselves.

Whatever the ultimate reasons for the big labels' loss of interest in Chicano music—and Texas-Mexican in particular—their withdrawal certainly left a vacuum in the commercial dissemination of such music. Actually, it seems surprising that American companies, which had so assiduously nurtured the fledgling market before the war, should turn their backs on that same market at a time when demand for a long-scarce music could be expected to rise. But abandon the field they did, a move that proved to be of benefit to a few far-sighted Chicano entrepreneurs—most notably Arnaldo Ramírez of Falcón Records and partners Paco Betancourt and Armando Marroquín of Ideal Records.

Thus, soon after the departure of RCA, Columbia, and the other American labels, a number of Chicano-owned companies had appeared in Texas and elsewhere. However, I must emphasize that, unlike their well-financed American counterparts, Chicano firms were without exception operated by small-time entrepreneurs whose access to capital resources was extremely limited. Besides the ones just mentioned, others included Globe, Corona, El Zarape, and Río, to name but a few tejano labels. Due to lack of capital, the equipment and facilities of these enterprises was often outmoded and of inferior quality. In addition, a haphazard system of distribution compounded the operating problems of most of these enterprises. Consequently, most Chicano recording operations were short-lived or achieved but limited solvency, despite the fact that a public hungry for music—and with more expandable cash than during the prewar years—was eager for the appearance of the music of their favorite artists.

Nonetheless, out of the various and for the most part marginal tejano-owned companies, two managed to achieve modest commercial success in their efforts to propagate tejano music. These were the aforementioned Ideal and Falcón. The latter actually assumed its leadership position after 1960; the 1940s and 1950s belonged to Ideal. A brief sketch of its rise to prominence follows.[2]

During the war Armando Marroquín of Alice, Texas, became keenly aware of the shortage of records for the jukeboxes he operated in the various cantinas, restaurants, and other business establishments in Alice. "During the war," he told me, "records were hard to come by, especially discos pa' la música de aquí" ("records for the music from here"). Toward the end of the war, when the scarcity became particularly acute, he finally decided to buy his own *aparatito*, which recorded live performances directly on acetate masters. But the volume of records he could turn out was extremely limited, and, furthermore, as he admitted, he knew nothing about distribution. Nonetheless, convinced of the potential for profit, he produced his first records in 1946. These were recorded in his own living room—a place, incidentally, that would serve as Ideal's recording studio throughout most of the company's existence.

The first Ideal recordings featured a female duet, Carmen y Laura, the latter none other than Marroquín's own wife. What is more significant is that they were accompanied by El Huracán del Valle himself, don Narciso Martínez. The results were more than encouraging: The first 200 records sold out rapidly. Marroquín thinks he knows why: "Como no había competencia lo que sacara uno estaba en demanda" ("Since there was no competition whatever you came out with was in demand"). Seeking a wider commercial outlet, Marroquín began searching for a more efficient way to put his products on the market. First, he found a firm in Los Angeles that could mass-produce his records; then, he contacted Paco Betancourt, owner of Rio Grande Music Company of San Benito, in the Rio Grande Valley, and proposed a partnership. The latter had had some experience in record promotion as well as contact with the broadcasting industry.

With Betancourt as a partner, Marroquín and Ideal Records were now ready to expand their operations. By 1947 the recording studio in the Marroquín living room, now equipped with new microphones and one-track tape recorders, had begun to bustle with activity. Besides Carmen y Laura prominent names of prewar years, such as Lolo Cavazos and Gaytán y Cantú, recorded for Ideal. Of these Narciso Martínez was the most productive, assuming the position of house accordionist who accompanied many of the singers Ideal recorded. In addition, a host of the most popular artists of the 1950s was launched by Ideal. These included Valerio Longoria, Tony de la Rosa, Paulino Bernal, and the "father" of modern *orquesta tejana*, Beto Villa (who teamed up with Martínez on "Rosita Vals"). In short, the Marroquín house became a full-fledged music studio, where musicians shuffled in and out of recording sessions almost daily. By 1950 Ideal had become the leading producer of Chicano music in the Southwest.

Many groups and individuals, veterans of the major label days, recorded for Ideal, though by far the most predominant ones were the vocal duets and conjuntos. In fact, the duet and the conjunto soon became inseparable after the war. One group, however, was conspicuous by its absence, and that was the string orquesta. Marroquín explained it quite simply: "Vino el acordeón y tumbó a todos esos grupos" ("The accordion came and toppled all of those groups"). Certainly he, for one, saw no point in resisting what to him was an irreversible trend. Instead, Marroquín and Betancourt responded to the new currents that were then "in the air," as Marroquín put it.

As mentioned, one of these currents was the union of the vocal duet and the accordion. Actually, the combination had been tried on occasion earlier in the 1930s (see Folklyric Records, *Texas-Mexican Border Music*, vol. 4), but no doubt since the accordion was then almost exclusively associated with instrumental music, no permanent trend had ensued. Now, however, Narciso Martínez was called upon to provide instrumental background for Carmen y Laura, Gaytán y Cantú, and others. Additionally, beginning with Valerio Longoria, the new generation of conjunto musicians included one or more singers as a matter of course, as the *canción ranchera* (usually in *vals* or polka tempo) became an increasingly indispensable part of the conjunto repertory.[3]

Here I should perhaps point out that in the postwar period not only instrumental but important repertorial changes took place as well. These changes formed part of the "currents in the air" mentioned by Marroquín, currents that Ideal was instrumental in promoting. In the case of conjunto, for example, stylistic change included the virtual disappearance of some older genres like the redowa, shottische, and mazurka from the repertory. Only the polka remained as a staple in the postwar period; however, by the mid-1950s even the instrumental polka, which had hitherto featured the accordion as the lead melodic instrument, was rapidly replaced by the sung *canción ranchera*, or *canción corrida* (today often called simply *corrida*), which, as several musicians pointed out, was nothing more than a piece in tempo di polka with lyrics added.

In such pieces the accordion still played solo introductions and fill-ins, but it functioned more as an obbligato counterpart to the singing (usually duets in parallel thirds) than as an exclusively melodic instrument. All the other elements of the polka remained the same; the bass patterns and the *bajo sexto* accompaniment were identical for both polka and corrida, and, later, when the drums were incorporated into the conjunto, they too executed in like manner for both genres. Perhaps the relationship between the polka and the *canción corrida* was best explained by Emilio Ayala (Pedro Ayala's son), who said, "Una canción corrida es como una polka, pero cantada" ("A *canción corrida* is like a polka, only sung") (personal interview, September 5, 1978). Ideal was, of course, highly sensitive to all of these developments; its survival was due in no small measure to its willingness to promote them.

Ideal was responsible for launching one more of the musical trends then taking shape—namely, *orquesta tejana*. It was Marroquín who first perceived the commercial possibilities that the increasingly popular wind orquesta—modeled after the American swing bands—might hold in store. He was proven correct, of course, though initially he was not so sure. According to Marroquín, the now legendary orquesta leader Beto Villa approached him one day: "Oye, quisiera que me hicieras un disco pa' mí, pa' oirlo" ("Say, I wish you would make me a record, for myself, to hear it"). Marroquín agreed, and Villa's group—himself on alto saxophone, one brother on trumpet, another on drums, Reymundo Treviño on piano-accordion, an electric guitarist, and contrabassist—recorded two selections, "Porqué te Ries" (a *vals*) and "Las Delicias" (a polka). This was in 1946. Marroquín recalled his thoughts at the time: "Dije, 'A ver si le gusta a mi compañero Betancourt' " ("I thought, 'Let's see if my partner Betancourt likes this' "). After some reluctance on the part of Betancourt—he did not think the group was "professional" enough—200 records were finally turned out at Villa's expense. Here, in Marroquín's words, is what happened:

> Entonces la sacó—Ah! Como al mes que la comenzó a man-
> dar [Betancourt], dijo, "Oye, dile que grabe más." La estaban
> pidiendo en cantidades. Era como un conjunto; no era ni or-
> questa todavía . . . Eran nomás cinco o seis . . . chiquitito, ar-
> rancherado . . . (So then the record came out—Boy! About a
> month after he [Betancourt] started sending it out, he said,
> "Say, tell him to record some more." They were asking for it
> in bunches. It was like a conjunto; it wasn't even an or-
> questa yet . . . There were only five or six . . . real small,
> ranchero-like . . .)

Of course, Villa was hardly interested in becoming another conjunto musician. Moreover, despite his overwhelming success with
Narciso Martínez, he eventually weeded out the "folk" musicians
in his fledgling orquesta and went on to organize a group more in
line with his personal aspirations.[4] This was the highly acclaimed
Orquesta de Beto Villa, whose fame, as Marroquín said, rested on its
ability to play both "high class" and ranchero. But ultimately, the
renown Villa achieved was in no small measure due to Marroquín's
entrepreneurial acumen, his intuition for what the tejano desired.
To a considerable extent the triumph of modern conjunto was also
indebted to Marroquín and Ideal, though, by all means, the in-
debtedness worked in the other direction, too. In any case, Ideal
Records played an important role in shaping modern tejano music
by helping to establish the dominance of conjunto and orquesta over
all other types of music in Texas.

The exact role of commercializers like Ideal requires consideration, since it is critical for the arguments I will raise later to understand to what extent conjunto music owed its emergence to forces
emanating from within the working class, as a function of its own
ideology, as opposed to market forces operating from without. Thus,
it is fair to ask whether the flowering of this artistic form was a
result of commercial exploitation by manipulative profiteers, as was
surely the case with Mexican ranchera music, a distinctly capitalist-
directed form of mass entertainment. Or were there counter balanc-
ing forces operating—that is, was the music first and foremost a
creation of and for the tejano working class? I suggest that the latter
is by far a more convincing alternative.

First, however, in summing up Ideal's participation in tejano
music, let us acknowledge once for all the company's undeniable
profit motives in promoting the music. In this respect, and despite

Marroquín's assertion that Ideal paid $3,000 in royalties to the composer of the famous "Rosita Vals," it is well to remember that the company did not make it a practice to sign contracts with its artists. None of the musicians I interviewed remembered ever receiving any royalties from Ideal, except, in a few instances, for recordings of their own compositions. The unflattering remarks of Reymundo Treviño sum up succinctly the complaints of other musicians on Ideal's not uncommon attempts to evade payment: "Marroquín," he said, "no le quería pagar a nadie nada" ("Marroquín didn't want to pay anybody anything") (personal interview, March 14, 1980).

As had been the practice during the major-label days, Ideal and the other Chicano outfits paid the musicians a flat fee per recording, which was sometimes as low as $2.50 (Tony de la Rosa, personal interview). Thus, one can certainly argue that Ideal exploited its artists, just as the American companies had done before. Moreover, Ideal had one additional resource from which it profited greatly —Marroquíns own intimate knowledge of tejano music and tejanos, a knowledge that helped him make some astute judgements about a changing public taste. The decision to market Beto Villa's music is a case in point. Decisions like that one made Ideal the most profitable Chicano recording enterprise of its time.

However, we still need to clarify whether Marroquín and Ideal engineered the changes that took place in tejano music in the late 1940s or whether they simply took advantage of "currents in the air," as Marroquín described the musical atmosphere of the time. To determine this we need to take into account Marroquín's own relation—both cultural and economic—to Texas-Mexican music and the musicians he and Ideal helped launch, for that relationship not only guided the judgments the company made, but ultimately determined the role of the commercial entrepreneur in the predominance that both conjunto and orquesta attained in the musical life of the Texas-Mexicans.

It is tempting to assign to Marroquín and others in his position the status of arbiters in matters of musical choice—the power to mold public taste to conform to their product—as is clearly the case in the American (and Mexican) mass-entertainment industry. However, among Texas-Mexicans the relationship between the producer and the consumer of musical entertainment has never been so predominantly dictated by the former. To take the example at hand, Ideal was never a monopoly in the sense that American giants like RCA and Columbia have been. It was rather a small, regional distributor that witnessed a measure of growth, all of this, incidentally, in the face of powerful competition from those same companies and their Mexican subsidiaries—as well as competition from its own local rivals.

In point of fact, it is more plausible to argue that Ideal's success was due to an a priori need for a tejano music outlet than to claim that it was a result of its own artificially created and sustained demand. In other words, the cultural context for a Texas-Mexican music had long existed. Marroquín and Ideal did not impose it from above. They merely responded to the demand, though they did of course capitalize on the existing musical climate, turning it to financial advantage by providing a commercial vehicle for the music's dissemination. And this is another point to reiterate: Ideal remained essentially a regional distributor for one kind of entertainment—*música tejana*. Whether by choice or constraint (more likely the latter), its musical and economic parameters—and, hence, its power to mold public preference—were circumscribed by that regionalism. On this factor hinges much of Ideal's success—and its failure. This factor also determines whether conjunto music is to be seen as a commodity imposed on tejanos through sheer commercialization or as an outgrowth of the evolution of a working-class esthetic. I think the evidence supports the latter explanation.

We need, finally, to recognize that Marroquín himself was by no means an "outsider," dispassionately calculating profit and loss margins and interested in directing the course of tejano music solely for his economic gain. I believe that in his system of values he had as much an ideological as an economic stake in the survival of that music. Whether the desire for economic exploitation may have competed with, or even overshadowed, Marroquíns cultural allegiance is not at issue here. Of course, he and Betancourt were no philanthropists; like any would-be capitalists they sought to maximize their investments. We have but to recall that contractual rights, such as they were, were entirely in their favor. Yet beyond (if not above) Marroquín's desire for profit was his obvious commitment to musical forms that coincided with his own sense of artistry, shaped and cultivated within the confines of a strong ethnic environment.

Marroquín was a Texas-Mexican, brought up, as he said, on tejano music: "Yo desde que estaba muy chiquito me gustaba la música, los discos que habían sido recorded en los twenties ... discos de corridos como 'Benjamín Argumedo,' 'Gregorio Cortez,' 'Jacinto Treviño' " ("Ever since I was a little kid I liked music, the records made in the twenties ... *corrido* records like 'Benjamín Argumedo,' 'Gregorio Cortez,' 'Jacinto Treviño' "). We can suggest, then, that in Marroquín economic motives and cultural commitments intertwined; the former were mediated by the latter. He was an ambitious entrepreneur, but never a full-fledged capitalist, because his business horizon was limited by his cultural outlook. And both were subject to the narrow limits inherent in an ethnic, regional music market. Marroquín did make money (though hardly a fortune), but he remained rooted in a tejano cultural network, with all the contradictions and limitations that a culture forged in the crucible of interethnic conflict imposes.

Ideal eventually fell into decline. Other competitors, who offered more money (particularly Falcón), drew the established artists away, and Ideal apparently did nothing to attract new ones. In the end the Betancourt-Marroquín partnership dissolved, furthering the company's decline. Marroquín started his own label, Nopal, but it never approached Ideal's scale of activity. The company's final demise came when Betancourt died, leaving the field to a surging Falcón Records.

Today Marroquín still operates Nopal Records out of a small, two-room frame house that he converted into a studio. But these days he treats recording more as a hobby than as a business, as he put it. He has no major recording artists. And he still lives in the same house-turned-studio that was once frequented by the best Texas-Mexican musical talent. It is in a modest neighborhood—not quite a barrio perhaps, but unpretentious by middle-class standards.

"Los Músicos Modernos"

While Narciso Martínez, Santiago Jiménez, and a few of the older accordionists continued to record for Ideal, Falcón, and other Texas-Mexican companies after the war, with the exception of the first two (and the newly introduced Pedro Ayala), the accordionists from yesteryear quickly faded from the public eye at the close of the 1940s. Changes taking place at the hands of a younger generation of musicians began to resonate strongly in the musical consciousness of a working class tejano society that itself was undergoing profound change. Old faces, such as those of Lolo Cavazos and Jesús Casiano, unwilling or unable to meet new musical challenges, all but disappeared from the commercial market after the war. One of the saddest cases was undoubtedly that of Bruno Villarreal, who was reduced to near beggary until sympathetic relatives finally took him in—a grimly ironic fate for the man who was the true "father" of recorded accordion music. Thus, the forging of the final, mature phase of conjunto music was left to "los músicos modernos", as Martínez called them, men like Valerio Longoria, Tony de la Rosa, Paulino Bernal, and Rubén Vela, to name a few of the most outstanding.

Before introducing these musicians I would like to make one or two general observations about the state of tejano music in the years following World War II. First, as I have already pointed out tejano recording activity was taken over almost exclusively by Chicano operators, most of whom remained small-scale distributors. The two exceptions were Ideal and Falcón, of which the latter became a relatively successful capitalist enterprise later in the 1960s. Secondly, with the resurgence of recording activity after the war, coupled with the modestly increasing spending power of the tejano worker, a new phenomenon appeared: the public, paid-admission ballroom dance.

The ballroom dance had actually made its appearance earlier during the war, but it did not become a permanent feature of Texas-Mexican musical culture until 1948 (Martínez and Ayala, personal interviews).[5] Thereafter, these public dances—at which first men, then in later years women, paid an admission fee—became an important forum for the commercial dissemination of both conjunto and orquesta music. As these dances gained popularity both in Texas and in the rest of the Southwest (and beyond), more and more of the new generation of musicians—that is, the most popular ones—turned to music as a full-time profession. The professionalization of conjunto musicians signaled an important socioeconomic change for them and, to some extent, for their clientele as well.

At the same time some of these musicians achieved the status of celebrities of a sort, in that they were able to attract packed houses wherever they played. It was during this period that a network of public ballroom empresarios sprang up throughout Texas, Arizona, California, and the Midwest. This network came into being as a result of the efforts of record promoters (many of whom, like Armando Marroquín, were also dance promoters) to market conjunto (and orquesta) groups, but it coincided with the institutionalization of the public dance among Mexicans in the United States generally, as this type of activity acquired a strong symbolic role in the changing society.[6] In the specific case of conjunto music, its spread to other parts of the country was tied to the increasing dispersal of tejanos and *norteño* Mexicans to farflung areas in search of better-paying jobs.[7] And wherever these workers traveled, their favorite performers went, as did the empresarios.

One more development took place in the last years of the decisive decade of the 1940s, and that was the appearance of a new style of dance grafted onto the by-now ubiquitous polka. I am speaking of *el tacuachito*, a dance that quickly captivated the popular imagination and forever changed polka dancing among Texas-Mexicans. Originating in the San Antonio area, the dance was identified as u-niquely native by metaphorically associating its name and gliding movements with another popular, native inhabitant—the possum.

According to veteran musicians like Ayala and Martínez, older polka dance styles among tejanos were very similar to those of the Germans and other groups they had observed—that is, they were probably imitations of the European styles universalized during the nineteenth century. The polka was danced *cancaneada* (probably from "cancan"), as Martínez put it, or *de brinquito* (jump step), as Ayala remembered it. However, *el tacuachito*, danced as it was in a swaying shuffle to a much slower tempo, changed all that, while at the same time establishing a peculiarly Texas-Mexican dance style. By the early 1950s the new style had become a standard feature of the equally common Saturday night dance. As a member of a migrant family I witnessed many of these dances during the 1950s in cities and towns from McAllen in the Rio Grande Valley to Lub-bock in the Texas Panhandle.

Later I want to discuss the significance of *el tacuachito* more ful-ly; here I only wish to suggest that all of these changes—in the ac-cordion ensemble, the introduction of public ballroom dancing, the professionalization of conjunto musicians, and, of course, the ap-pearance of *el tacuachito*—were interrelated, corresponding to the changes that took place in Texas-Mexican society in the years following World War II.

Any discussion of postwar conjunto music must begin with the names of two pivotal figures: Valerio Longoria and Tony de la Rosa. There were others, of course, who began their careers at this time—for example, Agapito Zúñiga, Daniel Garcés y Los Tres Reyes, and the Mexican duet famous in their own country and the United States, Los Alegres de Terán.[8] Most of these influenced the course of conjunto music in one way or another. However, Valerio Longoria and Tony de la Rosa were, by common consensus among conjunto musicians, the most creative and respected of the musi-cians in the decade immediately following the end of the war. More than any of the others they were responsible for initiating the changes that propelled conjunto music into its final phase. Only one group, El Conjunto Bernal—which nonetheless built on what Longoria and de la Rosa had initiated—succeeded in surpassing the accomplishments of these two.

Among conjunto musicians, special recognition ought to be given to one other person, guitarist Lorenzo Caballero from San Antonio—El Mago de la Guitarra ("The Guitar Magician"), as he was called. In a unique way he contributed significantly to the evolving music tradition, if not from a stylistic viewpoint at least in terms of what, for lack of a better label, we may refer to as "showbiz" aspects of performance. For example, I personally recall that to migrating farmworkers in the state of Texas the announcement of Lorenzo Caballero's appearance never failed to elicit excitement and anticipation. People delighted in seeing him perform his magic on the guitar. "Es un payaso, un mago" ("He is a clown, a magician"), people would say, because of the sleights of hand he executed while performing. These often included the maneuver wherein he would set his guitar on fire with lighter fluid. Another feat consisted of playing solos on his guitar with his tongue, while the accordion and the other instruments provided the instrumental background.[9]

In sum, perhaps more than anyone else, Caballero infused the conjunto ensemble with the kind of showmanship people associated with performers in *carpas de maroma* (tent shows). After Caballero most professional conjuntos, while not duplicating his more outlandish theatrics, nevertheless adopted a more choreographed approach, shall we say, toward their presentation. For example, besides wearing uniform outfits (an American influence, too, no doubt), conjuntos began to perform standing up, while at the same time the leader assumed the role of master of ceremonies. According to Pedro Ayala, who played with Caballero, this was done to lend the dances *ánimo*, or liveliness.

Valerio Longoria: Conjunto Music's Forgotten Genius

Probably the one person most responsible for moving conjunto music away from its earlier stylistic expression was Valerio Longoria, although until recently, when he returned to San Antonio after a twenty year absence, he was all but forgotten among tejanos. Among conjunto musicians, however, he was vividly remembered, and his name remains linked to "una nueva onda" ("a new wave"), as accordionist Oscar Hernández described it. From the time he began to record commercially shortly after the war, he evidently struck out in new musical directions, accomplishing things no one else had thought of or attempted before.

Longoria was born in 1924 in Kenedy, Texas, about sixty-five miles north of Corpus Christi on the road to San Antonio.[10] In terms of age Longoria falls between the older generation and younger musicians like Tony de la Rosa and Paulino Bernal. As a youngster he traveled with his divorced father on migrant treks that took them to places like Mississippi and Arkansas. As Longoria remembers it, "Andaba mi papá en los trabajos, en las labores. Siempre trabajó en las labores" ("My father was following the work in the fields. He always worked in the fields"). For this reason Valerio hardly ever attended school. As he explained, "Fui poco a la escuela. Era muy duro para mi padre; mejor me llevaba a trabajar" ("I had very little school. It was hard on my father, he would rather take me to work with him").

Despite his lack of education, Longoria exhibited an early talent for music, in reward for which his father bought him a guitar. Longoria was six at the time, and, as he said, "Le aprendí algo" ("I learned something on it"). At the age of seven he received his first accordion, a two-row model his father bought for $10. When Longoria began playing his first jobs, in the early 1930s, his predecessors were already firmly established. Thus in his early years he shared in that stage of the tradition. For instance, at his first paid performance—when he was a mere eight years old—the group Longoria played with was quite standard for the time. It consisted of accordion, guitar, and *tambora de rancho*. It was a wedding, a job that earned the young accordionist $3. This was in Harlingen, Texas, where Longoria and his itinerant father were staying.

By the time he was twenty-one Longoria had been married and widowed and was about to be drafted into the army. He served in Germany at the end of the war. Upon his return to the United States, the young veteran resumed his playing, an occupation he has since been engaged in exclusively. "Nunca he trabajado en otro trabajo," he said, "nomás en la música—y nunca he tenido hambre" ("I have never held any other kind of job, except music—and I have never been hungry"). Shortly after his return, Longoria was "drafted" again—this time by Corona Records of San Antonio. He recorded his first pieces in 1947, a polka entitled "Cielito" and a *corrido*, "Jesús Cadena." That same year he remembers recording one of his most successful songs, the *canción ranchera* "El Rosalito."[11] Longoria remained with Corona for about two years, then transferred to Ideal, where his fee was raised from $15 per record to $20. It was with Ideal, for whom he recorded for seven or eight years, that Longoria left his mark as the most innovative conjunto musician until that time.

Longoria's accomplishments are impressive. First, he apparently was the first accordionist to combine his singing talent with his playing. This was a noteworthy feat for the times, according to no less an authority of Texas-Mexican music than Armando Marroquín, who explained it thus:

> . . . Tenía su estilo para tocar . . . introdujo un estilo más diferente. Sí, lo que le ayudaba a él—tenía su talento, tenía regular voz. Porque lo que hace famoso a un conjunto de acordeón es que traiga buena voz, además que tengas tu estilo. Y Valerio tenía el talento de que componía sus acordeones; les sacaba sonidos diferentes. Las trasportaba a otros tonos . . . Valerio fué el que sacó eso de cambiarlas—más ronca . . . (personal interview, January 31, 1980) . . .
>
> . . . (He had his own style of playing . . . introduced a different style. Yes, what helped him—he had his talent, had a fairly good voice. See, what makes a conjunto good is having a good voice along; as well having your own style. Plus Valerio had the talent for fixing his accordions; he got different sounds from them. He would transpose them to other keys . . . Valerio was the one who came with this business of changing them—a huskier sound . . .)

What Marroquín meant by "más ronca" was Valerio's self-taught ability to alter the reeds on the accordion, enabling him both to transpose them to keys other than the original (e.g., from G to F) and to tune one of the double reeds that constitute each note so that it would vibrate at the rate of an octave lower. It was the latter type of alteration that lent Longoria's accordion the "sonido ronco," or "hoarse" sound (Broyles interview, April 16, 1981).

With reference to Longoria's singing talent, according to Marroquín, it was his group that popularized the *canción corrida* among conjuntos. Longoria was also responsible, incidentally, for the popularization of another type of *canción* in Texas-Mexican conjunto music, the *canción ranchera* in *vals* tempo. Like the polka, the latter was originally played as an instrumental composition by conjunto groups, but, beginning with Longoria, sung lyrics replaced the accordion as the melodic part. Again, these lyrics were usually sung in the form of a duet, with the second part commonly sung in parallel thirds below the melody.

Longoria distinguished himself in at least two more ways. He was apparently the first conjunto musician to record the bolero and perform it on a regular basis. This musical genre, originally of Afro-Cuban derivation, was "smoothed out" harmonically and rhythmically in twentieth-century Mexican music, becoming associated with a sophisticated type of *canción romántica*.[12]

Longoria's adoption of the bolero was a significant departure from tradition, first, because the genre makes greater demands on a musician's knowledge of harmony and rhythm, a knowledge earlier conjuntos lacked. Secondly, as the unrivalled epitome of the *canción romántica*, the bolero requires more singing finesse—better voice control, a smoother quality, and a more even vibrato—than folksongs such as *corridos* do, in order to adequately convey the passionately romantic message it conventionally carries.[13] The introduction of the bolero into conjunto music obviously signaled a broadening of the musical sensibility on the part of the tejano working class, since among Mexicans the bolero had hitherto been associated with genteel, sophisticated music. Its appropriation by conjunto musicians like Longoria would seem to be an attempt to lend respectability to their music and its constituency, though the possibility that this was another case of *gesunkenes kulturgut* cannot be ruled out.

Lastly, Valerio Longoria was evidently the first to make regular use of the modern dance band drums in a conjunto—surely the most radical innovation ever made within the tradition. Although such a move may not seem particularly original—since the *tambora de rancho* had been common up until the 1930s—the introduction of the drums created an entirely new dimension in that it altered the function of all the other instruments in the conjunto. As best as he can remember, it was in 1948 that Longoria used the drums for the first time on a recording (a date that corresponds more or less with the recollections of other conjunto musicians). However, the drums did not become a standard component of the conjunto until the early 1950s because many people in the business felt the drums were too overpowering, especially on recordings. Thus, for some years after they were first introduced, conjuntos continued to use drums only sporadically, relying on the accordion, the *bajo sexto* (occasionally the guitar), and the *tololoche*—though the latter was used mainly for recording purposes only.

Longoria's popularity—which, incidentally, was never as great as that of our next figure, Tony de la Rosa—began to decline when he left his adopted city of San Antonio for Chicago in 1959. He had been contracted to play in the latter city for three months, but, as he said, "Iba por tres meses y me quedé ocho años" ("I was going for three months and stayed eight years"). While in Chicago he continued his recording career with a company named Firma, but, unfortunately for him, the company did not market his records in Texas, and eventually, lacking the support of his tejano stronghold, his name began to fade in music circles. Later, Longoria moved to

Los Angeles, where he recorded for Volcán Records and a company from San José, Fama, but he was never able to duplicate his earlier successes, again because these companies did not distribute aggressively, especially in Texas, where Longoria's fame had originally been established. As he himself said, "Pero no distribuían discos pa' Texas . . . y me fui muriendo" ("But they did not distribute their records in Texas, and I began to fade"). Others soon moved in to take his place.

Tony de la Rosa: An Enduring Name in Conjunto Music

On a recent album in which he re-recorded some of his best-known polkas, Tony de la Rosa's accomplishments are described in the following manner:

> Tony ya cuenta con sus 35 años tocando profecionalmente [sic] y ha logrado sostenerse por muchos años . . . pero como dice la gente lo bueno dura y Tony lo ha confirmado al tocarles año tras año, ya que por tres décadas y media Tony de la Rosa a recorrido muchos lugares como Illinois, Indiana, Michigan, Florida, Colorado, Arizona, California y Nuevo México—en fin, en donde había raza amante a la música de acordión [sic] que es parte de la cultura tejana.
> (Tony counts on 35 years of professional experience and has succeeded in maintaining his position for many years . . . but, as people say, good things last, and Tony has confirmed this, playing year after year, having traveled for three and a half decades to such places as Illinois, Indiana, Michigan, Florida, Colorado, Arizona, California, and New Mexico—in short, wherever there was *raza* that liked accordion music, which is part of tejano culture.)

Such, indeed, has been de la Rosa's history as a musician. Alone among the members of the *nueva generación* that came into its own immediately after World War II, he has succeeded in maintaining, more or less intact, his popularity throughout the intervening years. As he himself remarked, "Si no estás al frente, rápidamente ya estás afuera. Así como te recuerda el público, así también te puede olvidar—rápidamente" ("If you're not out in front, you're quickly outside. Just as the public can remember you, it can just as easily forget you—fast").[14] That is a dictum de la Rosa apparently never forgot. Once he had established himself as a strong new force in conjunto music, he remained active, recording and traveling, always cultivating the public to whom he admits he owes all his success.

However, like almost all his predecessors, de la Rosa began his career under the harshest of conditions. He was born in 1931 in Sarita, twenty-five miles from Corpus Christi, then (as now) little more than a workers' hamlet in the vast King Ranch complex. His father was a field hand, though he was also a barber and at one time operated a restaurant. On work in the fields de la Rosa commented: "Todos mis hermanos anduvimos con él [mi papá]. Dime de pepino, azadón, tomate, cebolla—todo hicimos" ("All of us, my brothers and me, went out with my father. Tell me about cucumbers, hoeing, tomatoes, onions—we did it all").

By the time he was sixteen de la Rosa had set out on his own, though he had been playing "en bailecitos" ("at little dances") since he was ten. His father had bought him an accordion, which he had learned to play by listening to Narciso Martínez on the radio, and now, at sixteen, he decided to go to nearby Kingsville, where, he said, "había cantinillas donde tocar" ("there were *cantinillas* where I could play"). And he added: "Anduve mucho tiempo con el acordeón por un lado y el cajón de shine por el otro" ("I spent a lot of time with my accordion on one side and the shoeshine box on the other").

It was during this time that de la Rosa attempted to join Ideal Records, but Martínez had already been engaged, and he had to wait until 1949 for his first recording opportunity. That opportunity came with Arco, a short-lived label that Reymundo Treviño, erstwhile member of the Beto Villa orquesta, had established in Alice, Texas. De la Rosa's first recording featured, predictably, a pair of polkas: "Sarita" and "Tres Ríos." Soon, however, de la Rosa got his chance with Ideal, and in 1950 he began to turn out all the polkas that were to make his name a household word among the tejano working class. Among the most popular were "El Circo" (one of his first), "El Sube y Baja," "La Periodista," "Atotonilco," and many, many others. Beyond any doubt, by the mid-1950s de la Rosa's conjunto was the most popular accordion group in Texas. He toured widely, not only in Texas but in all the places mentioned earlier. With popularity came at least a degree of economic stability: De la Rosa never returned to the fields after 1950.

I mentioned earlier Valerio Longoria's pathfinding innovations and their effect on conjunto music. In his own way de la Rosa made his own contributions, and they merit recognition, if for no other reason than the fact that he was the best-known accordionist throughout most of the 1950s. If Longoria was the first to incorporate the drums into the conjunto, it was de la Rosa who ultimately standardized their relationship to the other instruments in the ensemble. In this respect I should mention that it seems likely that it was de la Rosa who sometime in the middle 1950s first introduced the electric bass and the electrified *bajo sexto* into the dance hall, two developments that completed the transformation of the conjunto style. With the addition of the P.A. system and microphones, used for singing and to amplify the accordion, the modern conjunto's spatial arrangement and musical organization were complete. The consolidation of all of these elements into a well-defined, normative style followed quickly, and in this El Conjunto de la Rosa, then at the height of its fame, played an important role.[15]

Clearly, the addition of the drums (which usually included a floor bass drum, snare, perhaps a tenor drum, cymbal, and high-hat), the electric bass, and P.A. system dramatically changed the acoustical nature of conjunto music. However, these changes did not always take place without some resistance, especially on the part of the public. For example, according to Tony de la Rosa, the drums were not immediately accepted when he introduced them at dances around 1950. He recalls that the people's reaction upon hearing the new instrument was one of mockery. They teased him for bringing the *convite* into the dance hall. A *convite*, of course, was originally a group of musicians who rode and played on a flatbed truck—or wagon, in an earlier time—by way of announcing a celebration, or *función*, that was to take place somewhere in the vicinity. Later, a *convite* came to be associated almost exclusively with a circus or *carpa de maromas*. In either case, the drums were a prominent and noisy feature of the *convite*, whose sound preceded the appearance of the musicians. In referring to the *convite* de la Rosa's clients were alluding to the noisiness of the new conjunto and the circus (i.e., *ludic-*rous) atmosphere the drums created.

Nonetheless, like the electric bass, the drums eventually became an indispensable member of the mature conjunto. And, like the bass, their utility was soon recognized by both performers and audiences. For performers, as de la Rosa pointed out, the drums "settled down" the tempo, especially for polkas, and thereby freed the *bajo sexto* and the accordion from the constant necessity of attending simultaneously to melody, harmony, and tempo. With the drums taking over the primary function of rhythm and "keeping time," both the accordion and the *bajo* were left to explore new modes of articulation. For audiences the drums added a much more solid pulse that in my estimation had much to do with hastening the adoption of the new dance style of *el tacuachito*.

De la Rosa's most important contribution to the rapidly evolving conjunto style resulted from the singular technique he developed in his performance of polkas. For, unlike Valerio Longoria, whose fame rested chiefly on his *canciones rancheras* and boleros, de la Rosa was best known for his superb polkas. And, while he recorded many *rancheras*, especially after 1955, it is in his polkas that his talent was stamped. Oddly enough, it was not until 1955 or thereabouts that de la Rosa's new technique became evident. In fact, in recordings prior to that date the influence of Longoria is clearly discernible.[16] In the polkas recorded after 1955, however, de la Rosa's technique quickly moved beyond the snappy, marcato style that Pedro Ayala best exemplified. Now de la Rosa evinced a strong, choppy, staccato quality that was enhanced by a considerably slower tempo than had been common up until then. An instrumental (polka) rendition of the *canción*, "Atotonilco," recorded in 1956 and featuring the new standardized four-instrument ensemble, demonstrates the dramatic changes that de la Rosa had wrought (see Appendix B., no. 7).

Out of Many, a Few

As happened with the emergence of conjunto music in the 1930s, the transformation of the style in the 1950s had many contributors.[17] It would lengthen this work unnecessarily to devote space to all but those few who are, by common consensus, the most prominent. However, in considering the best-known (if not always the most innovative) exponents, mention should at least be made of such well-recognized artists as Agapito Zúñiga, Los Tres Reyes, and Rubén Vela. Zúñiga, originally from Matamoros, across the border from Brownsville, began recording for Ideal in 1954, according to Longoria. Indeed, Zúñiga's first recordings featured him not as an accordionist but as a singer with Longoria's group. Only later did Zúñiga's own group, Los Desveladores, begin to record on their own. Consequently, Zúñiga's style is strongly reminiscent of Valerio Longoria.

Los Tres Reyes de Daniel Garcés were somewhat more influential. They are certainly well remembered and appreciated by conjunto musicians. Valerio Longoria's statements are perhaps representative of the general opinion: "Tocábamos aquí en el barrio, en San Antonio . . . Traían muy buenas canciones" ("We played together here in the barrio, in San Antonio . . . They had very good songs"). I personally recall that one of their songs, "Los Pizcadores" ("The

Cottonpickers"), was extremely popular in the early 1950s. The song dealt with the amorous overtures of a cotton-picker toward a female companion, who in the process tests the endurance of the suitor as he tries to keep up with her blazing pace. Despite its brevity, the song captured the atmosphere of the cotton field with unusual fidelity, a fact that, coupled with Los Tres Reyes's lively style, undoubtedly contributed to the song's appeal.

Finally, a somewhat less influential accordionist of the 1950s, though nonetheless a strong performer in his own right, is Rubén Vela, a native of San Antonio who was brought up in the Rio Grande Valley. Born in 1937, Vela left school when he was in the fifth grade to help support his family. He worked alongside his father and oldest brother on a farm in Relámpago, near the Mexican border. Vela organized his first conjunto when he was twelve. He remembered his first jobs: "Comenzamos a cobrar $12 por noche. Eramos tres—acordeón, guitarra y tambora. Nos costaba $2.50-$3.00 por noche para rentar el equipo—nomás un micrófono y una vocinita" ("We began charging $12 a night. It was three of us—accordion, guitar, and drums. It cost us $2.50-$3.00 a night to rent the equipment—just a microphone and a small speaker") (personal interview, May 9, 1980).

Vela acknowledges the influence of Narciso Martínez. As he said, "El fue el que comenzó con este estilito . . . De ahí puede que él nos dió la idea" ("He was the one who started this style . . . Perhaps it was he who gave the rest of us the idea"). Although he is self-taught, Vela remembers attending dances at La Villita, a dance hall in San Benito where Valerio Longoria, Tony de la Rosa, and Los Tres Reyes played. De la Rosa was his favorite, and Vela learned much from his style. That is evident in Vela's own recordings, which began in 1956, with Falcón Records. One of the most memorable of his early recordings is the polka "Adolorido." Although Vela did not break any new ground as far as conjunto music is concerned, his style did represent a strong synthesis of many of the changes that had taken place after 1950. And, like Tony de la Rosa, he has remained an active musician to this day, contributing to the survival of a style that has been relatively unchanged since the breakthroughs of the 1950s.

El Conjunto Bernal: The Early Period

The last of the major accordionists to make an impact on conjunto music was Paulino Bernal. Although Bernal's most far-ranging innovations came after the period being discussed here, by 1960 El

Conjunto Bernal had established itself as the most experimental group in the conjunto tradition. While clearly located within the generalized style dating back to the 1930s, el Conjunto Bernal had by this time begun to extend the music's horizon, even as the group had already perfected the features that dated from Narciso Martínez's initial emphasis on the treble end of the accordion to the standardization in the mid-1950s of the electrically amplified four-instrument ensemble. More specifically, what El Conjunto Bernal had done by 1960 was to exploit to an unprecedented degree the musical possibilities of each individual instrument, while at the same time paying close attention to such ensemble features as phrasing, dynamics, articulation, and general balance. The result was what tejano musicians described as a smoother, more polished sound than hitherto achieved by a conjunto.

El Conjunto Bernal was organized by the Bernal brothers—Paulino and Eloy—in Kingsville, Texas, in 1952, but it was not until the late 1950s that it began to distinguish itself as a leader in its field. It was in 1958 that the group recorded a remarkably different album (LPs having recently been introduced in tejano music) entitled "Mi Unico Camino" ("My Only Path"). The title song, a *ranchera* in *vals* tempo, was an unparalleled success, the more impressive because it marked the first time a conjunto had ever incorporated three-part harmonies. This was not a totally fortuitous accomplishment, however. Though new in conjunto music, the tradition was well established in Mexico by this time. In fact, several Mexican vocal trios, foremost among which was El Trio Los Panchos, were enjoying immense success in the United States. Bernal's decision to introduce stylistic elements from such trios, especially three-part harmonies, was based on his hope that this would generate a favorable public response while expanding the stylistic base of conjunto music.[18] The experiment worked; "Mi Unico Camino" not only broke new ground but established the prominence of El Conjunto Bernal.

With the powerful high tenor of Ruben Pérez, a young singer the Bernals had enlisted earlier, (with Eloy on second, Paulino on third), a new dimension had been added to conjunto music. El Conjunto Bernal's presence as a major new force in conjunto music was assured. Of course, not all of Bernal's music was geared toward the exploitation of three-part harmonies. The more traditional duet was continued; moreover, Bernal was very much interested in keeping the polka tradition alive. Indeed, one of the hallmarks of the mature Conjunto Bernal was the distinctiveness of its polkas. The polka and the duet (the latter often featured in *canciones rancheras* in tempo di polka) were the elements that linked El Conjunto Bernal to its predecessors. The exploration into three-part harmony was simply one of several efforts on the part of Bernal to seek new and diverse ways to sell his group.

Thus, Bernal's own accordion style was also expanding, as he searched for ways to "distinguish" himself, as he put it. However, he freely admits that at first other musicians helped shape his ideas:

> Después que empecé a tocar entonces empecé a oir y a buscar . . . Entre los músicas encontré a Tony [de la Rosa], a Daniel Garcés. En ese tiempo—pos, Narciso Martínez, también bastante popular. Entonces fue Valerio [Longoria], Tony de la Rosa, aquellos que me gustaban a mi mucho como tocaban.
> (After I started to play I began to listen and to search . . . Among the musicians I found Tony [de la Rosa], Daniel Garcés. At that time—well, Narciso Martínez, also very popular. And so, it was Valerio [Longoria], Tony de la Rosa, whose playing I liked very much).

And, in fact, Bernal's first polkas, while evincing a nascent idiostyle, are certainly reminiscent of Tony de la Rosa, in particular.

But someone—a disc jockey and dance empresario—had once given Bernal a word of advice that he took seriously. It was blunt but effective as far as Bernal is concerned. "Distínguete, aunque sea por idiota," he was told ("Distinguish yourself, even if it has to be as an idiot"). He began to experiment:

> Siempre me gustó escarbarle más y más a la acordeón. Me di cuenta que todos los tonos allí están, en la acordeón. Me propuse a tocar en tonos que no se tocaban. Empecé a tocar allí, y hacerlos los tonos principales para mí . . . Así es que fue la idea de distinguir al Conjunto Bernal, en primer lugar con tonos diferentes—que producen sonido diferente—y luego después irnos a buscar voces diferentes, estilo de música diferente.
> (I always liked to dig deeper and deeper into the accordion. I found out that all the keys are there, in the accordion. I set out to play in keys that were not used. I began to play in those and to make them my principal keys . . . And so, the idea was to distinguish El Conjunto Bernal, first by playing in different keys—that produce a different sound—and then by going for different voicings, a different style of music).

The summary effects of Bernal's experimentation were, indeed, to distinguish his group from those that had preceded it. First, in his own style Bernal developed a technical facility that was at least comparable to—though probably surpassing—that of any accordionist up to 1960. At the same time he succeeded in "perfecting," we might say, the staccato style first introduced by de la Rosa in that he was able to elicit it cleanly from all types of runs, whether they be eighth- or sixteenth-note patterns, or even more complex syncopated combinations. In short, more than anyone else before him, Bernal exploited the total range of the accordion, both rhythmically and melodically. However, it would be an injustice not to point out that of immeasurable help in projecting Bernal's virtuosity was the very substantial talent of Eloy Bernal, who has been recognized by many as the greatest *bajo sexto* player in conjunto music's history. Sensitive to the style's nuances and exacting in his own execution, Eloy's technique was in every way equal to the demands made by his brother. And finally, once the Bernals began to establish their reputation, they also began to attract exceptionally competent bassists and drummers. These, too, shared considerable responsibility for making El Conjunto Bernal the conjunto group par excellence that it became.

By 1960, then, El Conjunto Bernal, six years after its entrance into the commercial market, had established itself as the foremost group in conjunto music. Like Valerio Longoria, Tony de la Rosa, and others before them, Bernal and his group toured throughout Texas and beyond, filling ballrooms to capacity wherever they appeared.[19] I believe it is safe to say that in El Conjunto Bernal—at least up until 1960—the most ideal conjunto sound had been achieved. Its style became a kind of norm, emulated by many others, as Strachwitz has suggested (1978). In sum, Bernal had taken the various stylistic strands that had been coalescing around a uniquely fashioned tejano accordion ensemble, perfected them, and achieved a synthesis that marked the apex of conjunto music's evolution. His style was solidly ranchero, easily recognizable as part of a tradition that extended back to the 1930s, at least; yet it was also highly innovative, as my informants, both orquesta and conjunto musicians, acknowledged. But it was above all the group's discipline that enabled it to strike the ideal balance between the experimental and the traditional (see Appendix B, nos. 8 and 9).

Actually, the phenomenal success of El Conjunto Bernal was only beginning in 1960. Indeed, the greater part of that decade belonged to Paulino Bernal and his group. Things went so well for Bernal that by 1963 he was able to launch his own recording label, Bego (named after Bernal and a partner by the name of González), while at the same time he became something of a local television personality. However, post-1960 Conjunto Bernal presents special challenges whose discussion I postpone for the next chapter. Here I want only to add that these challenges have to do with the increasing resistance of most conjunto musicians and their audiences to change once the style had become standardized—that is, once the ensemble, its repertory, and its mode of performance had become set. Meanwhile, by 1960 Bernal had traveled a considerable social and economic distance from his first days as a conjunto musician.

Life had not been easy for the Bernal family during Paulino's childhood. The Bernals were no exception to the poverty that had visited Paulino's predecessors. Born June 21, 1939, in the Rio Grande Valley, Bernal moved to the town of Kingsville when he was a small boy. His parents had separated when Paulino was very young, and his mother, who became the head of the household, could hardly support the family of six that was dependent upon her. It therefore became necessary for Paulino and Eloy, who were the oldest, to leave school to help support the family. "Me salí del séptimo año," he recalled, "para irme a tocar, a tratar de ganar dinero y salir de la pobreza en que estábamos" ("I dropped out of the seventh grade, to go play and try to earn enough money to get us out of the poverty we found ourselves in"). But he was no stranger to the cotton fields: "Nos íbamos allí a Kingsville a pizcar algodón, pepino y cebolla" ("We would go to Kingsville to pick cotton, cucumbers, and onions").

Bernal had learned to play guitar earlier, however. As he recalled, one day a man came by the Bernal house selling a guitar. Despite the family's hardships the boys prevailed on their mother, and, guitar now at hand, both Paulino and Eloy began to explore their new instrument. Bernal learned enough on the guitar to team up with an old man, an accordionist, who played for nickels in the cantinas around Kingsville. He developed an interest in the accordion, borrowing it from the old man whenever he could. Afterward, a friend of his bought an accordion, but according to Bernal, Bernal himself was the chief beneficiary—it was he who did most of the practicing. Then,

> . . . en una de las venidas que veníamos para acá a visitar a mi papá—mi padre le compró un bajo sexto a Eloy, aquí en Reynosa. Entonces con el bajo sexto y la acordeón empezamos el conjunto que le nombramos los Hermanitos Bernal. Esto fué como el '52. Empezamos—Adán Lomas, un

tamborero, mi hermano Eloy y yo. Y entonces—no teníamos
instrumentos—batería, micrófonos, etc. Uno de los primeros
bailes que tocamos—le habíamos cobrado como $18. Lo
debíamos todo de puras rentas de micrófonos, batería . . .
(On one of the trips that we made to visit my father—he
bought a *bajo sexto* for Eloy, here in Reynosa. So then, with
the *bajo sexto* and the accordion we started the conjunto that
we named Los Hermanitos Bernal. This was around 1952.
We started—Adán Lomas, a drummer, my brother Eloy, and I.
And at that time—we didn't have any instruments: drums,
microphones, etc. One of the first dances we played—we had
charged $18. We owed it all on the rental of microphones,
drums . . .)

Los Hermanitos Bernal apparently displayed unusual talent from
early on. Not long after the group was organized it drew the attention of the enterprising Armando Marroquín of Ideal Records, who
brought them to Alice, at first for the purpose of providing instrumental backing for Carmen y Laura and other singers. Bernal
recalled the first time the group itself was featured:

Luego grabamos nuestro primer disco [1954]; fue un bolero, se
llamaba "Desprecio" por un lado, por el otro traía una canción que se llamaba "La Mujer Paseada." Era valseada, pero
me parece que la tocamos corrida. Gustó bastante, y nos
empezaron a llamar diferentes partes. Uno de los primeros
llamados fue de Dallas. Estuvimos en un salón que se
llamaba el Sky Club.
(Afterwards we recorded our first record; it was a bolero titled
"Desprecio" on one side, on the other was a song titled "La
Mujer Paseada." It was in waltz time, but I believe we played
it *corrida* [polka time]. It was well received, and we began to
get calls from different places. One of the first calls came
from Dallas. We played in a ballroom called the Sky Club.)

From this time on, the Bernal's days in the cotton fields were
numbered. By 1955 the brothers had turned fully professional.

The 1950s: A Summary of Stylistic Changes

As I have tried to make clear, the 1950s witnessed a series of
changes in conjunto music that in a dramatic way climaxed the

emergence and maturation of this tejano artistic expression. By way of highlighting the coming of age of conjunto music, I would like to summarize the most important stylistic changes that took place during this period.

First and most important was the virtually complete adoption by 1960 of the four-instrument ensemble: the three-row button accordion (tuned in various keys, e.g., F, G, C, etc., to accommodate specific melodic ranges), the *bajo sexto*, the electric bass, and the drums. The inclusion of the last two, in particular, had profound effects on the ultimate stylistic shape of conjunto music. Here is an outline of the changes wrought on conjunto music during the 1950s, as these were described by my informants and as they may readily be discerned by comparing the various recordings listed in the discography (and by comparing the transcriptions in Appendix B):

1. With the *bajo sexto*, electric bass, and drums providing solid harmonic and rhythmic accompaniment, accordionists of the 1950s came increasingly to neglect the bass-chord elements on the accordion. They simply did not develop a left-hand technique. The trend had, of course, been initiated by Narciso Martínez in the 1930s, but the left hand harmonic and bass support had continued to be used—in an increasingly random manner, to be sure—by accordionists up to Pedro Ayala's debut as a recording artist in the late 1940s. Thus, even Valerio Longoria had utilized the left end of the accordion in his early recordings. Now, with its almost total reliance on right-hand technique, the newer style of playing engendered a new crop of virtuosos who had divorced themselves almost completely from the style of their predecessors.

2. With the addition of the drums, polka and *canción corrida* tempos experienced a marked deceleration—from the earlier 125-135 beats per minute to a more leisurely 110-120 beats per minute. Whether the drums had the effect of "pulling back" the tempo, as de la Rosa once commented, or whether it slowed as a result of a changing conception of what "the right speed" should be is difficult to assess, though a combination of both seems plausible. In any case, the shift in tempos was an important development, one that also happened to correspond with changing dance styles, specifically the introduction of *el tacuachito*, which, according to Paulino Bernal, was perfectly suited to the slow tempo of the new *canción corrida*.

3. Another change concurrent with the decelerated tempo was the appearance of a far more staccato technique than hitherto heard, beginning with Tony de la Rosa. This new technique also served to distinguish the post-1950s accordion sound from that of an earlier day, though its relationship with the newer tempos is evident: the

slower speeds made it possible to detach the notes in a phrase—even in a sixteenth-note pattern—enough to create the choppy, staccato effect of Tony de la Rosa or a Rubén Vela. And once the new technique was accepted, it quickly established itself, after 1955 becoming the norm by which all conjuntos were gauged.

4. On the *bajo sexto* a different style of accompaniment for polka and *corrida* emerged with the addition of the bass and drums. Whereas earlier *bajo sexto* players, who usually had to carry the bass and rhythmic load alone (with some help from the accordion), tended to give at least equal emphasis to the bass patterns vis-à-vis the strum patterns, the younger players did not. With the bass providing the fundamental basses, the *bajo sexto* players began to neglect their own bass strings and concentrate on the treble, off-beat strums. This new technique was another identifiable constituent unit in the mature conjunto style of the 1950s. Figure 2 illustrates the differences I am referring to.

Figure 2: Differences in *bajo sexto* style

Old Style   New Style

5. As the modern conjunto style began to crystallize, the bass and drums began in their turn to develop their own technique. By its nature the *tololoche*, played pizzicato, as it was, had featured short, marcato, quarter-note patterns when accompanying polkas. This concept of articulation, deemed eminently suitable (we may recall that for a time the *tololoche* preempted the electric bass on recordings), was taken over by the electric bass—or at least a facsimile of the concept, since the acoustical effect of an electrically amplified bass could never possibly duplicate that of a contrabass. Thus, in its rather staccato articulation the electric bass paralleled to some extent the staccato patterns on the accordion, though of course it was restricted to playing for the most part simple, quarter-note fundamentals. The drums were the last to achieve a degree of stylistic standardization. Figure 3 illustrates some of the most common

Figure 3: Common rhythmic patterns used in polkas
and *corridas.*

rhythmic patterns used in polkas and *corridas*. (Note the accented double-sixteenth-note patterns; they are an important distinguishing characteristic of the conjunto drumming style for both the polka and *canción corrida*.)

6. Finally, in the latter part of the 1950s the instrumental polka gave way to the sung *canción ranchera*, or *canción corrida*, as it came to be known (and performed, again, in polka tempo). This happened at the same time that conjuntos had begun to adopt the bolero (as well as other related genres, such as the cha cha and an occasional *danzón*), even as redowas, schottisches, and other genres of an earlier day—the *huapango* excepted—were becoming increasingly rare. Thus, by 1960 the redowa and schottische had become novelty numbers, played only by special request. Even the instrumental polka had become less evident—often performed to show off the skills of good accordionists like Paulino Bernal.

In sum, by 1960 *la nueva generación* had completely asserted itself and its style of performance. There were links with the past, of course. For example, although the instrumental polka had given way to the *corrida*, the polka beat remained; and, while the accordion functioned less as a solo instrument and more as a counterpart to the singers, in its articulation—particularly in solo passages, such as introductions—it used the same technique as that used in the instrumental polka. The other instruments remained unchanged, whether for a polka or for a *corrida*. As the quintessential genres of conjunto music, the polka and *corrida* were consequently subjected to the most intensive elaboration as the younger musicians strove both to bring fresh variety to the newly forged style while maintaining what they perceived to be an established tradition that they knew extended back at least to the days of El Huracán del Valle.

But the differences between the old and the new cannot be ignored. The changes that had taken place were nothing short of dramatic. Nonetheless, just as dramatic was the conservatism that overtook conjunto music after 1960. The reasons for this conservatism are not too difficult to understand. I shall examine these reasons in the next chapter.

Notes

1. This is not to say that Mexicans in the United States have been totally excluded from the rosters of the major labels. They have not—as performers like Andy Russell, Freddie Fender, Vikki Carr, Richie Valens, and others have demonstrated. But these performers have for the most part adhered to mainstream American music currents.

Exponents of tejano music styles have never been considered by major companies for commercial exploitation since the pre-World War II days.

2. The following accounts are chiefly from a personal interview with Marroquín on January 31, 1980.

3.   According to Garrido, in Mexico the true *canción ranchera* gained currency in the 1930s. Previous to that time pieces with similar characteristics (i.e., associated with folk or folklike groups, such as the true *orquesta típica*) were designated simply as *canciones mexicanas* (Garrido 1974:70). Some of the recordings I have seen also referred to them as *canciones típicas*.

4.   Reymundo Treviño, the self-taught piano-accordionist who had played with Villa since the 1930s, recalled his ouster from the Villa orquesta: "... Los que no sabíamos leer música—we were fired ... Aquél [Villa] hizo un arreglo nuevo de músicos modernos ... y hizo la orquesta grande, muy moderna, como al estilo Luis Arcaraz, así" ("... those of us who did not know how to read music—we were fired ... He [Villa] made a new arrangement with modern musicians ... and he made the orchestra big, very modern, something like the style of Luis Arcaraz, like that"); (personal interview, March 14, 1980).

5.   This information is in accord with that which dance promoter and radio announcer Domingo Peña from Corpus Christi gave José Limón (1977). I should add that, while paid-admission dances became very common after 1948, many—if not most—were actually held not in ballrooms as such but in armories, on terraces (with flat roofs), in assorted buildings turned into dance halls, and even in the old-fashioned *plataformas*.

6.   For a discussion of the functional role of paid-admission dances in a specific context see my essay "Ritual Structure in a Chicano Dance" (1980).

7.   In this respect I should mention the massive displacement of Mexican cotton pickers in Texas, beginning about 1956, by mechanical harvesters. To my knowledge this displacement has never been documented to determine its social, economic, and demographic effects. These were certainly important; at least one effect was the permanent relocation of many of these workers, especially to the San Joaquín Valley of California (cf. Saragoza 1980:58) and to the Midwest. Predictably, these two areas have since become strongholds of conjunto music.

8.   *Los Alegres de Terán* (Eugenio Abrego and Tomás Ortiz), who now reside in the United States, are undoubtedly the most famous in the history of *norteño* music from an international perspective. This fame is surely due in no small measure to their connection with the powerful Columbia Records. However, their style, while sharing certain obvious characteristics with Texas-Mexican conjunto music (i.e., the use of the accordion and *bajo sexto*), is nevertheless more representative of Mexican *norteño* music. For example, they never integrated drums into the group, and in general their style is quite removed from that of, say, Tony de la Rosa.

9.   In the summer of 1979, while performing alone with his electric guitar in a Mexican restaurant in San Antonio, Caballero played the song "Spanish Eyes" with his tongue at my request, demonstrating that he had not yet lost his magic.

10.   This biographical sketch is based on two taped interviews conducted at my request by Yolanda Broyles of the University of Texas at San Antonio, April 16 and 26, 1981. Longoria's whereabouts were unknown to me when I did the field work for this study. He moved back to San Antonio in 1981.

11. Longoria must have recorded this tune twice, because I have in my collection the same song, recorded for the Ideal label.

12. Juan Garrido dates the emergence of the *canción romántica* in Mexico from 1896, when Miguel Lerdo de Tejada, whom Garrido considers a precursor, published his first compositions. Garrido writes: "Thanks to singers of note who have remained loyal to Mexican composers, our *canción* merits the attention of the most worthy exponents, and it marches forward on a plane of high excellence that encourages our national composers to excel . . . " (Garrido, 1974:12; translation mine). However, it is obvious that the *canción romántica* dates from a much earlier period, perhaps from the 1850s (cf. Mayer-Serra 1941).

13. Transcription no. 6 in the Appendix is representative of Longoria's boleros.

14. This and further biographical information on de la Rosa was obtained through personal interviews, December 6, 1979, and January 30, 1980.

15. The four-man conjunto ensemble may have been introduced into the dance halls earlier than the mid-1950s. Indeed, it is likely that it was, but in their totality all the elements—accordion, *bajo sexto*, electric bass, drums, and P.A. systems—probably did not become standardized until 1956. Certainly, in recordings, where a slightly different practice seems to have prevailed, the electric bass did not replace the *tololoche* until the late 1950s. Quite simply, the quality of the latter instrument was prized over the "deader" sound of the electric bass.

16. An explanation for the similarity may lie in the fact that Longoria once altered de la Rosa's accordions in a similar manner to his own (Broyles interview).

17. Again, I am excluding from consideration groups like Los Alegres de Terán and Los Gorriones del Topo Chico because, while they were popular on both sides of the border, they are part of a more generalized *norteño* music. A history of that music is impractical here. Moreover, as I have emphasized, while similarities did exist, Texas-Mexican conjuntos, especially in the 1950s, developed in a stylistic direction that tended to diverge considerably from that of the *norteño* groups proper. In my estimation these differences were not insignificant.

18. Biographical information on Bernal was obtained in two personal interviews, May 8 and 9, 1980. Some of the information on El Conjunto Bernal was obtained in the course of interviews with other informants; some comes from my own memory.

19. A short time later, between the years 1963 and 1965, while living in the vicinity of Fresno, California, I witnessed the success of El Conjunto Bernal in this area, particularly among tejano expatriates. The Sanger ballroom filled to overflowing capacity when Bernal and his group appeared.

4. Post–1960 Conjunto: The Limits of a Tradition

El Conjunto Bernal of the 1960s: "Twenty Years Ahead of Its Time"

The phrase "twenty years ahead of its time" was used by a well-traveled orquesta musician to describe El Conjunto Bernal's accomplishments after 1960. He was referring specifically to the wide-ranging innovations that Bernal introduced after 1963, innovations that challenged the stylistic limits of the music and that have not been matched to this day. Indeed, the surprising thing is that El Conjunto Bernal embarked on its radically new course precisely at a time when not only did it enjoy supremacy in the field, but the style had come of age and, in fact, was about to exhaust its potential for further evolution. How, then, can we explain El Conjunto Bernal's daring explorations in the face of a retreating tradition?

First, we need to understand that, with the notable exception of El Conjunto Bernal and a few of its imitators (none of which have even approached its renown), conjunto musicians since 1960 have been content to rework the stylistic ground laid out during the 1950s. This has met with strong audience approval, much to the chagrin of those musicians who would like to see the style move in new directions. For example, Esteban Jordán, the man many tejano musicians consider the most talented accordionist today, complained to me in the summer of 1980 that he was "tired," as he put it, of hearing the same *sonsonete* (singsong) from conjuntos everywhere. "No le cambian, bro," he said, with a note of exasperation in his voice, "el mismo n-ta, n-ta, n-ta" ("They don't change it, bro—the same n-ta, n-ta, n-ta"). Jordán was of course referring to the basic polka beat that characterizes much of conjunto music, as well as certain formulaic "licks" that are used time after time by modern conjuntos in their *canciones rancheras*.

The inclination is, naturally, to seek an answer for such a sudden turn toward conservatism after 1960, especially in light of the dramatic developments in the decade of the 1950s. It is apparent, however, from information I obtained from the musicians themselves (of which Jordán's was the most critical) that with the maturation of the ensemble—the standardization of the instrumentation, its basic sound, and repertory—came an increasing resistance to further change. This attitude was shared by both the musicians and their audiences, who became less and less receptive to new ideas. Thus, once conjunto reached its stylistic apex around 1960, further accretions, particularly in connection with the ubiquitous *canción ranchera* in polka tempo, became as rare as their acceptance. Pedro Ayala summed up the musicians' interpretation when he offered this explanation: "Así es como le gusta a la gente" ("That is how the people like it").

Ayala's explanation may sound simplistic at first hearing, but it begins to make sense when we recognize that once conjunto music achieved stylistic crystallization, or maturity, further change proved difficult because it had developed as far as it was possible, given the social, cultural, and economic constraints its exponents faced. Moreover, by 1960 the ensemble had attained a highly visible and identifiable musical structure with an equally accepted—or prescribed, actually—social context for its consummation. But most important, both musically and socially conjunto was an expression created by and for the working class, which saw it as *its* music and the performers as its own homegrown artists. In short, the process of change had run its course; the style had reached its cultural limits and was now considered a "finished" art form that eminently fulfilled its sociomusical design. Conjunto articulated the tejano proletarians' unique socioesthetic values—values that were in substantial opposition to those of the middle class in particular and of the larger American society in general. Further alterations could therefore only be seen as unnecessary, if not undesirable.

In reference to this last point we should keep in mind that the drastic changes that overtook conjunto music in the 1950s did so within the context of a more or less conservative folk tradition. By this time the accordion was already a traditional instrument among working class tejanos, and only the compelling forces of social change and conflict could cause such a corresponding modification in the music itself. Thus, once the stylistic changes were effected, or—what is basically the same thing—once the working class had wrought a style of music that addressed its esthetic needs vis-à-vis those of the middle class, a return to stability could be expected. (I shall elaborate on these points in Chapter 6.) The next twenty years, then (to the early 1980s), were to be a period of retrenchment, much to the dismay of adventuresome artists like Esteban Jordán, who were forced to conform to the prevailing public taste in order to stay in business.

However, as I have mentioned, El Conjunto Bernal was a major exception to conjunto music's conservative turnabout. Indeed, the group achieved its greatest exposure during the decade of the 1960s—this at a time when it was involved in some of the most remarkable experiments in conjunto's history. These experiments, as many musicians noted, distinguished El Conjunto Bernal from all others and, moreover, have not been equaled since that time. How could Bernal's innovations, which ran counter to the tradition's direction, receive public approbation?

But an outline of the group's experiments (see appendix C, no. 10, for an example) is in order. Surely the most radical of these took place sometime between 1963 and 1964, when Bernal broke ranks with his peers by not only adding a second accordionist to the group (in the person of the young but highly regarded Oscar Hernández), but at the same time following Hernández's lead in switching to the unheard-of chromatic, or five-row, button accordion. With this addition El Conjunto Bernal's break with past practice was accomplished in one stroke. The contrast between the old and the new Bernal was nothing short of radical, especially when viewed in the light of the musical climate of the time.

The new combination made possible a wide range of sonorities, as the Bernal-Hernández tandem combined to record such polkas as "Idalia," with its intricate execution and fast chromatic passages. Meanwhile, Bernal began to rely more and more on three-part singing, deliberately incorporating stylistic elements from Mexican trios popular at the time, particularly Los Tres Reyes, a suave, romantic trio that provided material for a number of Bernal tunes, especially boleros. Indeed, in addition to boleros, El Conjunto Bernal adopted many genres not normally associated with conjunto music, including *valses peruanos, mariachi sones,* and even American rock tunes. Of course the *canción ranchera*—mostly in polka tempo, though it was often done in three-quarter time as well—remained the staple genre, even for El Conjunto Bernal. However, even with the *canción ranchera* the group mixed solo and duet singing with three-part harmonies.

As I indicated earlier, Bernal's decision to change his style was motivated by his desire to "distinguish" his group, as he put it. It worked. In doing so—in becoming, in effect, more versatile and more polished—the group succeeded in capturing new segments of the tejano market. As Bernal explained to me, "Eso nos abrió otro público más—el ser un poco más moderno—que podíamos tener gente que en ese tiempo seguía a las orquestas" ("that opened up another public for us—our becoming a little more modern—so that we could have people who at that time followed orquestas"). Thus, what Bernal was trying to do, and succeeded in doing, was to broaden his social base, to win over at least some of the clientele that orquestas normally attracted. Bernal accurately judged that this clientele was ready for a more sophisticated conjunto sound, one that was still ranchero, yet capable of branching out into other types of music besides the *canción ranchera*. In the end, as Bernal explained, "Alcanzamos a agarrar dos públicos" ("We managed to gather in two publics"). This assessment was born out by every orquesta musician I talked to, all of whom agreed that El Conjunto Bernal was the only group of its kind to command the admiration of orquesta fans who would not normally support conjunto music.

Bernal succeeded in attracting both the traditional and at least some of the upwardly mobile workers for two reasons. First, the early 1960s was a period of instability for orquestas. A sizable portion of the population that had traditionally provided its support simply began to assimilate popular American music. Cognizant of this assimilation (because they themselves were caught up in its sweep), younger tejano bands at this time began to adopt names and styles inspired by American pop music. Throughout Texas, tejano groups with names like the Royal Jesters, Spider and the Playboys, Manny and the C.O.'s, Little Joe and the Latinaires, and Sunny and the Sunglows attempted to keep pace with the American music that the younger, more assimilated tejanos were irresistibly drawn to.

On the other hand, some orquestas, such as that of Isidro López, chose instead to encroach on conjunto's domain with some positive results, especially among those borderline workers who were ambivalent about the merits of conjunto music. By becoming more "rancheroized" these orquestas were able to capitalize on this ambivalence. Ultimately, of course, most of the younger groups—notably Little Joe and the Latinaires and the renamed Sunny and the Sunliners—turned to the more traditional *orquesta tejana* style, because they were simply unable (or unwilling) to compete in the field of American pop music. Forging a new, and more ranchero phase within the old orquesta tradition that dated back to Beto Villa, the new groups established themselves within a less Americanized constituency, a move that placed them in more direct competition with the more progressive conjuntos, especially that of Bernal. By this time, however (the mid-1960s), El Conjunto Bernal had established a formidable following. None of these orquestas offered a serious challenge.

Yet another and perhaps more compelling reason for the acceptance of Bernal's innovations was his keen understanding of the limits of the conjunto music horizon. He probed those limits, but despite a few spectacular exceptions—which, by his own admission, cost him some followers—his music seldom dissolved the fundamental elements of the style laid out during the 1940s and 1950s. Thus, while he did introduce some bold ideas, concealed beneath them was a solidly ranchero sound. In short, Bernal may have made unusual demands on his audiences's musical sensibilities, but he did so through a deft combination of complexity and *alegría*—the term used by the people themselves to refer to the basic qualities of the conjunto sound. In this way Bernal managed not to alienate but rather to intrigue his listeners. In sum, his success depended on maintaining a delicate balance between the novel and the traditional—for example, a sophisticated bolero sung in three-part harmonies immediately followed by a rousing *canción ranchera* sung in the traditional duet.

In assessing El Conjunto Bernal's eminence we must keep in mind that it was due in no small measure to a simple case of effective and talented musicianship. Bernal's musicians were all masters of the basic conjunto style that had been forged earlier. As I mentioned, Bernal was able to attract some of the most talented musicians available. There was Oscar Hernández, to this day recognized as the accordionist with the best technique in the history of the tradition. Other outstanding musicians and singers included the highly respected drummer Armando Peña, who later played with such notable orquestas as that of the Mexican Luis Arcaraz; the late Manuel Solís, a much admired tenor whose range was a hallmark of El Conjunto Bernal for the better part of the 1960s, as were the voices of soloists Juan Sifuentes and Cha Cha Jiménez. Additionally, when Bernal quit playing with the group in the latter part of the 1960s to concentrate on its expanding business, several very capable accordionists were brought in, including Ramiro Leyja, Ramón Treviño, and the piano-accordionist Beto Salinas. Lastly, there was of course Eloy Bernal, considered by most as the finest *bajo sexto* player in conjunto music's history.

In summary, El Conjunto Bernal was able to attract a broad range of Texas-Mexican people because its musicians, who were all intimately familiar with conjunto music, were able to enrich it through their virtuosity and their general mastery of the nuances that distinguish an outstanding from an ordinary musician. Backed by such musicians, Bernal was able to switch easily from traditional conjunto to more unconventional types of music, and sometimes to synthesize divergent styles. In the end, it was this unique blend of the traditional and the innovative that, in the words of one orquesta musician, made El Conjunto Bernal "the greatest and the only one of its kind."

The Post-Bernal Period

El Conjunto Bernal's influence began to diminish toward 1970, though it continued to exert its presence until 1977, when the group switched to Christian religious music. Paulino had become a "born-again" preacher in 1973, and the group had continued under the direction of Eloy Bernal until he, too, joined his brother in the traveling ministry. When Eloy Bernal joined Paulino and they organized the new, Christian music Conjunto Bernal, some of his fellow musicans—including Cha Cha Jiménez, accordionist Bobby Naranjo, and the late Manuel Solís's brothers, Juan and Joe—formed a new group known as Los Chachos. Los Chachos are still active today, carrying on in the old Conjunto Bernal tradition; however, neither they nor other similar groups, most of which Oscar Hernández has been involved with at one time or another, have been able to rekindle the creative spirit of El Conjunto Bernal or capture the hearts of the tejanos as that group had done.

Meanwhile, with the gradual decline of El Conjunto Bernal beginning around 1970, the more orthodox style of the 1950s regained supremacy—though it was never actually eclipsed, by any means, by El Conjunto Bernal. A number of conjunto musicians who were popular in the 1950s carried on with more or less vigor in the 1960s and even beyond that time. These included Tony de la Rosa, Agapito Zúñiga, and Rubén Vela, to name three of the best-known. Even some of the members of the older generation were actively promoting their music during these years, including Narciso Martínez and Pedro Ayala.

At this time, however, developments in the Mexican *norteño* music tradition began to complicate matters for conjunto music: *Norteño* groups were making substantial inroads into the conjunto market. This was due in no small measure to the fact that *norteño* recordings were aggressively promoted in the United States, while at the same time the musicians themselves had relatively easy access to the ballroom-dance circuit that had been established in the Southwest since the late 1940s. Tejano conjuntos, on the other hand, had an extraordinarily difficult time in distributing their records or making personal appearances in Mexico. Time and again the musicians cited the restrictive policies of Mexican customs officials, who either refused them permission to take their instruments across the border or else demanded exorbitant bribes. Yet, despite this imbalance—or perhaps because of it, since they may have perceived a need to adjust their style to the tastes of their north-of-the-border constituents—Mexican *norteño* groups came increasingly under the stylistic influence of the tejano conjuntos. Whatever the case, it is readily apparent that many *norteño* musicians popular in the 1960s—Los Tremendos Gavilanes, El Palomo y el Gorrión, Los Relámpagos del Norte, and others—had begun more and more to take their musical cues from the developments on this side of the border.

Los Relámpagos del Norte merits further comment, since it and its off-spring, Los Bravos del Norte, may well be the two groups that were the most successful in bridging the gap between *norteño* and conjunto styles. They also happen to have dominated the *norteño* music field in general from the late 1960s until about 1980. Organized in the mid-1960s by singer-*bajo sexto* player Cornelio Reyna and *bajo sexto* player-accordionist Ramón Ayala, Los Relámpagos was discovered in Reynosa, across the river from McAllen, Texas, by none other than Paulino Bernal. He had gone into Mexico to scout for *norteño* groups that he could sign up for Bego, a recording company he and a partner had recently formed. Once on the wax disc, Los Relámpagos achieved instant fame, rising quickly to overtake all the other groups of the time—*norteño* and conjunto alike.

However, in the early 1970s Reyna and Ayala went their separate ways, and it was at this time that Ayala decided to organize Los Bravos del Norte, a group that went on to supplant Los Relámpagos as the premier group in *música norteña*. Beyond that, however, Ayala is an important figure in the *norteño*/conjunto spectrum because, as Paulino Bernal observed, "está entre medio de los dos"—he is "in the middle" of the two styles, forming a link between the two. His style of singing, for example—more nasalized than that of modern conjunto singers and strongly reminiscent of the duets of the 1930s—is clearly in the mold of the Monterrey-based groups that long ago set the pattern for the *norteño* style and that until the 1960s were minimally influenced by the changing currents in conjunto music. His accordion technique, on the other hand, has from the beginning been much closer to that of the tejano accordionists, perhaps as a result of Ayala's intimate association with tejano musicians and recording companies. In any case, until

Los Relámpagos del Norte and Ramon Ayala's Los Bravos came along, no other *norteño*-style group had ever mounted a serious challenge against the supremacy of "homegrown" conjuntos among tejanos.

With respect to the popularity of Los Bravos and other later groups (e.g., Los Cadetes de Linares), one last point needs to be considered in relation to their competition with Texas-Mexican conjuntos. I refer to the unprecedented immigration of Mexicans not only from the north but from all parts of Mexico into Texas. This immigration has had an adverse effect on conjuntos (and even orquestas) in at least two ways. First, the influx of *norteños*, who have generally favored their own groups over conjuntos, has ultimately allowed *norteño* groups to overtake their tejano counterparts, especially outside of Texas. *Norteño* groups had always enjoyed a measure of popularity among tejanos, of course—Los Alegres de Terán are a case in point—but the heavy influx of Mexicans tilted the balance of public support in their favor. This tilt was also aided by the increasing cultural assimilation of second- and third-generation tejanos, so that at least some of the original base for conjunto music had eroded by the late 1960s.

Thus, beginning with the phenomenal appeal of Los Relámpagos del Norte, Mexican *norteño* groups gradually rose to overshadow their tejano counterparts. Today Los Cadetes de Linares and Los Tigres del Norte far outdraw a Tony de la Rosa or an Esteban Jordán anywhere in the Southwest, save perhaps in certain parts of Texas. Indeed, Texas remains, understandably, conjunto music's stronghold, particularly the area bounded by Austin, San Antonio, Alice, and Corpus Christi. The Rio Grande Valley, too, has its contingent of conjuntos, but *norteño* music from across the border offers stronger competition there.

Another way in which Mexican immigration has altered the musical culture of Mexican Texas—and in the process undermined conjunto music—is through the introduction of *grupos tropicales* (tropical groups)—ensembles that specialize in a Mexicanized, working-class variant of the South American *cumbia*, nowadays an international dance that derives from Afro-Hispanic origins. Today groups such as Perla del Mar, Rigo Tovar, and others that rely chiefly on a *cumbia* repertory have become a ubiquitous addition to the weekend dances that are held all over Texas and the Southwest. *Tropical* ensembles are especially popular with the so-called undocumented workers, though to some degree they draw their clientele from the tejano working class as well.

The popularization in the Southwest of *grupos tropicales* and *latino* music in general—for example, *música moderna* of the type popularized by the likes of Julio Iglesias and José José—has been facilitated by the immigration of Mexicans and Latin Americans, of course. But, as always, the large recording companies (which employ the big names), as well as radio stations and disc jockeys interested in promoting a generalized *latino* music purely for commercial gain, have had an immense influence in the universal propagation of such music. This is especially the case with so-called *música moderna*, where the financial backing of companies like RCA has no doubt been a most important factor in the music's widespread appeal. To this effect a statement by Gutiérrez and Schement on the programming practices of one Spanish-language radio station in the Southwest is worth quoting:

> The selection of music is heavily weighted toward the *música moderna* category. An analysis of the playlist for a six-month period revealed that 62% of the music was *música moderna*, 20% was *rancheras* and 18% *tropicales*. According to the program director this is the balance the station wants to maintain to attract the younger audience its advertisers desire" (Gutiérrez and Schement 1979:79).

On many Spanish-language stations in Texas, however, especially the smaller ones, conjunto music continues to garner its share of air play.

To summarize recent history: Conjunto music has been under considerable pressure in the last twenty years—from *norteño* and *tropical* music, as well as other types of a generalized *latino* persuasion. And, of course, orquesta music continues to present a challenge. Indeed, since the early 1970s orquesta music, now for the most part highly "rancheroized," has mounted a strong resurgence. In so doing, orquestas have become much more competitive with conjuntos, recapturing, for example, a good portion of the constituency that El Conjunto Bernal once held.

Yet the music has endured, and in the last few years the durable Tony de la Rosa, Rubén Vela, Flaco Jiménez (Santiago Jiménez's son), and others have enjoyed a modest resurgence. Rubén Naranjo, from Alice, Texas, whose style is solidly in the conjunto tradition, has achieved some renown; and, of course, Ramón Ayala, whose style for all practical purposes is now "tejanoized," continues to hold his on against both other conjuntos and their *norteño* counterparts. (Ayala now lives in Hidalgo, Texas, and presently records for the same company in Corpus Christi that Tony de la Rosa and others are connected with.)

One other development has emerged in recent years that on the whole bodes well for the survival of conjunto music. I refer to groups that have attempted to synthesize conjunto and orquesta tejana by combining (usually) two alto saxophones with the accordion to create a novel blend of the two styles. Roberto Pulido y Los Clásicos perhaps best personifies this synthesis. Pulido organized Los Clásicos in 1973. Recognizing the overwhelming appeal of the accordion among tejanos, yet wishing to maintain some of the features of the orquesta tejana, he decided from the beginning to include the two saxophones because, as he said, "It's a beautiful sound that gives you an orchestra flavor" (personal interview, April 2, 1980). "That's my style," he added, "está entre medio de orquesta y conjunto ("it is between orquesta and conjunto"). "I've got the horns, and I've got the accordion."

The combination worked. Although his first recordings, with GCP, a company from San Antonio, resulted in failure, Pulido did not give up, and in 1976 the more aggressive Falcón label decided to give Los Clásicos a chance. From that moment on, the group began its steady climb toward the pinnacle of tejano music. In fact, by 1980 Roberto Pulido y Los Clásicos was Falcón's best-selling group. In the words of Arnaldo Ramírez, head of the most successful Chicano recording company to date, "Los Clásicos are my bread-and-butter group right now" (personal interview, March 30, 1980).

However, despite Pulido's success and the possibilities that his experiment holds for an orquesta-conjunto hybrid that may replace its traditional predecessors, there has been no rush among tejanos—laymen or musicians—to cast the old music aside. In point of fact, as a music with its own highly developed style, based on the relationship between the accordion and the other instruments, conjunto is far from extinct. As Pulido himself admits, "That's the whole backbone of Chicano [tejano] music—la acordeón." Thus, today in Texas conjunto music still maintains a high degree of visibility, despite Esteban Jordán's complaints about its demise. The accordion remains "el instrumento del pueblo," as Arnaldo Ramírez put it, enjoying the preference of a sizeable portion of the tejano working class and reigning over celebrations large and small. Its continuity as an expressive form thus seems assured for the immediate future, especially since, as always, hundreds of amateur musicians carry on the tradition in scores of communities throughout Texas.

Lastly, conjunto music has received a boost from an unexpected direction—though its effect on conjunto's original, working-class orientation (and, hence, on its symbolic strength) is open to question, since the boost comes not from internal but external sources. I refer to the general curiosity that the popular film *Chulas Fronteras* has generated, as well as the interest that such institutions as the Smithsonian and the National Endowment for the Arts have shown toward ethnic folk traditions, including conjunto. As a result of these developments the music has suddenly found itself in the national limelight. Official recognition has come forth at an increasing pace in the last five or six years, as Narciso Martínez, Pedro Ayala, and others have been cited for their contributions in the preservation of this unique ethnic art.

American interest has in turn caused Texas-Mexicans to reexamine their relationship with this suddenly precious cultural resource. One suspects that many upwardly mobile, former proletarians (or their offspring), who in earlier times would have turned away from the music as a result of upward mobility, now feel that it is "respectable" to retain their allegiance to conjunto. On the other hand, even among erstwhile foes of the music, a new and sometimes romanticized interest is evident, to judge from the number of conjunto "festivals" that have sprung up in places like Corpus Christi and San Antonio, not to mention the number of media proposals on sundry aspects of the music that have been approved or are pending before various funding agencies.

In this way, a tradition that at its core has represented a counter-ideological response by tejano workers to their subordination under American politicoeconomic and cultural hegemony has been de-contextualized and "encompassed" by the institutions of that hegemony, in the process stripping the music of a vital chunk of its original symbolic force. And, through one of those ironies that only history can spring, all of this has happened even as well-intentioned Anglo-American "culture preservers" celebrate conjunto's entry into the ranks of venerable traditions that bear witness to America's multiethnic heritage. I shall have more to say about all of this in Part II.

A Working-Class Orquesta, ca. 1915, courtesy of the Houston Public Library.

Orquesta Típica Laredo, 1939, courtesy of José Compeán.

Narciso Martínez, Ideal
Records promo photo,
courtesy of Lalo Campos,
KVET Radio, Austin, Tx.

Narciso Martínez and Santiago
Almeida, *bajo sexto* player, ca. 1936,
courtesy of Narciso Martínez.

Ismael González, *tololoche*, Santiago Jiménez, accordion, and
Lorenzo Caballero, guitar, early 1950, courtesy of Santiago Jiménez
and Arhoolie Records.

El Conjunto Cielito, Austin, Texas, ca. 1950, courtesy of Lalo
Campos, KVET Radio, Austin, Tx.

Los Hermanos García Torres, New Braunfels, Texas, ca. 1950,
courtesy of Lalo Campos, KVET Radio, Austin, Tx.

Valerio Longoria and Valerio Longoria, Jr., ca. 1970, courtesy of Valerio Longoria.

Rubén Vela, accordionist, and Eduardo Vela, *bajo sexto* player, courtesy of Rubén Vela.

Johnny Degollado, accordionist, and conjunto members, Austin, Texas, 1980, courtesy of Johnny Degollado.

El Conjunto Bernal, ca. 1965, courtesy of Bego Records.

Los Relámpagos del Norte, Cornelio Reyna and Ramón Ayala, courtesy of Bego Records

Part II
The Evolution of a Style: Economic, Social, and Symbolic Dimensions

5. La Gente Pobre: The Social Base of Conjunto Music

In a recent paper on the Mexican *corrido*, John McDowell felt compelled to offer the caveat that, in mapping out the social context of the *corrido*, he was "indulging" in a "serviceable fiction"—assuming for the sake of argument the existence of "ballad communities" (1981:44). Such caveats are necessary neither for *corrido* nor conjunto music: The one's communities are as real as the other's. Indeed, the *corrido's* constituency has historically been the same as that of the conjunto's. Thus, although up to now I have taken the social context of the conjunto more or less for granted and assumed that a specific constituency with its own social, cultural, and economic characteristics formed the human environment for the music's development, at this point I would like to present a more concrete socioeconomic profile of that constituency. More specifically, I want to sketch the development of classes in Texas-Mexican society—particularly during the period from 1930 to 1960, when conjunto emerged as a fully stylized working-class musical expression. (Appendix A contains a fuller discussion of the class theories I have applied to Texas-Mexican society.)

A complete, multivariate analysis of the development of Texas-Mexican classes is impossible here, first, because that would actually require a study in its own right, and, second, because the research information that exists is far from complete.[1] Additionally, the data for the 1930s are particularly meager, since the 1940 census did not obtain socioeconomic information pertaining specifically to Mexicans. Nonetheless, at least a schematic profile is both possible and advisable for the purposes of this study, and should be enough to establish the empirical basis to substantiate my earlier statements on the working-class nature of conjunto music. There is enough evidence, both of a quantitative, socioeconomic nature as well as a qualitative one (based on oral histories), to draw such a conclusion. The data I will present, then, will serve as a general but valid reference to reinforce the many statements on the part of musicians that conjunto was the music of *la gente pobre* (the poor people).

In my analysis I shall, somewhat in the fashion of Wright's analysis of American classes (1976; see Appendix A), begin at the empirical (i.e., occupational) level with information drawn from the data to be found in the U.S. censuses from 1940 through 1970, and then proceed toward integrating that data into an analytical class structure. My main concern in this chapter is to delineate the features and parameters of a tejano working class as agains₍ those of the middle class and other segments which occupied "contradictory class locations" (Wright 1976). I leave for the next chapter a discussion of the conflict generated by the economic and ideological divergence between the working class and the middle class, and its implications for the development of conjunto music.

From Rural to Urban: Demographic Shifts and Social Change

I mentioned earlier the importance of the period surrounding World War II for the socioeconomic differentiation of tejano society. Indeed, the prewar period may be considered one in which Texas-Mexicans constituted as a whole a rural, mainly agricultural work force with strong ties to Mexican culture. Confined as they were to ranchos and other small enclaves—or to *colonias*, even in the larger cities—tejanos could not but maintain a strong sense of Mexican ethnicity. These feelings of ethnic differences vis-à-vis Americans have been noted by, among others, Paredes (1958, 1976), Foley (1977), Taylor (1934), and Mario García (1981). Complementing this difference was a more or less pervasive cultural isolation from American society. This isolation was not total, of course: Since the latter part of the nineteenth century Mexicans had increasingly been drawn into American capitalism's expansion into the Southwest, but it was marked enough to perpetuate the ethnic boundary between Mexicans and Anglos. Furthermore, a set of proscriptions governing relations between the two groups made cultural assimilation difficult, structural assimilation (e.g., intermarriage, acceptance in Anglo clubs, etc.) almost impossible.

The situation in Nueces County described by Taylor was probably representative of the tejanos' isolation. "Separation," wrote Taylor, "which distinctly characterizes the position of the Mexicans of Nueces County in education, domicile, class, and to a lesser degree, politics, is also a conspicuous feature of the social relations between

Mexicans and Americans" (1934:250). Taylor continues:

> A variety of social distinctions which penetrate even the realm
> of business make publicly manifest the desire of Americans to
> avoid social contacts with Mexicans. In commerce, where
> eagerness for contact is almost if not quite equal to the desire
> of farmers for Mexican laborers, sharp exception is made when
> the canons of American customs dictate, or are thought to dic-
> tate, that there shall be no contact (1934:250).

Coupled with this segregation from the rest of American society
was the notable lack of any class differentiation (see Barrera, 1979;
Richard García 1978). These twin conditions promoted the folk-like
existence that prevailed in Texas-Mexican society until the 1930s.
As I have indicated, this was evidently true even of those groups living in such cities as San Antonio, Corpus Christi, and Laredo,
though in these a small but well-established petty bourgeoisie with
perhaps a more urban orientation did exist (Taylor 1934; Mario
García 1981). In any case, the rural areas and small towns where
most tejanos lived up until 1930 were close-knit and relatively
homogeneous (cf. Foley 1977). (No more than 25 percent of the tejano population inhabited the four principal cities of San Antonio, El
Paso, Laredo, and Houston during the period 1900-1930, according
to Romo [1978:193]). This is not to say that no cultural or social
diversity existed. As mentioned, even in those earlier days there
was an incipient middle class of petty bourgeoisie and professionals
who considered themselves a cut above the common folk. In fact,
early Texas-Mexican music already reflected to some extent that
diversity (see Chapter 1). Moreover, it is unlikely that, given the
enormous distance between the Rio Grande Valley and El Paso, for
example, there would not be some degree of cultural diversity between two such regions.

Still, in its totality much of Texas-Mexican society of the nineteenth and early twentieth centuries exhibited at least some of the
characteristics of folk societies described by Redfield (1947). These
included such features as a strong sense of ethnic group identity,
relative isolation, extensive nonliteracy, a lack of labor differentiation in the capitalist, industrial sense—in sum, the features of an
agrarian society (cf. Paredes 1958:9-15). It was not, however, an
ideal folk society as described by Redfield, "in a little world off by
itself." The Mexican-American War of 1846-1848 had made tejanos,
and the Mexican immigrants who came later, subjects of a powerful,

aggressive nation whose capitalistic expansion into the Southwest was carried out literally "by the sweat of their brow" (Reisler 1976). But early contact with Anglo-American society up until 1910 was sporadic. It is true that it was traumatic, creating "deep disturbances" (cf. Bateson 1972) within Texas-Mexican society, but it did not immediately threaten to fragment the society or its culture through internal dissension. The threat was still external.

In fact, it was not until the early twentieth century that the situation began to change decidedly. As a result of greatly increased American economic activity in the Southwest, particularly agribusiness, Texas-Mexican society found itself under the increasing domination of American economic imperatives as more and more tejano workers were drawn into the network of agricultural and, later, industrial production (Taylor, 1934; Barrera, 1979). With increased participation in American economic activity, a corresponding exposure to capitalist relations of production and their social and cultural correlatives might be expected. By the 1930s the initial trauma and repercussions of conquest and interethnic competition were behind, as were the days of isolation. Now World War II was about to present tejanos with their most intense exposure to American life and its cultural hegemony (through military service or work in a wartime economy), and, with it, the most severe assimilative pressures in their cultural history.

Thus, the period 1900-1940 may be considered a prelude to change. It was World War II that marked a critical threshold in the social, cultural, and economic transformation of Texas-Mexican society. In one instance the war ushered in the final phase in the tejanos' movement toward a more completely urbanized—and, by extension, more acculturated—life in greater American society. It is of course undeniable, as Romo (1978) has demonstrated, that urbanization had been in evidence since 1910, at least. But as mentioned, in Texas even as late as 1930 only 25 percent of the Mexican population lived in the metropolitan areas. To complicate matters, even in urban areas tejanos were subjected to a set of restrictions affecting not only their economic but their social and cultural lives as well (cf. Taylor 1934; Landolt 1976). For example, in San Antonio, a city with a high Mexican population by the 1920s, the majority of workers surveyed in a labor study were either unskilled or semi-skilled (Romo 1978:188). Coupled with this limited occupational range was the fact that Mexicans in Texas (as elsewhere) lived overwhelmingly in barrios and *colonias* that one could argue functioned to preserve many of the older, rural traditions (cf. Achor 1978:38-46). In sum, even within an urban setting, Texas-Mexicans were more often than not segregated from the larger American society, an arrangement that fostered the retention of their ethnic culture.

Nonetheless, the transformation of tejano society was inevitable. Richard García (1978) has documented some of the changes already taking place in San Antonio by the 1930s. These, he says, "served to separate and crystallize the Mexican community in San Antonio into three distinct classes—a small Mexican bourgeoisie, a developing Mexican petit bourgeoisie and a vast Mexican working class" (1978:24). Each of these, in turn, was affected by disparate rates of cultural assimilation resulting from subjective status distinctions—the *jaitones* (high-toned) vs. the common people—and objective class differentiation. Furthermore, we may be reasonably certain that even greater social division ensued after World War II. With this qualification I would agree with García that at the root of social change was "the clash between urban and rural culture and Mexican and American culture" (1978:36). However, I would add that the process of class differentiation also contributed heavily toward cultural fragmentation.

Urban culture—that is, mainstream, American middle-class, "Anglo-conformity" culture (Gordon 1964)—had the upper hand (as it did with rural white America), particularly over those segments of tejano society that were absorbed, either occupationally or militarily, by the war effort and, later, by the accelerated economic activity that lasted well beyond the end of the war. As wages increased and work became both more available and more differentiated, tejano society responded. The norms that bound white-collar, petty bourgeois, and even blue-collar America into a broad-based conformity group had their impact on a developing tejano counterpart. It was at this time that tejanos became irrevocably split between middle class and working class.

Forming an integral part in the split of Texas-Mexican society were the divergent values and attitudes that the various status groups in the society ascribed to themselves and to others. Of particular interest here were those that upheld or challenged the traditions and values of the earlier rural, more folk-like, and Mexicanized society, for these contributed significantly to the appearance of new and often contradictory forms of symbolic expression. Orquesta music is a prime example. We may note also the awkward attempts on the part of Americanized tejanos to anglicize their names, much to the scorn this aroused among the more Mexicanized people (cf. Limón's comments on *agringado* joking [1978]). I should also mention Paredes's observations on the confusion of labels that newly Americanized Chicanos spawned in their search for respectable

American citzenship, no matter how hyphenated (Paredes 1976: 158-160).

Ultimately, for those tejanos who achieved one degree or another of upward mobility, urbanization, and acculturation (the three often occurred simultaneously) important changes took place, marked by the following: (1) increased education, (2) an improved standard of material life, (3) heightened involvement in political activity (4) increased acceptance of English, though often accompanied by a high rate of code-switching, and (5) a generalized tendency to acquire the sentiments and attitudes, or normative patterns, of the dominant American society. In short, upwardly mobile Texas-Mexicans found themselves sharing more and more of the core values of a generalized American society: They were becoming culturally if not structurally assimilated (cf. Gordon 1964), even as they were abandoning, forgetting, or even repressing the norms of an older Mexican and Texas-Mexican culture.

On the other hand, for the mass of unskilled, working-class tejanos, who have been seen by some as a colonized or semicolonized reserve pool of cheap labor (Barrera 1979; Montejano 1979), the opportunity for both socioeconomic advancement and cultural assimilation remained beyond their grasp. In this respect we must not overlook the constant reinforcement of workers—and with them, Mexican culture—that immigration from Mexico provided. This immigration, aside from all the political problems it involved, surely had an enormous impact on the maintenance of Mexican culture, at least on the part of the working class in the United States (cf. Gamio 1971; Grebler et al. 1970; Cardenas 1977).

Of course, total structural assimilation into American society, achievable primarily through exogamous marriage (and other types of primary contact), remained virtually nonexistent for all segments of Texas-Mexican society. A powerfully restraining ethnic boundary, congealed into place by post-conquest conflict, made such assimilation almost impossible. Cultural assimilation, however, especially in its ideological aspects (e.g., the "super-Americanism" of LULACers [Paredes 1976:158]), could not be avoided—not in the long run. Yet in the short run we would expect that Anglo-Mexican cultural contact, even when it intensified after 1910, should not immediately result in the loss, or even diminution, of Texas-Mexican culture. Such was indeed the case, though some aspects of tejano culture were adversely affected.

Musical production, for example, seems to have suffered, not in terms of a decline in output but in a qualitative way. That is, adequate musical training and instruments were difficult to obtain, thereby inhibiting the development of permanent ensemble styles in particular. Thus, while there is ample evidence to indicate that musical activity was intense among the Texas-Mexicans (see Chapter 1), this activity seems not to have led to any stylistic breakthroughs comparable to the impressive achievements of conjunto and orquesta during the years surrounding World War II. We know that as a result of conquest and subordination the bulk of Texas-Mexican society remained locked for a long time at the bottom of the American occupational structure. (After 1910, Texas-Mexicans were captives, really, of a labor-repressive system that effectively prevented upward mobility, at least for the bulk of the unskilled workers [cf. Montejano 1979:132].) Were these factors—social and economic repression and the absence of a powerful overarching style of conjunto's magnitude—related? We cannot be certain, for stylistic development may not always be linked in a cause-and-effect relationship with the rate of social change. Nonetheless, the evidence suggests such a relationship and, in any case, the conditions present at the time of conjunto music's emergence were of a special sort, absent during the earlier periods.

Those conditions were linked to the rapid changes that took place beginning at the end of the Depression of the 1930s and culminating with the Korean War, by which time significant demographic, social, and economic developments had altered the cultural makeup of Texas-Mexican society. The principal catalyst for change was World War II; however, the transformation of the society had been set in motion earlier. But more important, the repercussions that socioeconomic division triggered at the cultural level did not create their full impact until the 1950s. And that, as I have contended, was the critical moment for the final emergence of conjunto music. In the next pages I would like to present a socioeconomic profile of Texas-Mexican society to 1960, to demonstrate in an empirical manner the changes I have been discussing. Later, in Chapter 6, I will draw the analytical connections between these changes and the emergence of the music itself.

An Analytical Class Model

Since I will be utilizing a model borrowed from E. O. Wright to analyze Texas-Mexican classes, I want to introduce in a highly abbreviated form Wright's conception of classes in modern capitalist societies (see Appendix A for further discussion). Briefly, while Wright is reluctant to allow for the existence of a middle class—especially one that is autonomous from the bourgeoisie—he nonetheless recognizes the existence of an "ambiguous" intermediate stratum. This stratum is made up of managers, semiautonomous workers, and small employers. Wright assigns this group of occupational categories to "contradictory class locations" between the bourgeoisie, petit bourgeoisie, and the proletariat. Wright describes his scheme in the following manner:

> An alternative way of dealing with such ambiguities in the class structure is to regard some position as occupying *objectively contradictory locations within class relations.* Rather than eradicating these contradictions by artificially classifying every position within the social division of labour unambiguously into one class or another, contradictory locations need to be studied in their own right (Wright, 1976:24).

For Wright, then, the bourgeoisie, petit bourgeoisie, and the proletariat are the three properly constituted classes in capitalist society, insofar as they stand in unambiguous relation to the means of production. To account for the contradictory locations mentioned in his model, Wright provides slots that are placed along the axes that link the three main classes. Managers, who have some control over the means of production but who are nonetheless wage workers, occupy a contradictory location between the proletariat and the bourgeoisie, so they are placed along the relational axis between these two major classes.   Semiautonomous employees (teachers, professionals, craftsmen, etc.), on the other hand, who retain rather high levels of control over their immediate labor process, should be located on the relational axis between the proletariat and the petty bourgeoisie. Finally, small employers occupy a contradictory location between the bourgeoisie and the petty bourgeoisie and are so located. Figure 4 illustrates Wright's model.

Wright's typology is useful not so much because of its formal clarity, but because, as he rightfully claims, it is based on the "real stuff of class relations in capitalist society." Thus, the contradictory nature of managers, semiautonomous wage earners, and small employers is tied to three processes in the relations of production, namely: control over the physical means of production (whether by ownership or by decision-making power), control over individual labor power, and control over capital in the form of investments and resources and their allocation (Wright, 1976:28). On these three processes Wright argues:

When we speak of the fundamental class antagonisms between workers and capitalists, what we mean is that these
two classes are polarized on each of these three underlying
processes: the capitalist class has control over the entire apparatus of production, over the authority structure as a whole
and over the overall investment process; the proletariat is excluded from each of these . . . The petty bourgeoisie, on the
other hand, constitutes the unambiguous location within simple commodity production: they have full economic ownership and full control over the physical means of production,
but control no labor power (1976:29).

The groups which occupy contradictory locations have varying access to these processes, as Wright demonstrates.

Figure 4: The relationship of contradictory class locations to the
basic class forces in capitalist society.

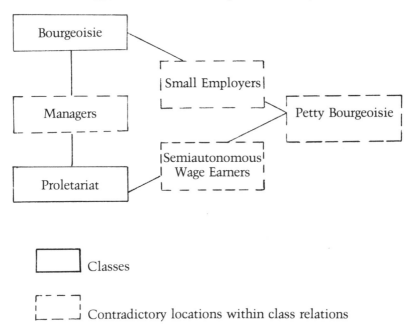

Source: Wright, 1976.

Social Classes in Texas-Mexican Society

In organizing the socioeconomic profile of Texas-Mexican society during the 1930s, 1940s, and 1950s I have more or less followed Wright's model, insofar as this was possible on the basis of census data, which are not collected according to Marxian categories.[2] I have, however, made some modifications to accommodate what I believe was the social and ideological reality of that society, especially after World War II. Thus, in contrast to Wright I have not hesitated to make use of the concept of the middle class, which is a useful heuristic device intended to account for the presence of a group of people—most of them white-collar workers—who were culturally removed from the tejano proletarians, recognizing at the same time the contradictory location that some of these people occupied in the total American class picture. I also use the term for convenience sake to avoid using absurd phrases such as "agents in contradictory locations allied with the (petty) bourgeoisie."

Meanwhile, I accept Braverman's word of caution that if we are to call managers, semiautonomous workers and others the "new middle class, we must do so with certain reservations" (Wright 1976:33). I should therefore point out that as a politicocultural group the Texas-Mexican middle class actually included members who did not occupy contradictory locations at all, in Wright's terms (i.e., in their relation to the means of production), but were actually a fraction of the working class that nonetheless espoused a middle-class ideology.

In this sense these workers, like the rest of the tejano middle class, could be said to have behaved very much according to the Warnerian conception of class as a prestige-status group. Like Hollingshead's class IV people, who avoided contact with Class V whenever possible (1953:220), white-collar tejano workers sought to solidify their middle-class status by dissociating themselves from the common workers. As Grebler et al. wrote with respect to all middle-class Chicanos: "Middle-class position is still precarious and beset with apprehensions over status maintenance and the grim consequences of sliding back" (1970:343). I would go so far as to propose that this fear of "sliding back" was a most important dynamic in the cultural lives of the tejano middle class, especially the low-level white-collar workers, whose foothold on middle-class status was the most precarious of all.

The true bourgeoisie—except insofar as the American bourgeoisie cast its shadow over all of Mexican Texas—was not a significant factor in the class structure or the culture of Texas-Mexicans.

To reduce my conception of tejano social classes to a schematic representation, I offer the model shown in Figure 5 and illustrated by Table 1. Unlike Wright, my decision to include low-level white-collar workers (e.g., sales clerks) stems, again, from the evidence that in the period being discussed here these workers evinced a considerable amount of estrangement from the rest of the working class (Rubel 1966:22). As Madsen wrote, "The middle class [i.e., white-collar workers] regards manual labor as degrading and a reflection of the lack of intelligence" (1964:36). Moreover, upwardly mobile tejanos in general displayed sentiments and attitudes that clearly emulated those of the Anglo-American middle class. This is not surprising in a state such as Texas, where Mexican nationality and proletarian status were as congruent as they were stigmatized and where the attainment of "Spanish" status was possible only by distancing oneself culturally and socioeconomically from the mass

Figure 5: Distribution of Texas-Mexican classes
and contradictory locations.

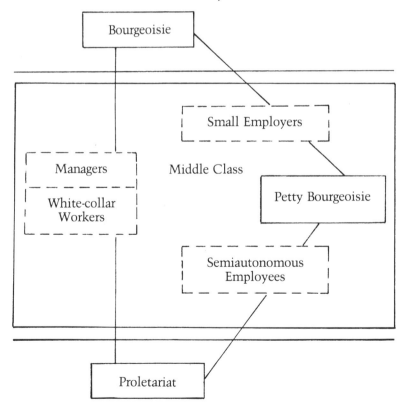

of workers. This may be one reason why Simmons, in his study of the early 1950s, concluded that in South Texas "class lines are much more distinct and sharply drawn within the Mexican group than in the Anglo group" (Grebler et al. 1970:345). In this respect, then, and contrary to their position in the actual relations of production, Texas-Mexican white-collar workers could be said to occupy a contradictory location within these relations.

One other factor often mentioned in stratificational studies of Texas-Mexicans ought to be noted here—the rural-to-urban demographic shift. As I have already indicated, beginning in the 1930s the urbanization of tejanos proceeded at a rapid pace. By 1960 over 78 percent of the tejano population was urban (Grebler et al. 1970: 113). However, while urbanization contibuted substantially to the socioeconomic differentiation of Texas-Mexican society, it should be placed in proper perspective. That is, it is clear that during the

Table 1: Some Texas-Mexican Occupations Considered
Contradictory and/or Middle-Class

Class/Location	Occupations
Petty Bourgeoisie	Family-run dry-goods store proprietors; physicians; lawyers; pharmacists; labor contractors
Small Employers	Restauranteurs; supermarket, garage/service station, and slaughterhouse proprietors
Managers	Foremen; white-collar supervisors
Semiautonomous Employees	Teachers; craftsmen (e.g., radio & TV repairmen; tailors; musicians; plumbers)*
White-collar Workers	Bookkeepers; salesclerks, insurance salesmen

*Wright's list of contradictory locations includes craftsmen in the semiautonomous category. Given the existence of a "dual labor market" in Texas (cf. Fogel 1967:147-48), where tejanos have historically gained access only to the lowest-level, lowest-paid crafts, it is my estimation that many such craftsmen would be located within the working class itself, except perhaps under conditions described below, where women enter the employment picture.

period being discussed here—particularly the postwar period—the urban-rural dichotomy became less important than emerging class differences. To be sure, symbolic distinctions remained (e.g., *lo ranchero*), but after World War II there was little difference, for example, between an urban and an agricultural worker. Indeed, many an urban dweller from, say, San Antonio spent his working life in agriculture (Grebler et al. 1970:299).

The decade of the 1930s presents the most difficulty in obtaining exact data on the socioeconomic composition of Mexicans in Texas, because the primary source for such data, the 1940 U.S. census, did not gather that kind of information. However, from the little information the census did compile, as well as that scattered in other reports, an unmistakable picture emerges: Texas-Mexicans in the 1930s were overwhelmingly poor. Moreover, in this respect the Mexican population of the 1930s was rather more homogeneous than it was by the end of the 1940s, and much more so than it was after 1960. As I have mentioned before, the ethnic isolation of tejanos was certainly one contributing factor (Grebler et al. 1970:300-301), but the homogeneity was further strengthened by the commonality of class.

The homogeneity of tejanos can thus be traced to two major factors: the folk, agricultural, and proletarian background that had recently characterized the bulk of Texas-Mexican society (including northern Mexican immigrants) and a strongly active discrimination that up until the 1930s relegated Mexicans almost exclusively to what Mario Barrera has described as "subordinant class segments [within the proletariat] based on the interrelated factors of race and ethnicity" (1978:168). Barrera attributes such subordinate class segments to the existence of a dual labor market, wherein the "primary" sector offered good pay and working conditions and the possibility for advancement. Secondary market jobs offered the opposite and "might be termed deadend jobs" (1978:168). As the preceding biographical sketches demonstrate, historically— especially in the years prior to World War II—Chicanos have had access mainly to the latter market.[3]

Despite the general lack of quantitative data on Texas-Mexicans for the 1930s, enough exist for at least a schematic profile. The U. S. census tabulated a few facts based on a survey of nativity and parentage that are useful. Table 2 summarizes these facts.

Even with no other available data, from the numbers in the table we can see that slightly over one quarter of the Mexican population in Texas resided in rural-farm areas. From what we know about

Table 2: Persons of Mexican Nativity and
Parentage in Texas, 1940

Total Mexican Stock	Urban	Rural-Nonfarm	Rural-Farm
484,306	275,223	86,981	122,102

Source: U.S. Bureau of the Census, 1943, p. 70.

Texas-Mexicans of the period, we may assume that the preponderant majority of these were propertyless, agricultural wage earners, inasmuch as few Mexicans owned farm property. In this respect the example of Nueces County is probably representative: In 1928 only twenty-nine tejanos owned farm acreage in that county (Taylor 1934:179). Furthermore, it is highly probable that a large number of the rural-nonfarm residents were also employed in agriculture. In any case, we have more detailed data on the occupation of Mexicans from Walter Fogel. And, although Fogel's figures are for 1930, it is not likely that the socioeconomic picture had changed very significantly by the end of the decade.   Fogel's data actually include all of the Southwest, but no variations may be expected that would change the Texas picture in any significant way.   Table 3 illustrates Fogel's analysis.

Clearly, by simply adding the figures in the "farm labor" and "laborer" categories, we can see that an overwhelming majority—over 63 percent—of the Mexican population in the Southwest consisted of proletarian workers. Furthermore, as Barrera (1979) and Grebler et al. (1970) have pointed out, even in the other occupations, Mexicans tended to cluster in the lowest-paid jobs of most occupational categories, so that most of the service, operative, and even some crafts categories would be solidly located within the working class, augmenting its ranks even more. Note, however, that as early as 1930 a small middle class ("significant," according to Taylor [1934:176]) of managers, proprietors, sales and clerical workers, and professionals—comprising approximately nine percent of the occupations—was in evidence.[4] As I have indicated, there is no reason to assume that these figures changed appreciably over the next ten years. Indeed, as Fogel pointed out, "the Great Depression of the 1930s was not conducive to the occupational upgrading of minorities" (1967:70).

By 1950, however, marked socioeconomic changes had occurred

Table 3: Occupational Distribution of Mexican American
Males in the Southwest, 1930

Occupational Category	Percentage
Professional	1.2
Managers and Proprietors	2.8
Clerical	1.3
Sales	3.2
Craft	5.9
Operative	10.0
Service	7.5
Laborer	25.8
Farm Laborer	32.9
Farm Manager	8.5

Source: Fogel, 1967, p. 63.

in the Texas-Mexican population. In fact, as I have proposed, there is evidence that the 1940s were a watershed period for Mexicans in the United States in terms of their opportunities for socioeconomic advancement and the cultural changes that entailed. And, while the expanded opportunities during and after World War II did not by any means mark the end of marginalization and economic subordination for tejanos, undeniable occupational changes took place that increased the socioeconomic and cultural diversity of the population. As Grebler et al., noted, "The World War II period brought a rather impressive improvement in the occupational position of Mexican Americans" (1970:199).

Fogel, meanwhile, readily acknowledged the dramatic economic strides made by California Chicanos during the 1940s, but he is more cautious in his assessment of tejanos' progress. Nonetheless, there are strong indications that substantial occupational upgrading took place among tejanos, too, especially the native-born, but their economic improvement was masked in the statistics by the harsh conditions of the 1930s. Thus, as Fogel put it, tejanos' gains in the 1940s, while significant, were "not sufficient to do more than offset the retardation which occurred during the 1930s" (1967:72). Nonetheless, taking all these considerations into account, we may justifiably propose that the socioeconomic improvements made by tejanos in the 1940s were substantial enough to allow a significant number to achieve at least marginal middle-class status, an accomplishment that set them apart socially and culturally from their less fortunate peers. The proletarians, of course, continued to maintain their preponderance in Texas-Mexican society, as indicated by the percentages in Table 4 for laborers, farm laborers, and operatives.

As can be determined from Table 4, there had been a considerable drop in farm labor employment between 1930 and 1950, a direct result of an expanding wartime urban labor market. As Grebler et al. summed up, "the onset of World War II brought improving opportunities for urban jobs" (1970:302). With urban jobs came the final push in the urbanization of tejanos: In 1950 over 78 percent lived in urban areas (1970:113), as compared with approximately 57 percent in 1940 (U.S. Bureau of the Census 1943). Additionally, middle-class occupational categories (male) had risen from just over 9 percent in 1930 to 24.9 percent in 1950, if we count the skilled craft (semiautonomous) occupations. Lastly, it is worth noting that 23.5 percent of the employed Texas-Mexican women in 1950 were in the sales and clerical categories (Barrera 1979:132).

In fact, although women did not play as prominent a role in the tejano labor force as men,[5] they apparently were not an insignificant segment in determining the class composition of the society. This

Table 4: Occupational Distribution of
Texas-Mexican Males, 1950

Occupational Category	Percentage
Professional	1.6
Managers and Proprietors	4.4
Clerical/Sales	6.5
Craftsmen and Foremen	12.4
Operatives	16.3
Laborers	18.8
Service	6.5
Farm Laborers	25.4
Farmers and Farm Managers	5.1
Occupation Not Reported	1.0

Source: Barrera, 1979, p. 132.

is because from early on they were conspicuously present in certain types of employment, particularly sales and clerical jobs, and were present even in professional occupations.[6] For example, by 1930, according to Taylor, "a large proportion, in Corpus Christi a majority, of the clerks were young women" (1934:177). And, as one Anglo businessman told Taylor: "I have two Mexican [women] clerks. They are a good class of Mexicans and speak good English . . ." (1934:176). Thus, it is very likely that women employed in sales and clerical jobs had an impact not only on a family's income but on its ideology as well. That is, these women adopted to some extent the sentiments and values of their Anglo superiors, in this manner distancing themselves socially and culturally from lower-status proletarian workers, who had little or no contact with middle-class America. Clearly, it was this distance that in the eyes of the Anglo businessman qualified the clerks as "a good class of Mexicans."

I know of no studies of Texas-Mexican working women's impact on the social, economic, and cultural life of their families. However, my own experience in South Texas up until the early 1960s would indicate that many women in the sales and clerical areas came from families in which the men were engaged in occupations other than that of "stoop" labor. Rubel's descriptions about my own hometown tend to substantiate this personal impression. Speaking of upwardly mobile Mexicans in Weslaco, Texas, who had moved up the socioeconomic ladder and across to the Anglo side of town, Rubel writes:

> The great majority of those who have moved . . . are veterans of either the Second World War or the Korean conflict . . . The young men are all bilingual, but some of their wives speak only Spanish. None of these south-side Chicanos work as "stoop" laborers in agricultural season labor, and their annual income ranges from $2,400 to $20,000 . . . In many families both husband and wife work . . . Those who move south of the tracks and others who seriously comtemplate the action share significant objective indicators of social-class status. They have completed elementary or high school, are employed in "clean" occupations, and boast dependable incomes . . . (1966:18-19).

Moreover, according to Rubel these tejanos "aspire[d] to a life goal of equality with Anglos, whose status symbols they had acquired" (1966:22). These symbols included "English-language skills, high school and college education and possession of such status markers

as automobiles, refrigerators, television sets and barbecue 'pits' "
(1966:12). But crucially important in the operation of the cultural
dynamics that set one group of tejanos against another is Rubel's
remark on "clean" occupations as a symbol of distinction. For
ultimately, in the status distinctions that tejanos recognized, a
"clean" occupation was the ideological determinant for admission
to the middle—or at least "respectable"—class, even if, as often happened, the occupation itself was objectively located within the
limits of the working class in terms of its relation to the means of
production. But most significantly, for many families admission to
the "respectable" occupational category was established on the
strength of the women's employment.

Perhaps an actual case will serve as an illustrative example. A
couple I knew were both employed, he as a service station mechanic
who moonlighted as a musician, she as a sales clerk in a local store.
In many respects their cultural outlook certainly evinced many of
the middle-class characteristics described by Rubel—including one
not mentioned by Rubel, a dislike for conjunto music. Many such
families have undoubtedly existed throughout Texas since the
1930s in which the occupation of the wife (or daughters) not only increased the family's income, but contributed to its "respectability,"
and certainly to its middle-class outlook. In this way, as a result of
the women's employment, the Texas-Mexican middle class (or at
least a bloc with a middle-class ideology) has historically been
augmented beyond the small percentages indicated when we take
only the employment of the males into account.

By 1960, then, Texas-Mexicans had made strong, if not dramatic,
gains socioeconomically in comparison to the 1930s. Noting that
Chicanos improved their economic lot considerably between 1930
and 1949, Fogel adds, "summing up, Mexican-Americans did
achieve slight improvement in their incomes relative to those of
Anglos between 1949 and 1959" (1967:55). Using census data, Barrera (1979) computed the occupational distribution of both males
and females in Texas for 1960 in terms of percentages. The results
are reproduced in Table 5.

It should be apparent from the foregoing data that the
socioeconomic characteristics of Texas-Mexican society changed
considerably between 1930 and 1960. It is, of course, basic to the
thesis advanced in this work that these socioeconomic changes
were vitally interconnected with the musical changes I have
described. In this respect one especially relevant fact stands out: A
clear majority of tejano workers was still solidly proletarian in 1960,
although a much more visible middle class, drawn to a great extent

Table 5: Occupational Distribution of Texas-Mexicans
by Sex, 1960

Occupational Categories	Percentage	
	Male	Female
Professional	3.1	5.3
Managers & Proprietors	4.5	2.8
Clerical	4.6	15.9
Sales	3.8	9.3
Craftsmen	14.7	1.0
Operatives	22.3	20.3
Laborers	14.6	1.2
Service	7.3	32.2
Farm Laborers	14.2	5.7
Farmers & Farm Managers	3.2	.2

Source: Barrera, 1979, p. 132.

from white-collar workers and craftsmen, had emerged. Converting the 1960 census data into the class schema I proposed earlier results in a class composition as illustrated by Figure 6.

Looking beyond 1960, we observe that the Texas-Mexican middle class (as I have defined it here) continued to grow. By 1970, if we include the professional and technical, the manager and the clerical and sales classifications, we find that 26.4 percent of the males and 42.9 percent of the females were in middle-class types of occupations (Barrera 1979:132). If we also include the males in the skilled-craftsmen classification, the figures (for males) jump to 43.2 percent. Thus, taking the various factors that influenced a person's ideological position (e.g., "clean" vs. "stoop" labor), we may calculate the limits of the tejano middle class to fall within the 30 percent to 40 percent range by 1970. By the same yardstick, however, the proletarian class still held a commanding numerical advantage, comprising 60 percent to 70 percent of the population.

The percentages that I have ascribed to the three main classes in this brief sketch make no pretense to represent absolute limits. To begin with, as I have already ponted out, census occupational classifications very often do not elicit the kind of information that

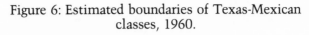

Figure 6: Estimated boundaries of Texas-Mexican
classes, 1960.

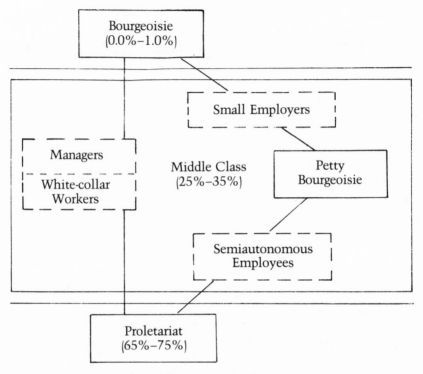

would enable us to make even the simple distinction between owners and non-owners in the production process, let alone to make the crucial one between proletarian workers and those who occupy contradictory locations. In the absence of such data-based distinctions, inferences—and sometimes outright guesses—are inevitable. For this reason the percentages in Figure 6 represent nothing more than high and low estimates of the distribution of Texas-Mexican classes.

In any case, my primary objective here has been to profile the tejano working class, with an outline of the middle class serving only contrastive purposes. With such limitations acknowledged, I believe that for the purposes I have in mind a useful profile of the working class has been drawn, and a reasonable distinction between it and the middle class established. These two features will form part of the framework for the interpretation I will undertake in the next chapter, which examines the social and symbolic significance of conjunto music.

Notes

1. Besides the U.S. census, Fogel (1967) and Grebler et al. (1970) provide the most extensive data on the socioeconomic characteristics of Mexican-Americans generally, Texas-Mexicans specifically. Barrera (1979) provides a good account, and useful information may be found in Richard García (1978) and Foley (1977). As always, Paul Taylor's seminal work (1934, 1968) contains valuable information.

2. An example of the potential anomalies that occupational census classifications can create is the designation "healer" under the "professional, technical, and kindred" listings. Presumably among Texas-Mexicans both physicians and *curanderos* would fall under this designation; yet neither form an economic viewpoint nor, much less, from a cultural one can these two types of "healers" be conceived as similar or identical. Under almost any circumstances the *curandero's* life function lies within a wholly proletarian ethos as a sort of "organic intellectual" (Gramsci, 1971) who, no matter how inarticulately, speaks for the proletariat's interests. The physician, on the contrary, in most cases would in fact be a small employer whose interests may be expected to be allied with the bourgeoisie. Conjunto musicians, who are also in the "professional"classification, would, of course, be in the same situation as the *curandero* vis-à-vis the physician. I will have more to say about this in the next chapter.

3. Evidence for this statement comes from a myriad of sources. Besides Barrera, see, for example, Taylor (1934), Montejano (1979), Richard García (1978), Foley (1977), Briggs et al. (1977), Landolt (1976), and Reisler (1976). Of course, the overwhelming employment of Mexicans in the secondary labor market cannot all be blamed on outright discrimination. A constant flow of unskilled workers from Mexico since 1940, especially, inflates the figures.

4. According to Taylor, at this time in Nueces County Mexicans were "generally found in chain stores of all types, department stores, groceries, hardware stores, lumber yards, clothing and shoe stores and one or two [were] in banks" (1934:176). Furthermore, "Mexican businessmen were also becoming numerous" (1934:177).

5. Fogel (1967) observed that nearly twice as many men were active in the labor force as women at any given time. Actually, the 1950 census reveals a ratio that is closer to four to one; the 1960 census, a three-to-one ratio.

6. Fogel has broken down the numbers into percentages. In 1950, 26.2 percent of the employed women were in clerical and sales jobs; 27 percent were so employed in 1960.

6. Social and Symbolic Dimensions of Conjunto: From Ascendancy to Decline

Now that I have traced the stylistic development of conjunto and sketched a profile of Texas-Mexican classes, I would like to turn in this final chapter to an interpretation of the social and symbolic dimensions of the music. I shall focus on the period of the music's ascendancy, but will also devote space to an assessment of its decline since the 1960s. That conjunto is historically the music of *la gente pobre* should be a self-evident fact, but, as I proposed from the outset, it has been more than a casual or desultory entertainment item in the cultural fare of the Texas-Mexican working class. Indeed, the evidence clearly indicates that, especially in the 1950s and 1960s, when conjunto reached its zenith, it possessed a substantial measure of cultural significance among the tejano workers.

I do not want to argue that conjunto music has been a master symbol that in some way functioned as an organizing principle for tejano culture (cf. Ortner [1973] on "key" symbols). Few, if any, musical symbols exert that kind of influence over a collective consciousness, and whatever strengths they are endowed with are usually most evident when brought into play during condensed, episodic events of festive and/or ritual nature (Blacking 1967; Manning 1973; Wasson et al, 1974). Of course, like ritual, music's expressive energies are not exhausted in its consummation as event; its effectiveness lives on in people's memories and may, moreover, be metaphorically linked with other domains of social life to create complex bundles of meaning, affect, and action.

Conjunto music's power as a symbolic expression derives from such a metaphorical link with and contribution to other symbolic domains that in their totality have circumscribed the cultural world of the Texas-Mexican workers during a specific period in their history. Thus—and I am referring in particular to its period of ascendancy—while the music was customarily actualized in designated settings of an episodic nature (principally dances), the symbolic statement each of these events enacted carried over and was absorbed into the everyday experience of the tejano worker. In other words, the musical events were a special sort of rhetorical play form (cf. Abrahams 1968, 1976; Burke 1969) that both defined symbolically what a tejano was and prescribed how he or she should behave culturally. And, in a wider sense, this definition of working-class, ethnic identity was governed by sociocultural dynamics that I believe are analyzable in terms of both class and ethnic conflict. It is to the task of interpreting those dynamics that I want to devote the remainder of this work.

As I have done up to now, I shall pay special attention to the twenty-year period following the war, because this was the historical moment when conjunto reached its limits as an artistic expression whose impact on working-class life was most pronounced. By focusing on the 1950s and 1960s I do not mean to suggest that the music's symbolic energy has been exhausted. However, as an expressive instrument of working-class ideology its galvanizing force has weakened considerably. I shall have more to say about this later.

A Sociohistorical Assessment

From the very inception of this study I stressed the interplay among several factors in the development of conjunto music—some of an empirical, others of a more abstract or subjective nature. In the former category would fall urbanization and occupational differentiation, as I described them in Chapter 5. Under the latter we may include the concepts I discuss in Appendix A: ethnicity, cultural assimilation and its ideology, and class. I would suggest that the processes of urbanization and occupational differentiation[1] necessarily precede and should be considered catalysts for the latter, although ethnic consciousness surely existed in a more purely crystallized form before urbanization set in. What urbanization did—and the class differentiation it fostered—was to complicate this ethnic consciousness, as more and more tejanos attempted to conform to "American citizenship" (Taylor 1934:242). Once urbanization was an accomplished fact (by 1950), it was the interaction between the ideology of cultural assimilation, ethnic resistance (on the part of both Anglo and Texas-Mexican), and class that helped shape the course of Texas-Mexican society and culture.

Thus, in the early years of the twentieth century, when tejanos were still largely confined to ranchos and other small enclaves, and their occupations restricted chiefly to agriculture, an awareness of their Mexicanness could not but occupy a prominent place in their world view. Furthermore, as I have repeatedly stressed, despite their increasing absorption into an expanding capitalist economy, tejanos remained culturally isolated from the rest of American society, as a result of ethnic prejudice and segregation.   Under such circumstances the retention of Mexican culture was inevitably encouraged.

Clearly, most of the folk traditions of tejanos up until the 1930s were of Mexican provenience, even if through the passage of time they had acquired a distinctive Texas-Mexican or more general *norteño* characteristic—for example, the border *corrido*. This would naturally apply to other musical traditions as well—even those of more recent European extraction, such as accordion music and salon music generally.   As I pointed out in Chapter 1, the music extant in Texas up until the 1930s was indistinguishable from that of northern Mexico, which was also acquiring its own characteristics (see Paredes [1963] on the *polca tamaulipeca*).   In the specific case of the accordion, which by the 1920s had begun to challenge other types of instruments for supremacy among the tejano proletarians, an unmistakable ethnic character had begun to be stamped on its music, as witnessed by such emergent stylistic elements as the accordion-*bajo sexto-tambora* combination and the ethnosemantic alteration of originally European genres, e.g., the redowa transformed into the *vals bajito*.

It is important to reiterate, however, that in addition to the ethnic transformation accordion music was undergoing, it was already, by the early twentieth century, a music associated with the working class. Thus, symbolically, it was attaining *both* an ethnic and class character.   However, its symbolic weight had a double valence: While it registered positively among the proletarian worker, already it had incurred a negative value from the viewpoint of the middle class and, especially, the Anglo. Indeed, this symbolic association dates from an even earlier period, if we are to judge from the attitude expressed in the *San Antonio Express* in 1881, an attitude that bears repetition: "These fandangos are become so frequent they are a great curse to the country. The respectable class of Mexicans do not attend them."[2]   In another article a short time earlier the *Express* had written about another "fandango" in Del Rio with the same disapproving tone, referring to the Mexicans in attendance as "natives," as opposed to the "respectable class" of Mexicans who avoided such events (June 18, 1881, p. 4). (In this case the accordion was specifically mentioned as the instrument providing the music for dancing.) Among the Mexicans themselves the recollections of Armando Marroquín are perhaps illustrative of the middle class's attitude:

> Pos realmente cuando comenzó la acordeón lo que apoyaba la música esa eran las cantinas. Todos los grupos de ese tiempo andaban en "rat traps"—las cantinas más humildes. Qué los iban a ocupar en un baile de sociedad. (Well, in truth, when the accordion started, it was the cantinas that supported that music. All the groups of that time hung around in rat traps—the humblest cantinas. No way they were going to be hired for a society dance) (personal interview, January 31, 1980).

Marroquín's statements correspond with my earlier remarks on the accordion's association with the disreputable *baile de negocio*. From the foregoing it is also evident, as I mentioned, that by the 1920s accordion music's symbolic significance had gravitated toward two poles: Among the working class its popularity was gradually eclipsing other ensembles as a musical expression, especially for dancing; among the "respectable" class of tejanos it was acquiring a negative association. Even so, despite the accordion's popularity in early Texas-Mexican working-class society, it had ample competition among the sundry ad hoc groups I mentioned earlier. But more importantly for the interpretation I shall soon offer, we should note that no particularly powerful stylization had been achieved as late as 1948. That did not take place until conditions became more propitious. I shall discuss these conditions shortly.

Meanwhile, beginning in the 1930s, as the process of urbanization and class differentiation began to accelerate, the old cultural isolation and, with it, traditions that fostered ethnic solidarity began to undergo an increasing amount of erosion. For example, in Corpus Christi by 1930 a few tejanos, "mainly of the middle and professional classes" (Taylor 1934:249), had begun to push for the "Americanization" of Mexicans. The League of United Latin American Citizens (LULAC) was especially active. As one LULACer expressed it:

> The world war taught us a lesson. We had thought we were Mexicans. The war opened our eyes . . . We have American ways and think like Americans. We have not been able to convince some [American] people that there is a difference

between us [and the old Mexicans] . . . (Taylor 1934:245;
brackets Taylor's).

The statement of another middle-class tejano summarized the intraethnic cleavage that the middle class's espousal of the ideology of
cultural assimilation was precipitating. (The "old Mexicans" in
reality included not only recent arrivals, but the less assimilated tejano proletarians as well.) In reference to the "task of lifting the
cultural level" of his people, a Texas-Mexican remarked, "We tell
our people, 'If you have not been treated like you should, or have not
the standard of living, it is your own fault. Before asking for your
rights under the constitution you must be prepared' " (Taylor
1934:247). But perhaps the most poignant statement was made by
another urbanized, middle-class Texas-Mexican, whose remarks
underscored the dominant presence of Anglo hegemony: "The Mexicans say we're trying to Americanize, and get away from Mexican
patriotism. We have to be American citizens whether we want to or
not" (Taylor 1934:242).

In this way, then, through urbanization and the emergence of a
middle-class, the erosion of ethnic homogeneity among tejanos was
hastened. Especially after World War II, unmistakable class
cleavages appeared that irrevocably divided Texas-Mexican society.
I have already discussed some of the effects of class differentiation
on this division, and will discuss further implications in reference to
conjunto's development below. Here I want to reiterate that by and
large, while "inexorable," as Richard García argued (1978), the
cultural absorption of tejanos into American life proceeded at highly
disparate rates. Due to confinement in barrios, poor education, and
low-paying occupations with minimal contact with Anglos, the proletarian masses remained far less accessible to American culture
than the emerging middle class, a fact that played a prominent role
in the ideological rift between the two classes.

This rift was expressed in many ways: in manners, attitudes
toward Mexican traditions and beliefs, choice of language—in short,
in differences on the observance of the norms that governed social
behavior. To cite linguistic usage as an example, the middle class's
dismay and antagonism toward the (usually) less Americanized proletarians may be discerned in some of the epithets that were common by the 1950s. These included such expressions as *el peladaje*
(from pelado: stripped, i.e., lumpen), *la plebe* (from plebeian: common people), *gente corriente* (common, vulgar people), *animal de
uña* ("clawed beast," i.e., beastlike, uncivilized), and any number of
more or less pejorative terms. Of course, *la plebe* was not at a loss

for a counter-response. Thus, at its disposal were such verbal slings as *jaitón*, (high-toned), *ay sosiégate* (a bilingual word play on the Spanish "oh, settle down" and the English "high society"), *agabachado* (from gabacho, a pejorative term for the Anglo), and, for maximum effect, *gringo fundillo prieto* (dark-assed gringo). To be sure, many of these refer to ethnic, not class-motivated scorn, but since proletarian workers had few pretensions about becoming too Americanized, the slurs were obviously aimed at upwardly mobile, culturally assimilated tejanos.

It would not be surprising if the class differences manifested through linguistic expression carried over into the realm of musical evaluation. Such is, indeed, what I have been proposing all along. In fact, while both groups had inherited a common musical tradition, by the 1950s conjunto and its rival style, orquesta, had emerged as the musical counterparts to the verbal cross fire that marked the class conflict. The two musics articulated the ideological split that the linguistic terms marked off. The musics were, to borrow Bauman's terminology, expressions of differential identity, "where the contrasting identities of the participants [i.e., proletarian and middle class] are directly relevant to the structuring of the situation and to their understanding of it" (Bauman 1972:292). This statement aptly describes the relationship between the middle and working classes, as it was expressed in their attitudes toward music generally, conjunto and orquesta in particular. The latter two were understood by the respective groups to be symbolic markers for their social differentiation. Narciso Martínez stated his understanding of this differentiation perfectly well: "La orquesta era pa' high society," he said; "el conjunto era pa' la gente ranchera" ("orquesta was for high society; conjunto was for the rural people").

As a culturally sanctioned symbolic expression, then, almost from its beginnings conjunto music was part of a larger response by the working class to the challenge posed against it by an increasingly Americanized middle class. How that response included and was translated into the symbolic language of music is explored in the next few pages.

Conjunto, Orquesta, and Social-Symbolic Polarization

As I have pointed out, while accordion music had from early on been appropriated by the tejano working class, no strong moves had been made prior to World War II toward the adoption of a well-integrated ensemble with fixed relationships between socially approved, regularly combined instruments. This did not happen until the 1950s, when the ensemble attained a high degree of stylization, as well as deep and widespread acceptance among the workers. It is now time to attempt to answer once for all the question set forth at the beginning of this work: Why did this musical style not reach maturity as a social, cultural, and artistic expression until the post-war years? Moreover, since we know that this maturation coincided with a deepening polarization between the proletarian and middle classes, can we reasonably claim that events at the artistic and social levels were linked? Or, to state the question differently, was conjunto music, as I have contended, a cultural solution on the part of the workers to the social problem of intraethnic class cleavage—particularly as manifested by the middle class's growing disenchant-ment with traditional Texas-Mexican culture?

To address these questions I think it is best to turn now to the statements collected from the musicians themselves—as well as others—on what the music means to them and to their consti-tuents. To this end I would like to begin by citing a few commen-taries on how polarized tejanos were on the merits of conjun-to—especially prior to the 1970s. I have already cited evidence on the early attitudes; from the interviews I had with musicians and others, it appears that polarization reached its peak in the 1950s and early 1960s.

To begin with a personal observation, I recall that in the late 1950s in my native city of Weslaco, Saturday-night dances were common in the town plaza, or *la placita*, as everyone called it.[3] At this time conjunto music reigned supreme at *la placita*, and per-formers like Rubén Vela, who were very much in demand, were regularly featured. These open-air dances attracted large crowds of *pachucos*, young men who had adopted what Paulino Bernal called a "rebellious" lifestyle: They had a distinctive way of speaking, ac-ting, and dressing (long, Vaseline-groomed ducktails, tattooed crosses on their hands, baggy slacks with ankle-tight cuffs, and double-soled, shellacked shoes). Moreover, since *pachucos* were universally drawn from the working class, the dances evinced what "respectable" people used to refer to as a low-class, *animal de uña* atmosphere. This atmosphere was enhanced by the *tacuachito*-style dance, which was considered ideal for the slowed down tempo of the late 1950s polka. As I recall, it was understood by young men and women *de buenas familias* (i.e.,of middle-class orientation) that they were to avoid such affairs.

I had an opportunity many years later to confirm my early impres-sions. As part of the research for this study I went back and spoke to

Delia Gutiérrez Pineda, who had been a featured singer in her father's orquesta in the 1940s and 1950s. Eugenio Gutiérrez's orquesta had played regularly at *la placita* in the late 1940s, and Pineda remembered quite well the changes that had taken place in the 1950s. The following is a partial transcript of our conversation (July 7, 1979):

Peña: "Now, your father was playing in *la placita* in the late forties?"

Pineda: "Yes."

Peña: "And by the late 1950s the atmosphere had changed, am I right?"

Pineda: "Yes."

Peña: "What kind of music did they have in the late fifties *en la placita?*"

Pineda: "Acordeón."

Peña: "It seems to me the atmosphere had changed—iban muchos pachuquillos (many *pachuquillos* went)."

Pineda: "Sí, sí."

Peña: "Can we discuss that? What . . . (interrupted)?"

Pineda: "Bueno, at the time when we were playing la placita, no había muchos salones (there weren't many dance halls)—very few places where they could make dances. So, afuera (outside), la placita was the dance hall. And then all of the families would gather there. It was just like a family deal. Los papaces iban a oír y los muchachos y las muchachas iban a bailar (The parents went to listen and the young men and women went to dance). At that time our fun consisted of drinking Cokes and going to dances—very simple. As time changed, ya después no podías ni ir a los bailes porque se juntaba pura pachucada (afterward you couldn't even go to the dances, because only the *pachucada* gathered). The families stopped going."

There are two subjects in this exchange that are worth exploring further. First, there is the matter of the *familias*. While Pineda did not insert the adjective *buenas* before the noun, I do not feel we are distorting her meaning by suggesting that such a qualifier may be inferred from her general tone and, specifically, the phrase "the families stopped going." In any case, the point is that, as Pineda stated later, the people who patronized her father's orquesta were generally more "sophisticated" than those who supported conjunto music. They had, as Pineda remarked, "better occupations." Indeed, in Weslaco every time they turned out to hear Eugenio Gutiérrez, some of the better-established families enjoyed the privilege of seeing their names inscribed on the stone benches they had donated to add grace to *la placita*.

In sharp contrast to the *familias* was *la pachucada*. While the *pachuco* has become somewhat romanticized as a result of the Chicano power movement,[4] in the 1940s and 1950s he was decidedly abhorrent to middle-class tejanos and was even frowned upon by the more "respectable" working-class families. This is not the place to explore the *pachuco's* social role, but it is undeniable that socioeconomically he belonged to the working class. In fact, as Pineda's comments imply, he represented the "lowest" elements of tejano society—*lo más raspa* (the lowest scum), as I personally heard people say more than once. It is also common knowledge that until the 1960s, among tejanos the most avid supporters of conjunto music were the *pachucos*—working-class youth who aspired, as Paulino Bernal put it, "to be social class rebels" whose cultural idiosyncrasies were designed to distinguish them from the rest, whom they considered "square" (personal interview, May 8, 1980). Bernal's statements are worth quoting more fully for what they reveal about the social division that the relationship between *pachucos*, conjunto and orquesta signified:

> Yo me crié en el barrio . . . entre so-called pachucos. Todos mis amigos eran así. Nos vestíamos y andábamos así como pachucos. Toda nuestra idea era, "Pos yo me junto acá con los que nos llamamos los pachucos, porque aquellos son muy square. Y a ellos les gusta la música de orquesta." A nosotros nos gustaba la música de conjunto. Allí había la división otra vez. (I was raised in the barrio . . . among the so-called *pachucos*. All my friends were like that. We dressed and went around like that, like *pachucos*. Mostly our idea was, "Well, I hang around over here with those of us who call ourselves *pachucos*, because those over there are too square. And they like orquesta music." We liked the music of the conjunto. There again was the division.)

Another example of the social perception of conjunto music comes from the city of Corpus Christi. The wife of a deceased orquesta leader who had been prominent in the 1940s and 1950s recalled for me the kinds of dances her husband played for: "Eran de gente decente," she said; "la gente corriente no se arrimaba" ("They were for decent people; the vulgar people did not come near"). By way of expanding on her statements, the bandleader Freddie Martínez, also from Corpus Christi, explained that "in the past orquesta and conjunto did not cater to the same people . . . Valerio Longoria, Tony de la Rosa—they used to play cantinas" (personal interview, March 13, 1980). This view was confirmed by Eddie Galván, another orquesta musician: "Conjunto was designed for a certain category of people [the migrant workers]." And, as he explained, "the so-called upper crust"—for example,those who belonged to the Cotillion Club, for whom Galván's twelve-piece orquesta regularly played—"demanded big bands for their dances" (personal interview, February 29, 1980).

Perhaps the statements of two men deeply involved in the tejano music business, Falcón Records' Arnaldo Ramírez and the famed conjunto musician Paulino Bernal, best illustrate how strong conjunto music's negative symbolic value was among orquesta's clientele. Speaking of El Conjunto Bernal's mixed success in the 1960s in its attempt to expand its constituency beyond *la gente migrante* (by becoming more "sophisticated"), Bernal emphatically pointed out:

> Mira, en ese tiempo [the 1950s] había una división, que él que le gustaba la orquesta odiaba el conjunto. Así era: "Quién va a tocar, conjunto? ¡O, no!" Los que iban con Balde González [orquesta] no iban a ir acá con conjunto (Look, at that time there was a division, that he who liked orquesta hated conjunto. That's the way it was: "Who's going to play, a conjunto? Oh, no." Those who went with Balde González were not going to go over here with a conjunto) (personal interview, May 9, 1980).

Ramírez's comments were even more graphic: "La acordeón era instrumento del pueblo. [A la gente de posición] mencionar la acordeón era mentar la madre" ("The accordion was an instrument of the folk. To mention the accordion to [people of position] was to call their mother a name) (personal interview, March 27, 1980). Lastly, these statements were echoed by my own father's assessment of conjunto music. "La música de acordeón," he said, "era considerada música del arrabal, música arrabalera" ("The accordion was considered music from the outskirts; it was music of the riff-raff") (personal communication).

One final comment from Paulino Bernal on the social significance of conjunto, vis-à-vis that of orquesta, deserves quoting, because of its lucid perception of the basic socioeconomic differences that orquesta and conjunto embodied:

> Siempre había entre la raza, entre los Chicanos, lo que llamábamos nosotros, "N'hombre, te crees muy 'high society.' " O sea, había una clase entre los Chicanos de gente que era más high y quería vivir como el americano, y vivir mejor. Claro, ya habían alcanzado alguna posición más alta económicamente, y todavía había mucha raza que apenas estaba llegando, y con mucho—struggling all the way. Entonces sí había la división; y allí es donde se dividía no tan solo la posición social o la posición económica, sino que también se dividía la música—el de la orquesta y el del conjunto (personal interview, May 9, 1980).
>
> (There was always among *la raza*, among the Chicanos, what we used to call, "No, man, you think you're really high society." That is, there was one class of people among Chicanos that was higher, and they wanted to live like the American, and live better. Of course, they had already reached a higher position economically, and there was still a lot of *raza* that was just arriving, and with a lot of—struggling all the way. So there *was* a division; and that is where not only the social or economic position was divided, but the music was divided as well—that of orquesta and that of conjunto.)

The comments I have quoted do not begin to exhaust the number of testimonials I obtained on the dichotomic differentiation of orquesta and conjunto during the period of ascendancy for both: i.e., the late 1940s and the decade of the 1950s.[5] It should also be apparent from the foregoing statements that a sociocultural assessment of conjunto music must inevitably take some account of orquesta music as well. Although orquesta music, in all its complexity from the most *ranchero* to the most sophisticated, deserves its own separate study, it nevertheless enters necessarily into a discussion of conjunto music because of the structural relationship between the two. Indeed, in many respects historically they form a symbolic pair in opposition to each other: The one depends on the other for its social definition. This definition, as I have said, is analytically reducible to a dichotomy based on class division, at least for the period up until the mid-1960s.

However, I want to stress once more that class differentiation among tejanos was complicated by the formidable and constraining ethnic boundary that has long existed between Mexicans and Anglos. Thus, while orquesta and conjunto reflected the reality of socioeconomic cleavage between middle and working classes—e.g., the assimilative aspirations on the part of the former, ethnic resistance the latter—on another level of consciousness they seemed to have reinforced a common ethnic identity vis-à-vis that of the Anglo (see the Introduction). In this respect conjunto and orquesta—the latter particularly in its most *ranchero* (i.e., tejano) guise—may be considered paired styles that inevitably interacted and shared certain stylistic features, just as the middle-class and working-class tejanos' destinies overlapped in their confrontation with a hegemonic yet alien Anglo culture.[6]

But the assimilative effects of American cultural hegemony were felt much more strongly by the tejano middle class, partly as a result of its contradictory relation to the means of production, partly because of its ideological desire for cultural assimilation. Thus, no doubt reflecting the ambiguous position of the middle class, orquesta tended to respond to and oscillate between Mexican, American, and the more conservative conjunto style in turn. Here it is worth recalling the remarks of Delia Gutiérrez Pineda on the attempts of *orquestas tejanas* to amalgamate Glenn Miller, Mexican boleros, and conjunto polkas into a single repertory. In short, orquesta music expressed the cultural duality of the Texas-Mexican middle class (cf. Marks [1974] on cultural duality in Afro-American music). It functioned as a kind of symbolic style-switching, somewhat comparable to Blom and Gumperz's concept of "metaphorical switching" among Norwegian *Bokmal-Ranamal* speakers (1972), that allowed Texas-Mexicans access to both Mexican and American sociomusical systems. The proletarian workers, meanwhile, danced to the beat of the much more traditional and monocultural conjunto.

So far, the assessment of conjunto music I have drawn has, on the whole, tended to emphasize the Americanized middle class's reaction to the music. I have not presented the proletarian side, so to speak. I did this to stress the fact that the musical expression of class cleavage among tejanos requires the identification of two alternative styles—orquesta and conjunto. Having presented the middle class's response, I want now to explore more fully how the working class defended its position vis-à-vis the antagonism of the middle class, as well as that of American society generally. In the process of doing this, I want to delve deeper into one of the central themes of this work: the counter-ideological aspects of conjunto music.

A Proletarian Expression: Conjunto Music as Counter-Ideology

In his brief but provocative essay on the application of Gramsci's theory of cultural hegemony to white country music of the 1930s, Patterson (1975) sketches some ideas that have a certain affinity with tentative conclusions I had arrived at independently in an early assessment of conjunto music (Peña 1981). These ideas have to do with what Patterson considers "making the crucial connections between music and society" (1975:261). While Patterson candidly admits to the programmatic nature of his proposals, these include the notion that the proletariat, as a class, might be capable of exerting some degree of cultural autonomy vis-à-vis the bourgeoisie's hegemonic ideology by creating alternative forms of cultural expression that either explicitly or implicitly defend its class interests vs. those of the bourgeoisie (cf. Abercrombie, Hill, and Turner 1980). Patterson contends that in the early days of country music a "white underclass in the South," a predominantly rural, agricultural population, steadily experiencing pressures toward proletarianization, expressed through its music the latent "resentments of a class" (1975:283).

A key feature of Patterson's analysis is his reading of Gramsci's theory of cultural hegemony, especially that part which refers to the function of "organic intellectuals" (Gramsci 1971) in the maintenance—or supersedure—of particular social orders. For Gramsci "all men are intellectuals" (1971:9); thus,

> each man . . . outside his professional activity, carries on
> some form of intellectual activity; that is, he is a philosopher,
> an artist, a man of taste, he participates in a particular con-
> ception of the world, has a conscious line of moral conduct,
> and therefore contributes to sustain a conception of the world
> or to modify it, that is, to bring into being new modes of
> thought (1971:9).

However, "not all men have in society the function of intellectuals" (1971:9). Thus, in all places and all times where there appears a new class, one emerging out of "an essential function in the world of economic production" (1971:5), a breed of individuals will also appear who holds a special relation to the socioeconomic order and who carries a special share of responsibility for protecting the interests of that class. These individuals serve their class by imparting to it "homogeneity and an awareness of its own function not only in the economic but also in the social and political fields"

(Gramsci 1971:5). Furthermore, for Gramsci the activities of the intellectual "can no longer consist in eloquence, which is an exterior and momentary mover of feelings and passions, but in active participation in practical life, as constructor, organizer, permanent persuader . . . " (1971:11). In sum, as Adamson points out,

> It is important to recognize how much broader this definition of *intellectual* is than the one in current everyday usage. For while Gramsci certainly meant to include the scholar, the writer, and other men of letters, he was referring generally to anyone whose social function is to serve as a transmitter of ideas within civil society and between government and civil society (Adamson 1980:143).

In his analysis of white country music, Patterson includes the folk musicians as organic intellectuals, because, while these musicians did not constitute any sort of "vanguard," "they were one important segment of the 'brain' of this pre-industrial proletariat, at a time when it had not yet become part of a class which could operate decisively and successfully in the political arena" (1975:282). In this respect the country musicians shared one crucial characteristic with their tejano counterparts: There was "no sharp dividing line between performer and audience, and with most musicians and singers gaining their incomes not from music but from the same agricultural occupations as the rest of the class" (1975:281). I do not know how accurately Patterson's assessment reflects the role of white country musicians or to what extent these were "permanent persuaders" and "transmitters" of proletarian ideas. In any case, this is precisely what I have proposed for conjunto music and musicians.

As propagators of a symbolic expression that at its core was (and continues to be) "anti-bourgeoisie," they offered a counter-challenge—at least in the form of symbolic resistance—to American cultural hegemony generally and to the *agringado* segments of tejano society specifically. It is also my contention that conjunto musicians fit the characteristics of the organic intellectual, because, although it would be absurd to consider them "the vanguards of a revolutionary class," they did "express the conditions and resentments of a class." They did this by projecting and defending a music that encapsulated a tacit awareness on the part of the tejano workers of their class position, and an explicit awareness of their ethnic subordination. The latter was especially evident in songs that ridiculed the American and/or the Americanized Texas-Mexican.

But linguistic content aside, *as a musical style*—that is, as a cultural system—conjunto could not but be symbolic: It signified something.   And that something was a set of perceptions, beliefs and attitudes rooted in working-class traditions and embodied in a shared musical esthetic, traditions that were pitted against a competing set of attitudes and beliefs identified with both the *agringados* and a generalized Anglo culture.

However, as a potential source for grounding a well-developed proletarian class consciousness, conjunto music inevitably remained that—a potentially powerful but inchoate symbol that defined an equally inchoate cultural strategy.   That strategy was the legitimation of a changing but nonetheless folk, working-class, tejano culture.   The reasons for conjunto music's failure to bring about a sharper focus on working-class strategy are not difficult to understand.   In brief, I propose two.

First, there was the hegemonic presence of American culture in all its ideological manifestations.   Admittedly, by the end of World War II American sociocultural and politicoeconomic institutions were already interwoven into the cultural fiber of Texas-Mexican society.[7]   Thus, there was, on the one hand, the middle-class *agringado* Texas-Mexican, who was convinced that cultural assimilation was the only alternative for the survival of the Mexican in the United States (cf. Taylor's comments, above).   But even among the more Mexicanized proletarians, there was a basic (if grudging) respect for the social machinery that maintained progress and "efficiency" in American society.   Whatever misgivings these tejanos might have about the way Americans treated them, given the opportunity most of them would have sacrificed important elements of their culture to share in the American "way of life."   In yielding to the dominant presence of the American social order, most tejanos undoubtedly shared the attitudes of the Mexicans in North Town described by Foley.   To them this was the way things were in America. It was the Anglo's game; he knew all the rules to succeed, and the Mexican did not (Foley et al. 1977:49-52).

Under these circumstances tejano sociocultural institutions generally (symbolic expression specifically) were under incessant pressure,[8] a fact that reduced (if not eliminated) their potential for the effective mobilization of a counter-hegemony.   For that matter, it is unlikely that there were many tejanos who possessed an adequate understanding of the human forces whose economic actions held most of them hostage within a proletarian status.   And if there were, it is equally unlikely that even a highly organized politicocultural activity would have achieved much result—

especially prior to the 1960s. Tejanos had no choice, then, but to adapt, as well as they could, to the conditions American life imposed upon them.

This is not to say that tejanos were oblivious or fatalistic toward their oppressed condition. In the first instance, having been relegated exclusively to secondary labor markets the tejanos of the 1930s, 1940s, and 1950s were too intimately acquainted with the harsh reality of economic uncertainty and deprivation to entertain any false illusions about their position in American society. In the second instance, tejanos did undertake action to secure social, economic, and cultural justice (see Limón 1974; Nelson-Cisneros 1975). However, except for limited victories in the field of civil rights, efforts at politicocultural sovereignty have not, even to this juncture, been very successful.

The second point I wish to make with respect to conjunto music's role in the development of a proletarian class consciousness is this: A full awareness on the part of the tejano workers about class dynamics in American capitalism and their status as a subaltern group could hardly be achieved on the strength of their music alone. Had a counter-hegemonic thrust been possible, conjunto music *as* music could only have played an auxiliary role—one response linked to a wider social and cultural network. Obviously, as a symbol conjunto music was "incomplete"; its field of reference was limited. Unlike language, whose referential capacity is much better developed, music *as* music can never address specific issues. Rather, its power lies in its capacity to create associations, although these can then be conceptualized and transformed into action. In the case of conjunto, while it did contribute toward the articulation of incipient feelings of class solidarity, its conscious *use* was governed by esthetic, not political motives. Moreover, its symbolic significance was deflected by the textual messages that became an integral part of the music in the 1950s. The linguistic messages simply did not carry their share of the load. In short, the words got in the way, as song lyrics invariably dealt with nonpolitical themes, almost always involving unrequited or betrayed love.

Of course, not all songs were dominated by such romantic lyrics. *Corridos*—including those dealing with Anglo-Mexican conflict—became staples in the conjunto repertory. And a few topical songs included descriptions or even laments about working-class life—for example, "Los Pizcadores" by Los Tres Reyes. Sometimes interwoven with the love theme were statements about poverty, such as "No me quieres porque soy pobre" ("You don't love me because I'm poor"). In fact, I am convinced that a fruitful study of the *canción ranchera* would be one that interprets the cruel, fickle woman, so bitterly denounced in many of these songs, and alcohol, so ready at hand, as symbols that scapegoat for social and economic oppression. Titon (1977) suggests a somewhat similar interpretation for downhome blues.

The reasons for the sentimental content of most songs in the conjunto repertory are not difficult to explain. First, there was in Mexican music generally a long tradition of love songs. Secondly, the ideology of American (and Mexican) commercial music, with its strong aversion to controversial messages and preference for "safe" statements about personal but abstract sentiments, had its impact on tejano music. This ideology was further reinforced when radio broadcasting began to expand the conjunto music market. At this time it came under the control of Anglo commercial interests, who owned the radio stations. These were certainly not about to entertain music with openly seditious—i.e., anti-American or class-conscious—content.

I do feel, however, that beyond their power of censorship over linguistic content, the owners of these stations should not be assigned any direct influence in determining the stylization of conjunto music itself. The stations helped popularize it, of course, but even to this day the tejano market has remained a marginal one. In the early years stations that catered to a Texas-Mexican clientele devoted only limited air time to Mexican music, and that was commonly sold in blocks to tejano "brokers" (Gutiérrez and Schement 1979:6-11). Thus, contrary to what happened in country music, no commoditized, big-name artists sponsored by big capital ever emerged in conjunto music. Even in later years, when the conjunto market did expand, artists such as Tony de la Rosa, Paulino Bernal, and others remained "organically" linked to their working-class constituency, even though in fact the most popular artists no longer relied on proletarian occupations to support themselves economically. Just as importantly, their less successful epigones, who were as responsible as their first-line colleagues in the propagation of the music, were usually weekend musicians who labored in the fields or pursued other common occupations the rest of the time.

In order to discover the symbolic import of conjunto as a musical style we need to examine its musical, rather than its linguistic message, for that is where its real counter-ideological power resided. Given the lack of a well-developed class consciousness among the tejano workers—and the inevitable censorship of Anglo-controlled radio stations—it could not have been otherwise. As such, like other cultural mechanisms of its kind (e.g., "stupid American" jokes), conjunto's contribution toward the maintenance of a tejano cultural autonomy should be interpreted within the framework of a *defensive*, not a hegemonic strategy. Within this framework the increasing influence of the tejano middle class must not be underestimated, because, as subscribers to the ideology of Americanization, they contribute, however unwittingly this may be, toward neutralizing any social action the working class might take in defense of its cultural position.[9] Thus, for the most part only symbolic expression remained as a viable channel for protest and resistance (e.g., the *corrido*) and as a means to maintain some degree of sociocultural continuity and autonomy in the midst of rapid change. A product of that change, conjunto music was an example of defensive, counter-ideological, symbolic expression.

It was in the struggle to maintain politicocultural continuity that working-class tejano intellectuals served a critical function. Keeping Gramsci's conception in mind, I would certainly include strike leaders and other social activists, but more importantly, in everyday barrio life there must have been many others of a different persuasion—for example, those gifted in the performance of folklore, in all its varieties. These would include *curanderos*, among whom at one time must have been the epitome of the organic intellectual, don Pedrito Jaramillo. Of course, conjunto musicians (as well as other folk musicians and singers) should also be included, because there is no denying that their art invested them with a special prestige.

One other point that is crucial and worth reconsidering is the fact that these musicians had an intimate relationship with their participant audiences. As I demonstrated earlier, among conjunto musicians there have never been "stars" in the mass-industry sense, whose marketability is promoted by keeping them away from their public and turning them into objects of fantasy and glamor. To this day, economically, socially, and culturally the vast majority of conjunto musicians have been homegrown proletarian artists who are organically linked to their constituency. Thus, as far as their music is concerned, Patterson's remarks on early country music performers are applicable: Historically there has been "no sharp dividing line between performer and audience."

Lastly, if it is the special duty of an organic intellectual to voice the ideas of his class, the conjunto musicians I came to know were certainly at no loss for words. In fact, it is through their statements that we can gain a glimpse of what conjunto has accomplished, as a cultural expression, in the lives of the tejano working class. True, it is one thing to elicit statements after the fact, another to have observed the musicians actively invoke their art in the cause of their constituents, especially in the critical period of its gestation, when Texas-Mexican society was experiencing the turmoil of rapid change. Still, for the musicians to have articulated their feelings about conjunto music with such conviction required that they bring an a priori awareness of the music's impact. That awareness can be traced back to the theme at hand, namely, the musicians' tacit recognition that their music represented a defense of their culture in the face of a social challenge that threatened its legitimacy.

As a starting point on the musicians' perception of their art, we may recall the words of Santiago Jiménez on the resistance of his early San Antonio comrades to American music: "At that time people my age didn't pay much attention to American music." Clearly, this was nothing short of a snub. And, when we also recall don Santiago's sober indictment of an American educational system that condemned Mexicans to illiteracy and poverty, we can begin to appreciate why his people "didn't pay much attention to American music." By the simple act of ignoring that music and opting for their own, the musicians were choosing an alternative mode of artistic expression, one that was consonant with *both* their ethnic and class position.

If Jiménez's statements are somewhat oblique vis-à-vis the role of conjunto music and musician-as-intellectual, the words of Martin Rosales, a longtime disc jockey and a great favorite among tejanos, put the matter of the music's role in the tejano's defensive cultural strategy in a clearer perspective. Speaking on the maintenance of tejano music in the face of ethnic discrimination and economic exploitation, Rosales offered the following assessment:

> Entonces el americano es el que ha explotado al méxico-americano, y le ha creado ese sentimiento de discriminación. Para que lo vamos a negar? No podemos tapar el sol con el dedo. No podemos cerrar los ojos a la realidad de las cosas. Entonces el méxico-americano tiene que hacer algo para identificarse, y con ello vienen los costumbres, y parte de eso es la música (personal interview, March 8, 1980). (So, it is the American who has exploited the Mexican-American, and has created in him that feeling of discrimination. Why should we deny it? We cannot screen out the sun with our thumb. We cannot close our eyes to the reality of things. So, the Mexican-American must do something to identify himself, and with that come his customs, and part of that is the music.)

The articulate Paulino Bernal came very close to making the link between the dramatic changes in conjunto music of the 1950s and the "rebellion" of the working class against the snobbery of the middle class. I have already quoted part of his statement on *pachucos* and the working class. I quote here additional remarks for the light they throw on intraethnic class conflict and the strategies of the working class. Speaking of the *pachuco* fashion and *el tacuachito*,[10] Bernal made the following observation:

> Otra vez venía la rebeldía entre clases sociales. El más pobre, la raza más—de no alta posición económica y de otra manera—empezó como una cierta rebeldía [lo del pachuco] . . . A nosotros [los pachucos] nos gustaba la música de acordeón. A ellos [los "square"] les gustaba la orquesta . . . Allí había la división otra vez. Entonces, en esa época del pachuco se tocaba la música más despacito . . . (Here again came in the rebellion between social classes. The poorest, the *raza* most—not of high economic position of otherwise—it started as a certain rebellion [the *pachuco* trend] . . . We [the *pachucos*] liked accordion music. They [the "squares"] liked orquesta . . . There was the division again. And so, during that era of the *pachuco* the music was played slower . . .)

It was in such ways, then—the *pachuco* mode of dress, which was so prevalent among working-class youth, the dance style of *el tacuachito*, the conjunto's distinctive rendition of the polka and *canción corrida*, particularly the slowed-down tempo—that conjunto music and dance signified the working class's "rebellion" against its middle-class critics.

Perhaps the most trenchant observation about the working class and its reliance on music for "escape" from its oppressed condition was offered by Roberto Pulido, whose group Los Clásicos much later, in the 1970s, successfully combined elements from both conjunto and orquesta to create a highly popular sound. The following is a partial transcript of a conversation I had with Pulido (April 2, 1980):[11]

> Peña: "Socially speaking, did orquesta cater to a different crowd than the conjunto?"
>
> Pulido: "Yeah, the orchestra catered to a little bit more educated crowd—más—se creían más chingones (they thought of themselves as more big shot), money-wise and every-wise. Y el conjunto no, el conjunto siempre it caters to la gente

más trabajadora de la labor, la gente mas chingoteada, la gente más olvidada (And conjunto didn't; conjunto always caters more to the people who work in the fields, the most ass-busted people, the most forgotten people)."

Peña: "You actually worked as a farm worker at one time, right?"

Pulido: "Yeah, I did; I used to migrate to California a trabajar durazno, la uva, tomate, algodón (to work the peaches, grapes, tomatoes, cotton)—you name it, I did it. Trabajo de la labor, I did it all."

Peña: "Would this have something to do with your sympathy for playing for la gente trabajadora (working people)?"

Pulido: "Yeah. Me da lástima, me da gusto también al mismo tiempo que la gente trabajadora que va y se chingotea diariamente, ir a ganarse unos cuantos dolares, y luego ir a darse gusto, para olvidar las penas. Y van y gastan—te voy a decir—la gente mexicana es una gente que no tiene miedo gastar. El mojado—más. Sort of makes you wonder why people do that. (I feel compassion, I feel joy at the same time, that the working people, who go and work their asses off daily, go to earn a few dollars, and then go have some fun, to forget the sorrows . . .)."

Peña: "Maybe they have a need for it."

Pulido: "Right, they need an escape."

Aside from the keen understanding Pulido demonstrated toward the hardships of the tejano worker, his remarks are illuminating for their tacit recognition that conjunto was (and remains) an inseparable part of proletarian life. I would suggest, however, that in light of other evidence available, the working class's relationship to its music is not so much in the nature of an escape from life's drudgery as it is an "adventure into reality," as Blacking wrote about Venda music and dance (1973:28; cf. Keil [1966] on blacks and their music). More so than today, in the two decades following the war this reality was defined by the conventional setting of the dance, within whose ludic atmosphere the tejano workers symbolically reasserted their cultural independence. The music-and-dance event, in turn, was part of a larger response to the social pressures of a rapidly changing environment, a response through which the workers became "more aware of themselves and of their responsibilities toward one another" (Blacking 1973:28) and whose ultimate aim was to preserve and defend the working class's sense of integrity and cultural solidarity.

Finally, perhaps the comments of Pedro Ayala on the place of conjunto music within tejano culture will serve as a simple but effective illustration of the music's counteracting force to the alternatives demanded by the middle class. In comments that echoed sentiments I heard many times as a youngster among the tejano workers, don Pedro defended his music:

> . . . la acordeón es una música muy clara que se entiende perfectamente bien. Precisamente como la toca Narciso, como la toco yo, Tony de la Rosa, Rubén Vela—como tocamos todos. Se entiende la música que estamos tocando. Y la gente le gusta bailar cuando entiende la música bien. Cuando hay muchos pitos y que agarra uno por un rumbo y otro por otro, que se hace borlote, pos no, no le haya la gente . . . (. . . the accordion is a very clear music that is perfectly understandable. Exactly as Narciso plays it, as I play it, Tony de la Rosa, Rubén Vela—as we all play it. The music we play is understood. And people like to dance when they understand the music well. When there are too many horns, and one goes this way and the other that—when they make a jumble—that's it, the people can't figure it out . . .)

As for the accordion:

> No, la acordeón es música tradicional, por muchos años . . . y la gente la lleva en el corazón, y no se les borra de la cabeza, porque es tradicional. La tocaban sus abuelitos, sus padres, y ahora sus hijos. (No, the accordion is traditional music, for many years . . . and the people carry it in their hearts, and it will not be erased from their minds, because it is traditional. Their grandparents played it, their parents, and now their sons.)

And this was Pedro Ayala's final assessment:

> El día que a la gente le toquen otra música no se les paran ni las moscas (The day they play a different music for the people not even the flies will stop in) (personal interviews, November 4 and December 1, 1978).

It was in this manner, then, on the one hand defending their music as a cherished tradition, and, on the other, as a tradition constantly denigrated by a snobbish, Americanized *gente jaitona*, that the musicians spoke—organic intellectuals that they were—in behalf of their constituency. Other testimonials could have been included, but the ones I have presented should make it abundantly clear that, especially during its rise to prominence, conjunto music fulfilled a quite specific function in tejano culture. It was (and to a large extent remains) a social marker, of course, but more importantly, it was a unique art form that epitomized the perseverance of a working-class tejano culture besieged by an overpowering American cultural hegemony on one side and an intransigent tejano middle class on the other. This intransigence reached its peak in the 1950s and early 1960s, when the socioeconomic opportunities engendered by World War II and the Korean conflict began to have an impact on tejano society—when a sufficient number came under the influence of American middle-class ideology.

It was at this time that the middle class became cohesive enough to mount a real campaign against the old-fashioned values and traditions of the working class, fearful perhaps that the latter's "un-American" ways might possibly reflect adversely upon its own new-found status, especially since only recently it too had been proletarian. The working class was aware of all this, of course—else why the need for the scorn in "se creen muy jaitones" ("They think they're very high-toned")? And it responded, in different ways and with different strategies, to the challenge of the Americanized middle class against its fundamental cultural values. It was this response, in my estimation, that spurred the rapid changes and subsequent crystallization of conjunto music.

For their part the musicians, who were vital participants in working-class culture, played their own key role. Clearly, their music, coupled with the solid support of their audience, represented a strongly symbolic though unverbalized counter-ideology to American hegemony, a de facto attempt at the legitimization of tejano working-class culture. Musical activity was part of a complex of symbolized strategies designed to maintain cultural continuity within the group, even if the conjunto did change in the process of mediating the conflict between the working class and more Americanized segments of Texas-Mexican society. And finally, although lacking a specific political philosophy, the artistic efforts of the musicians, which were consonant with their constituency's world view, may be thought of as "organically" motivated. That is, the men who forged this unique style were attempting to create an art form that was faithful to proletarian esthetic principles, which were in turn based on traditional ethnic norms. In sum, conjunto musicians fit well the conception of the organic intellectual as described by Adamson:

> In the case of a subaltern class like the proletariat, organic intellectuals seek to inspire its self-confidence as an historical actor and to provide it with social, cultural, and political leadership (1980:143).

Viewed in this light, the changes that Tony de la Rosa, Valerio Longoria, and others introduced in the late 1940s and that culminated around 1960 take on added meaning. These shifts in tempo, articulation, and so on symbolized the reactions that were taking place socially. In other words, the musical developments transcended the universe of musical discourse and interacted with developments occurring at the level of social discourse. In short, there was a critical connection between music and society. Clearly, changes in the social structure were being transformed into changes in the musical structures—except that the latter were under the conscious control of the working class, even if they were in response to external circumstances.

Thus, the innovations of the *nueva generación*, while clearly in a musical line that extended at least back to Narciso Martínez, nonetheless reflected the maturation of a musical esthetic which objectified the traditional proletarian ideals being called into question at that time by a middle class that was increasingly accommodating in its desire to be accepted by the larger American society. In sum, the move toward assimilation by the middle-class segments of Texas-Mexican society was countered by a corresponding move by the proletarian workers to strengthen their own cultural position. And conjunto musicians and their innovations symbolically gave expression to this move.

Conjunto after 1970: Stylistic Retreat and Symbolic Decline

As I previously explained, from a stylistic viewpoint conjunto music's remarkable push toward a full-blown artistic expression came to an end with the experiments of El Conjunto Bernal in the 1960s. Since that time, conjuntos have settled into a pattern of imitation and repetition. The "instinctual inertia" (Ackerman 1962:228) that sets in when a style reaches its limits has overtaken conjunto music. The maverick accordionist Esteban Jordán summed it up in terse words: "Nobody wants to explore anymore." To restate what I proposed earlier, the turn toward conservatism was a necessary corrective to the rapid changes of the 1950s. Conjunto musicians had, after all, wrought an expressive form that eminently fulfilled the esthetic needs of the proletarian workers. Consolidation was now essential in order to stabilize the gains that had been accomplished, and the 1960s provided the requisite social climate for the new style to settle in and establish itself.

However, as Ackerman perceptively observed, a style can never be completely static; "when it is not vital, it actively degenerates" (1962:228). Such, at any rate, has been the case with conjunto music since about 1970, when purely conventionalized techniques and ideas became the norm and, through sheer overuse, have drained the music of much of its former freshness and vitality. But that is what a conservative public demands and recording companies encourage. Thus, groups that adhere to the stylistic baseline worked out in the 1950s and 1960s (with a few minor modifications here and there) continue to dominate the scene, while those that do not soon find themselves wihout an audience.

An intriguing question arises: To what extent is conjunto's stylistic retreat, or even degeneration, from the creative vitality that characterized its ascendancy in the 1940s and 1950s related to its diminished stature as a symbolic vehicle of working-class ideology? Clearly, a correlation exists, but I have found it difficult to measure—more so than assessing the close connection between the music's rise to prominence and the working class's search for an artistic form that would give voice to its cultural strategies. Nonetheless, certain variables can be sorted out of the confusing relationship between conjunto and social developments since 1970—variables that can begin to clarify the diminished role of the music in tejano society. At least four are worth considering.

First, as I pointed out in Chapter 4, the intense commercialization of other types of music has cut deeply into the tejano music market. As Gutiérrez and Schement have demonstrated (1979), vigorous mass-media promotion, especially of *música moderna* and other international styles, has had an inescapable effect on audience preferences—even that of the tejano working class. Simply by saturating the air waves with the music that serves their own interests, broadcasters and the recording industry exert a suasive power—if not outright control—over the types of music that audiences will or will not have access to. This has unquestionably worked against regional musics like conjunto, though even against such overwhelming competition the conjunto has managed to hold its own. But it has not emerged untouched; mass-market music has taken its toll, weakening not only the appeal but, more importantly, the organic relationship that it once enjoyed with its working-class supporters.

A second variable operating in the decline of conjunto music is the lack of a coherent ideology that could have integrated conjunto music into a larger program of politicocultural action. As I suggested earlier, as a cultural system without a specific, verbalized conceptual referent, the style in and of itself could have only limited utility in a counter-ideological thrust. True, the music carried a potent message that could, under the proper circumstances, easily have been transformed into a direct statement of working-class solidarity, but it needed a political program to give it conceptual direction—that is, to ground it in social action. Lacking such a program, the propitious historical moment—the 1960s, when a general Chicano political mobilization stirred—slipped by. Regrettably for the working class, the Chicano movement, as Limón has contended (1981), failed to develop legitimate, organic connections with the workers. Instead, by failing to mobilize potentially unifying cultural resources—of which conjunto music is an outstanding example—or, in some cases, by misappropriating others (cf. Limón 1981), the movement inadvertently alienated itself from the working class. Not surprisingly, it drew little active support from this most crucial group.

A third and extremely important variable enters into the discussion of conjunto music's decline. As I indicated earlier, with the mechanization of cotton harvesting, the thousands of workers who had depended on this crop lost a critical source of income for their livelihood. Many flocked to urban centers like Houston and Dallas in search of work, but thousands also scattered throughout the United States, especially the Midwest and California—the "El Dorado for Chicanos," as Briggs, Fogel, and Schmidt (1977:18) referred to this prosperous state. By the mid-1960s, then, the resident ranks of the tejano workers had been considerably thinned, as stories of better conditions in California and elsewhere circulated, encouraging an ever-increasing number of workers to emigrate. No one knows exactly how extensive this exodus of workers was, although it was unquestionably a sizeable one. In fact, Texas became the "largest exporter of migrant labor," according to historians Meier and Rivera (1972:221).

The consequences of this mass exodus of tejano workers for conjunto were not as beneficial as they might have been. Since the music did in fact follow the workers, firmly establishing itself in

California's San Joaquin Valley, for example, we might expect a renaissance of sorts to take place in its new setting. Such was not the case, however, as musicians transplanted to new locales (as well as new initiates to the style) have merely continued what their tejano counterparts have been doing: imitating, often in degraded fashion, the accomplishments of the 1950s and 1960s. Meanwhile, contributing to the decline of the conjunto in Texas has been the heavy influx of undocumented Mexican workers who replaced the emigrating tejanos in proletarian occupations. This influx, as Briggs et al. pointed out, "has, since the mid-1960s, assumed epidemic proportions" (1977:82). These workers, of course, have no particular allegiance to conjunto music. On the contrary, it is through their unwavering support of *grupos tropicales*—or *grupos cumbieros*, as they are sometimes called—that the latter have become so prevalent in Texas (as elsewhere). More to the point, these have posed a substantial threat to the economic health of conjunto by encroaching deeply into the crucial public-ballroom dance circuit.

Finally, as I mentioned previously, the attention that films like *Chulas Fronteras* and institutions like the Smithsonian have focused on the Texas-Mexican conjunto has admittedly brought a measure of respectability and even prestige to the music. An unintentional effect has been the popularization of the music with segments of Chicano society, in Texas and beyond, that in earlier years most emphatically did not form part of its social base. I am referring to those upwardly mobile people who are aware of the music's newfound respectability and who have developed a nostalgic attachment to it. But the summary effect of the popularization of conjunto beyond the historical confines of the tejano working class has been the dilution of its class-derived symbolic power. In short, as a result of its cooptation by American "culturalizers," it can no longer claim to be the exclusive property—nor the symbolic banner—of tejano workers.

Having set forth the proposition that conjunto music has suffered a decline both in its stylistic (formal) and social-symbolic (cultural) dimensions, let me insist that this decline is not to be equated with demise and that, despite the contravening circumstances, it is apparent that it continues to maintain an essentially folk, proletarian character. Moreover, even to this day—at least in its working-class context—it remains an artistic creation that negates, however implicitly, the hegemony of American mass culture. This latter, as Luis Valdez (1972) trenchantly pointed out, continuously bombards Mexican communities everywhere with the debris of its mass-market commodities, specifically the "entertainment" fare that pours out of television, stultifying dissent while pacifying the masses.

As a symbolic expression conjunto may not be as powerful as it was in the days of its unquestioned supremacy, but hidden away in its traditional setting it is still brought to life on Saturday nights in little-known places like Beeville, Mathis, and Edinburg to remind us that at the very heart of the Sun Belt, the nation's most "American" region, the voice of a different cultural order may be heard.   The voice is purely symbolic, lacking a specific sociopolitical program. But tejanos are multiplying, and they are organizing.   Lately, religious proselytizers—including Paulino Bernal—have discovered the power of the music in converting tejano neophytes.   It does not seem beyond the realm of possibility that in the future the music may be subjected to a renewed creative surge that will link it to a broader tejano politico-cultural movement.

Notes

1. Properly speaking, in my theoretical approach occupational differentiation is an empirical category, class differentiation an analytic one. Though obviously based on occupational factors, the latter incorporates both structural (in relation to the means of production) and politico-ideological relationships.

2. Although the *Express* article mentions only the beating of drums, it is almost certain it was referring to the *tambora de rancho*, prevalent in early Texas-Mexican music and a frequent companion instrument for the accordion.   The *Express* always used a more approving tone when reporting on orquestas, as, for example, in a news feature of September 16, 1886, where the *fiestas patrias* were said to be enlivened by "two string bands and two rooms of dancers . . . going on at once."

3. *La placita* was located on the "Mexican" side of town; at this time, like many other communities in South Texas, Weslaco was divided socially and spatially between an Anglo and a Mexican "town" (see Rubel, 1966).

4. See, for example, José Montoya's poem "El Louie" (in Valdez and Steiner 1972). In his play (now a movie) *Zootsuit*, Luis Valdez has turned the West Coast *pachuco* (zootsuiter) into a mythical, romanticized character, and the basic sales strategy of magazines like *Q-Vo* and *Lowrider* seems to revolve around the romanticization and commercialization of a composite *pachuco/lowrider/cholo* image (Plascencia, 1983).

5. Again, I am not including here the substantial changes that overtook orquesta after the mid-1960s, when it converged considerably upon conjunto. I am currently completing a study on orquesta's own development.

6. This fact helps explain why Beto Villa and Eugenio Gutiérrez did not hesitate to combine their talents with Narciso Martínez and Pedro Ayala. They were no doubt aware that as long as they maintained a sufficiently cosmopolitan repertory, their "back-to-the-roots" gesture would not endanger their popularity with the middle class. At the same time their collaboration with conjunto musicians gave them access to the much larger working-class audience, without whose support orquestas

could not hope to attain widespread attention.

7. Writing in a nationalistic vein, Luis Valdez described the Chicano's cultural subordination in the face of American hegemony in a rather acerbic but essentially accurate tone:

" . . . the barrio is a colony of the white man's world. Our life there is second hand, full of chingaderas imitating the way of the patron. The used cars, rented houses, old radio and TV sets, stale grocery stores, plastic flowers—all the trash of the white man's world mixes with the bits and pieces of that other life, the Indio life . . . " (1972:xvi).

8. Cf. McWilliams's statements to this effect:

"Above all it is important to remember that Mexicans are a 'conquered' people in the Southwest, a people whose culture has been under incessant attack for many years and whose character and achievements, as a people, have been consistently disparaged" (1968:132).

9. There were exceptions, of course. Sometimes in the face of blatant racism against Mexicans generally the middle class was willing to step in and defend the total group's position (see Limón 1974; Peña 1982).

10. According to Valerio Longoria, 95 percent of the people who went to his dances dressed in the *pachuco* style in the 1950s (Broyles interview April 26, 1981).

11. Pulido's collapsing of past and present in discussing conjunto music indicates that he is aware that the social context of the music has not changed appreciably over time—i.e., it is still a working-class music.

Appendix A
A Theoretical Framework

"Methodology," writes P. Pelto, "refers to the structure of procedures and transformational rules whereby the researcher shifts information up and down the ladder of abstraction in order to produce and organize increased knowledge" (1970:4). The real world presents many obstacles for the scientific investigator in the search for "true and useful information" (1970:1). As Pelto argues, knowing "with some assurance" that a researcher's claims and propositions are "valid" or "reliable" is not always a matter of simply looking at the "facts." For, as González Casanova has argued, a researcher's selection of facts or data to be studied depends "upon the perception from which he views the set [the collection of data], the system being studied . . . ," and his "political position" (1981:11-12). Thus, the best we can strive for is a theoretical framework that sorts out and organizes the phenomena we observe in the most coherent, verifiable, and truthful manner. To do this we need to spell out wherever possible the relationship between our selection of data, our methodology, and the theories from which the research enterprise springs. In the next few pages I propose to do just that.

Broadly speaking, besides certain accepted assumptions about the nature of music—e.g., that it is innate in basic human brain processes—there are at least four other theoretically developed areas that I have explicitly drawn from in the organization of this work. These areas are related to the concepts of culture, ethnicity, assimilation, and class. Two additional analytical concepts, linked here closely with culture and class, round out the theoretical framework I have used. These are ideology and hegemony.

First, from anthropological thought I have accepted as axiomatic the proposition that there is an entity, culture, that embodies at both the visible and conceptual levels the interrelationships between the structure of ideas and the structure of society (Singer 1968—for example, that between music as cultural symbol and class as a social reality (cf. Seeger 1934; Béhague 1973). These inter-relationships are, of course, *to be discovered.* This proposition is such a long-standing, widely accepted "metatheory" in anthropology (Pelto 1970) that I need not delve into it at length here; however, a few pertinent remarks are offered below in connection with my discussion of ideology and hegemony.

Secondly, I have drawn extensively from the literature on ethnicity. It is abundantly clear that a sense of ethnicity, "emically" conceived, is a very real force in the lives of many groups, even in modern societies like that in the United States. Expressible in "notions of common descent and of an essential, though frequently indefinite, homogeneity" (Weber 1958:173), the existence of ethnic difference has often been the friction that sets off the spark of conflict in intercultural contact (Paredes 1958; Eidheim 1969; Van den Berghe 1981). In point of fact, the concept of ethnicity is as old as both disciplines, anthropology and sociology. As Barth noted, "Practically all anthropological reasoning rests on the premise that cultural variation is discontinuous . . ." And, "since culture is nothing but a way to describe human behavior, it would follow that there are discrete groups of people, i.e., ethnic units, to correspond to each culture" (Barth 1969:9). It comes as no surprise, then, that many of the case studies in cultural anthropology, for example, take as their starting point discrete groups that may be considered ethnic in character (e.g., Madsen's *The Mexican Americans of South Texas* and Hart and Pilling's *The Tiwi of North Australia*).

The third theoretical principle that enters into my discussion of conjunto music is that of cultural/structural assimilation.[1] A common occurrence in interethnic contact, the phenomenon of assimilation as well as its corollaries—adaptation, syncretism, and reinterpretation—has been the object of study and discussion for some time (cf. Beals 1943; Herskovits 1948; Foster 1960; and, especially, Gordon 1964). Although not without argument (cf. Aguirre Beltrán 1970), the problem of culture contact, "the significant and rapid restructuring of one or both of the cultures in contact" (Beals and Hoijer 1965:736), is an inescapable fact of human life, especially in situations of conquest and colonialism (see Foster 1960; Memmi 1967). The most comprehensive statement on assimilation may be found in Milton Gordon's classic, *Assimilation in American Life* (1964). McLemore (1980) has applied Gordon's concepts to several minorities in the United States, including Mexicans (cf. also Murguía 1975). I have relied on the work of these scholars in my use of the concept of cultural/structural assimilation.

Briefly, Gordon views assimilation, particularly where a dominant "host" society absorbs various ethnic groups, as a series of stages, or subprocesses, rather than a unilinear process or result (1964:70). Specifically, in the case of the United States the host society is that of the Anglo-Americans, who form the "core" population whose culture all other ethnic groups, whether we consider them immigrant or "colonized" (Blauner 1972; cf. McLemore 1980), have been under pressure to adopt and into whose social order these groups have been more or less welcomed. The assimilation subprocesses form a continuum along which the various ethnic groups are ranged vis-à-vis the Anglos, depending on such considerations as the nature of the contact (i.e., immigration or conquest), its length, and most important, the receptivity of the host group.

Gordon divides the assimilation processes into seven stages; I list only the first four, since these are the most applicable to my analysis. The four stages, or variables, are reproduced in Table 6.

Table 6: The Assimilation Variables

Type or Stage of Assimilation	Subprocess or Condition
Cultural Assimilation	Change of cultural patterns to those of host society
Structural Assimilation	Large-scale entrance into cliques, clubs, and institutions of host society, on primary group level
Marital Assimilation	Large-scale intermarriage
Identificational Assimilation	Development of sense of peoplehood based exclusively on host society

Source: Gordon, 1964, p. 71.

For my purposes, I have collapsed the four variables in Table 6 into two: cultural and structural assimilation, as the last two are far less critical in discussing Anglo-Mexican interaction. I do this because, first, cultural assimilation is an antecedent stage to all the others. Moreover, it is undeniable that, given time, the vast majority of Mexicans in the United States have variously absorbed not only the basic communicative apparatus of American society but its norms, values, and beliefs—in short, its culture. Thus, during most of the period covered here, especially the postwar years, cultural assimilation in the form of a set of ideological attitudes about "Americanization" was clearly evident, being cast in sharp contrast to the antiassimilation forces operating both within Texas-Mexican and Anglo societies. Second, despite long and continuous contact with Anglo society, tejanos as a group have experienced little *structural* assimilation, though this subprocess, upon which the remaining types of assimilation are predicated (Gordon 1964:81), serves as the contrasting element in formulating the interethnic equation. That is, though the prospect of structural assimilation of Mexicans in American society remains in doubt, its role—especially in relation to the ideology of *cultural* assimilation—makes its consideration unavoidable.

Some researchers have favored the notion of ecological competition/adaptation over that of assimilation in their studies of intercultural contact (Achor 1978; Barth 1969). I have no quarrel with the fact that in human societies "there is continuous interchange between culture and environment" (Achor 1978:167). Indeed, with other primary life forces, such as biological needs, the ecology must be considered a fundamental determinant of human sociology. I do feel, however, that in modern industrial societies, where the most pressing problems of elementary subsistence have been overcome (i.e., a successful mode of production established), the natural environment recedes into the background as a focal point for cultural activity. For example, fetishes originating in an earlier period from the relationship between people and natural phenomena (e.g., totems) give way to fetishes connected with human relationships—particularly economic relations (e.g., commodity fetishism; cf. Marx 1977, I: 163-177, 982-983, 1003-1004).

This is not to argue that ecological competition and adaptation are not present in modern industrial societies. However, ecological problems directly related to survival are not nearly as critical in day-to-day cultural activity as ideological issues related to the acquisition and maintenance of politicoeconomic power by one or more groups over others. In the United States this is where cultural phenomena like the ideology of assimilation play their most important role. For one thing, the popular belief in assimilation—that every newcomer must embrace the "American way"—imposes conformity on diverse and potentially disruptive populations. At the same time, the ideology of assimilation extends the hope, especially to subordinated minorities like the Chicanos, that the way to achieve equality, socioeconomic status, and all the perquisites of "citizenship" is through assimilation, beginning with the espousal of those patterns of thought and action that are unique to the

"American national character."[2]

In sum, in the study of pluralistic, capitalist societies we need to pay close attention to the mechanisms, such as the ideology of the American national character, whereby the ideas of one group exert their hegemony over other groups, so that certain social arrangements—of domination and subordination, for example—maintain their continuity. I would agree with Vayda and Rappaport's observation that "a science of ecology . . . does not entail any appreciable sacrifice of traditional anthropological interests" (Sahlins 1976:90). Thus, in the study of American-Mexican interaction and its consequences for Mexicans in the United States, an ecological model is clearly applicable in early contact and competition. However, once the American expansion into the Southwest was consolidated (by the end of the nineteenth century), ecological competition was practically ended. For interethnic relations thereafter, an analytical model that incorporates the dynamics of assimilation outlined above seems to me to be a more fruitful theoretical tool.

As I have indicated, then, closely linked in this study with the concept of culture are those of ideology and hegemony. However, unlike the "metatheoretical" acceptance of the former, these two share a measure of controversy and require some clarifying remarks. It is not my intention to attempt an exegesis of ideology and hegemony; that would be impractical, anyway. Nonetheless, since I believe the concepts possess explanatory value, I want at least to work out a basic definition so that no confusion will arise when I refer to them in my discussion of the symbolic role of conjunto music in tejano society.

The relationship between culture and ideology has not been adequately resolved and remains problematic. Indeed, as Abercrombie, Hill, and Turner observed, the concept of ideology "has given rise to more analytical and conceptual difficulties than almost any other term in the social sciences" (1980:187). Despite this, most Marxist scholars seldom use the term "culture", even when it seems called for, preferring "ideology" and, in a broader sense, "superstructure." On the other hand, non-Marxist anthropologists, for whom the concept of culture is a theoretical cornerstone, have only recently begun to pay serious attention to the relationship between culture and ideology. (Edward Sapir demonstrated an early, though inchoate, awareness of culture vs. ideology in his essay "Culture, Genuine and Spurious" [1949].) One such anthropologist is Clifford Geertz, who, in agreement with Fallers, assigns to ideology a specific place within the larger domain of culture. Geertz subscribes to that concept of ideology defined by Fallers as "that part of culture which is actively concerned with the establishment and defense of patterns of belief and value" (1973:231).

But this is not a particularly illuminating comparison between culture and ideology. A more useful conception is that adopted by Dolgin et al. (1977; cf. Lefebvre 1977), who, at least implicitly, view culture as a more or less "neutral" system of symbols and their meanings for organizing social life. Culture can conceivably serve as a true mediator between human thought and action and can thus reveal the objective nature of social organization, providing a relatively undistorted interpretation of human relations. Of course, in such a case culture would coincide with science, if by the latter we understand a true theoretical conception of reality. However, as many have argued (Marx 1977; Lefebvre 1977; Godelier 1977), some infrastructures—specifically those of capitalism—are far less conducive than others to the development of "undistorting" cultures. Under capitalism, culture long ago ceased to account for the full consequences of social relations, but operates instead to conceal or distort at least some aspects of these. It creates, in effect, a "false consciousness" about the world: It has been transformed into ideology.[3]   Furthermore, as false consciousness, ideology does not restrict itself to the limited domain staked out for it by Geertz;

> rather, ideology comes to be seen as the system of representations whereby everyday life is produced, and understandings of it represented as "natural" and about which, as it has been frequently remarked, those who believe in the ideology are not self-conscious exactly because ideology is obvious to those who are "inside" it, to those who believe in—and through—it (Dolgin et al. 1977:39).

In short, ideology usurps the place of a "genuine" culture; it becomes a "way of life," which, moreover, does conform to Geertz's view of ideology as a symbolic system whose purpose is the "defense of patterns of belief and value." But it does so in a much more pervasive manner than Geertz seems willing to admit. Of course, it would be inaccurate to claim that *all* communication under capitalism is ideological. Furthermore, within a broader theoretical framework for the study of culture, ideology should still be subsumed under the larger generic term "culture," since it is, like the rest of culture, a "system of symbols and their meanings." But it is its pervasiveness in modern capitalist society (cf. Miliband 1969)—the way it unconsciously permeates so many areas of social activity—that makes it such a formidable component of culture (see Barthes [1972] on its mythical dimensions).

How this pervasiveness comes about merits further comment. I have indicated that culture may be viewed as a conceptual system mediated by symbols and their meanings (cf. Schneider 1976). Another way of approaching the matter is through Eco's suggestion that "the whole of culture *should* be studied as a communicative phenomenon based on signification systems" (1976:22). An additional point that needs to be brought up is the universal organization of these systems of signification around "patterns for action," or norms (Schneider 1976). Expressible in terms of "values," "attitudes," "traditions"—in short, of shared beliefs and their sanctions in a given society about the nature of human relations and the world in general—these patterns often assume an immutable quality and thereby become a powerful force for social control. It is their immutability that makes these patterns for action so amenable to ideological manipulation (as Eco demonstrates), for once they take root in the collective consciousness (and unconscious), they become increasingly resistant to change.

Yet one more way of conceiving culture is to extend the notion of signification to include praxis, or to think of it as the "complex unity of thought and action, meaning and intention . . . ," whereby "people understand their world, themselves, and their actions" (Dolgin et al. 1977:37). Within this complex, symbols may play a normative role, impelling and directing action, or, again, they may play an explanatory role through "which the world is imagined, understood, and expressed" (Dolgin et al. 1977:36). As a function of praxis—the unity of thought and action that enable people to define experience and at the same time control it—culture may be subjected to a wide range of adaptive strategies in social relations. These cultural strategies may reflect the relatively "transparent" social relations found in primitive societies, or they may promote (and be promoted by) the highly "opaque" relations in modern productive systems. In either case, one point needs to be emphasized: Although a concomitant to praxis, culture is not in a cause-and-effect relationship with the productive process. It is not "determined" by production, any more than it is "an immediate expression of the [infra]structure" (Gramsci 1971:407). Culture possesses a certain autonomy.

Nonetheless, Marx, for one, maintained that the degree of complexity in the organization of production had a powerful if not determinative impact on the relative "transparency" or "opacity" of a society's social relations—and hence on its culture (superstructure). I should add, however, that transparency is not to be confused with simplicity (cf. Dolgin et al.: "There is probably no such thing as a truly or wholly transparent system" [1977:42]). To Marx capitalism was the most complex of productive systems, one riddled with built-in contradictions between base and superstructure. It was, consequently, an "opaque" system. But more than that, according to Marx, capitalist culture as mediator (like all cultures) in social relations was a dismal failure insofar as the kind of behavior it engendered. It is in his ethical stand that we may fruitfully compare Marx's notion of transparent vs. opaque superstructures—and the results they lead to—with Sapir's ideas about the genuine and the spurious culture.

Like Marx, Sapir contended that certain productive arrangements lend themselves to the development of genuine cultures—or their opposite, spurious cultures. Precapitalist and even caste societies, which Marx labeled transparent, Sapir would call genuine, as long as no efforts to mask basic social relations ideologically are in evidence. Of course, this is not to suggest that either Marx or Sapir would condone unmediated, nonideological oppression. Such a state of affairs would surely have been repugnant to both. But since systems based on domination and oppression almost always require the defense of the indefensible, some form of ideology seems inevitable for their long-run survival. In any case, speaking of the genuine culture (in a manner Marx surely would have approved of), Sapir boldly states:

> The genuine culture is not of necessity either high or low; it is merely inherently harmonious, balanced, self-satisfactory . . . It is not a spiritual hybrid of contradictory patches, of watertight compartments of consciousness that avoid participation in a harmonious synthesis. If the culture necessitates slavery, it frankly admits it; if it abhors slavery, it feels its way to an economic adjustment that obviates the necessity of its employment. It does not make a great show in its ethical ideals of an uncompromising opposition to slavery, only to introduce what amounts to a slave system into certain portions of its industrial mechanism (1945:315).

What Sapir was hinting at, and Marx openly attacked, was that in modern capitalist societies, where the productive process is based, first, on the expropriation by the capitalist of the worker's labor and second, on the alienation of the worker from that labor (e.g., Sapir's telephone girl [1949:316]), cultural structures that mediate social relations cannot but be "spurious"—or, in Marxist terms, "opaque." This is so because the culture—the bundle of concepts, symbols, and patterns for action that regulate society—is often in direct contradiction with the structurally generated inequalities of capitalism, wherein the capitalist dominates and exploits a numerically much larger working class. Thus, to maintain this arrangement, capitalist society (whose prevailing ideas are those of the bourgeoisie) marshalls a potent array of symbols built upon "fuzzy concepts" (Eco 1976) in order to perpetuate and legitimize a system of privileges whose nexus is capital accumulation through the exploitation of labor (cf. Miliband 1969; Roemer 1982).

But to be effective the symbols must be opaque, too. They must, in short, succumb to ideology in order to mystify the structural inequalities inherent in capitalism. Mystification is facilitated by the "conceptual displacement of contradiction" (Dolgin et al. 1977:41), wherein potentially disruptive counter-cultures (or, more likely, counter-ideologies) are defused—"encompassed," by being coopted by the dominant bourgeois ideology. This cooptation is

> the encompassment and recruitment of people through the appropriation of their symbolic forms to an over-arching, encompassing structure which is the property of a dominant group, is universal, and at the root of the stability of culture and its extension throughout a population . . . (1977:42).

In American society encompassment is facilitated by the ideology of cultural assimilation—a system of universally accepted symbols and norms clustered around the popular concept of "the American creed," which is held up as a mirror to the best-of-all-possible-worlds that American democracy represents (cf. Myrdal 1962). Thus, as Kenneth Burke observed, when conflict rooted in class exploitation threatens to burst upon the social consciousness, "you are likely to confuse the issue by ideals that give a semblance of national unity" (1969:108). That is, you invoke the principles of "equal opportunity," "self-determination," or, to quote Burke once more, those of " 'liberty,' 'dignity of the individual,' 'Christian civilization,' 'democracy,' and the like, as the motives impelling at least *our* people and *our* government . . . " (1969:108).

But this is precisely when a cultural system becomes ideology: when the actions and symbols that are invoked in the name of democracy or liberty come into conflict with social reality—with the actually existing relations of domination and exploitation that govern a capitalist economy. Ideology thus emerges out of the dislocation between the structure of ideas and the structure of society—or between the superstructure and the infrastructure. The former obscures rather than reveals the latter. Under these circumstances social relations assume a contradictory quality, as does cultural expression. In sum, ideology is a distorted reflection of reality. As Lefebvre observed, "Every ideology is a collection of errors, illusions, mystifications, which can be accounted for by reference to the historical reality it distorts and transposes" (1977:257). However, every ideology has a starting point in reality, but it is a "fragmentary, partial reality . . . [Ideologies] refract [rather than reflect] reality via preexisting representations, selected by the dominant groups and acceptable to them" (Lefebvre 1977:259). And lastly, as Lefebvre notes, "every ideology worthy of the name is characterized by a certain breadth and a real effort at rationality" (1977:260).

Finally, as long as a given ideology holds sway over the majority of the people, the reigning social order will survive. It does this by permeating the most important sociocultural institutions, a large part of whose legitimation is assigned to more or less specialized "ideologists"—priests, jurists, politicians, philosophers, artists, etc. These are the "organic intellectuals" spoken of by Gramsci (1971), whose task it is to maintain that ideology's hegemony. This brings us to the concept of hegemony; briefly, it may be defined as

> an order in which a certain way of life and thought is dominant, in which one concept of reality is diffused throughout society in all its institutional and private manifestations, informing with its spirit all taste, morality, customs, religious and political principles, and all social relations, particularly in their intellectual and moral connotations (Williams 1960:587).

It is always possible, of course, that a counter-ideology (or, less likely, a "genuine" culture) will rise to challenge the prevailing one. This counter-ideology may be strong enough to topple the existing order (as capitalism did with feudalism), or it may, on the other hand, be encompassed. The point is that it is likely that in many times and places incipient counter-ideologies have gained enough of a foothold to challenge a dominant class's supremacy.

That in capitalist societies no serious challenge has been offered is due to various factors, not the least of which is the strength of bourgeois ideology. I would nonetheless agree with Tim Patterson that the working class is capable of mounting at least limited resistance, of exerting some degree of cultural autonomy, of striving, as Charles Seeger once proposed, "to be as unlike the bourgeoisie as possible and therefore to eschew, among other things, bourgeois music" (1934:122). Often this resistance has been purely symbolic, communicating alternative experiences and feelings rather than calls for direct action, but, as we see in the case of conjunto music, it is there for anyone who wishes to discover it. In some cases, such as that of white country music, an incipient class awareness is articulated; in the case of blacks and Chicanos ethnic awareness intervened as well (cf. Paredes 1976; Keil 1966).

Lastly, the concept of class. In my study of conjunto music I have assumed as valid the postulated existence of classes in American society. Since the concept is such a critical analytical construct in my interpretation of conjunto music, a few explanatory remarks are in order. I offer these remarks because the expressive power of conjunto derives from a dynamic that can be properly interpreted only within the framework of class (as well as ethnic) domination and conflict. Furthermore, the nature of the class conflict can best be analyzed within the framework of a Marxian theoretical perspective, although I do not wish to discount the non-Marxist, i.e., Warnerian, conception altogether. My reliance on a Marxist analysis stems from my conviction that as a symbolic expression conjunto music (as well as orquesta) embodied, however inchoately, certain cultural strategies that can ultimately be traced to the conflict generated by tejanos' participation in the American capitalist economy. I believe the evidence I have presented supports my assessment that one result of that participation was a deepening estrangement between the working class and an emerging, increasingly Americanized middle class.

Of course, it is unlikely that tejanos conceived of this estrangement as in any way related to the contradictions that American capitalism had introduced into their midst. Nor is it likely that they were conscious (any more than most Americans were) of the complex manner in which American social, cultural, and economic institutions justified their subordination. I am not suggesting that tejanos were not conscious of ethnic discrimination against them; of that they could not help but be highly sensitive, especially after World War II. But what they almost certainly did not comprehend was that ethnic prejudice and economic subordination were structurally linked to a set of economic imperatives, especially the capitalists' need for cheap labor, that facilitated—indeed, demanded—the continuation of such an arrangement, as Montejano

(1979), Mario García (1981), and others have demonstrated. Thus, tejanos lived and worked in a system they conceived in terms of a hierarchy in which people were ranked as socially superior (*jaitón*: high-toned) or inferior (*rascuache*: low-class) according to whether their occupation was "clean" or "dirty."

Tejanos did have a sense of class, then, but, like that of most Americans, it corresponded with the "class" awareness Warner had discovered in American society. It was based on a subjective, or "sociopsychological" (Page 1953), conception of social stratification, that is, of "distinctions made by the people themselves in referring to each other" (Warner and Lunt 1941:xiii). This was an emic, cultural category in American society that acquired increasing significance for Texas-Mexicans as greater numbers of them were assimilated into American life and its status distinctions. The Warnerian notion of "middle class" was particularly attractive to upwardly mobile tejanos (though they surely had never heard of Warner), because in subscribing to it (or Mexican variants, such as *la gente decente*) they felt a sense of affinity with the mainstream American middle class, whose culture they wished to share. This is a distinction that must be kept in mind in studying Texas-Mexican society, because, as I have indicated in connection with orquesta music, class differences, whether conceived culturally, as Warner did, or infrastructurally, as Marxists do, played a crucial role in the ideological development of post-World War II Texas-Mexican society.

My own reliance on a Marxian concept of class is based on evidence that the conflict and contradictions embodied in the conjunto-orquesta relationship—at least in the twenty years or so after the war—were a clear reflection of the conditions at the infrastructural level of tejano society.[4] Moreover, the contradictions that beset the Texas-Mexicans cannot be explained by appealing to functional models that utilize the kinds of status distinctions so central to the American sociology of class best exemplified by Warner. By "infrastructural" I mean the relationship of tejanos to American capitalism's productive forces. As long as they remained isolated and confined to a proletarian work force (whether rural or urban), they retained many of the elements of an ethnic, folk society. However, once a sufficient number of tejanos were absorbed into occupations that we may assign to "contradictory class locations" (Wright 1976)—that is, occupations with a different structural relation to the process of production—then the ethnic solidarity was shattered and class antagonism emerged as a dividing force.

In short, with their integration into the American politico-economic system, tejanos succumbed to the same ideological dynamics that characterize American society—except that the ethnic factor remained as a stumbling block to full (structural) assimilation.

I want now to discuss briefly the Marxist concept of class in order to clarify the model I have used in Chapter 5, on the social base of conjunto music. This concept is based on a structural principle of capitalist society, namely, the objective position people occupy in relation to the means of production. In brief, in capitalist society there are those who own and/or control the productive resources and those who do not, despite the widely accepted argument that in "postindustrial" societies such a distinction is no longer valid, because of the separation between ownership and control (cf. Dahrendorf 1959; Miliband 1969). This means that at a fundamental level capitalist society divides itself into Marx's two "great camps"—the bourgeoisie and the proletariat. For Marx and Marxists this distinction between workers, who neither own nor control anything but their own individual labor power, and the capitalists, who own the resources for commodity production, is a fundamental, incontrovertible reality in capitalist systems.

Now this productive arrangement is both economic and social. It is economic because it involves a specific, historically determined mode of production; it is social because, like all modes of production, it brings people into a set of unique relations among themselves. These relations constitute the relations of production, which give rise to but are in turn mediated by culture and all its institutions. These institutions, as Lukacz writes, "start by controlling economic relations between men and go on to permeate all human relations (and hence also man's relations with himself and nature)" (1968:48). Culture, then, is no mere epiphenomenon of the productive process. Indeed, it is the *total* autonomy that human beings bestow on it, through "idealist," reified conceptions of their world, that makes possible the rise of ideology—of native, "homemade" models for explaining their social existence. Only a rediscovery of the true nature of class relations, based on rational thought and action, can uproot the ideological, homemade notions of socioeconomic relations that now prevail.

In its emphasis on "etic," or nonnative, analytical models, the Marxist conception of class shares certain affinities with French structuralism. In its analysis of social class it views it as a social structure "not immediately visible in the 'concrete reality' " (Levi-Strauss 1963:304). Nor is its existence or significance likely to be grasped, at least initially, by the members of the class because of "false consciousness," or, in structuralist terms, because "conscious models, which are usually known as 'norms,' are by definition very poor ones, since they are not intended to explain the phenomena [e.g., class exploitation] but to perpetuate them" (Levi-Strauss 1963:281). The affinity between Marxian and structuralist theory can be perceived by comparing the quote from Levi-Strauss just cited with this one from Marx: "All science would be superfluous if the outward appearance and the essence of things directly coincided" (Althusser 1972:249).

However, even the "eticist" Levi-Strauss recognized the importance of attending to native categories when he warned against "dispensing" with "homemade" models. Responding to that warning, I have attempted whenever possible to integrate emic categories, such as *jaitón* and *raspa* (scum; dregs[?]) into my analysis. This is why the Warnerian scheme is useful, because it brings to light attitudes that are important in understanding the role of ideology, particularly with respect to prestige-status distinctions, precisely of the sort that *jaitón* and *raspa* (or other social markers) represent.   Now these distinctions may be at variance with economic reality—certainly with that of Texas-Mexicans. But they merely demonstrate how ideology can distort the reality of class domination—for example, by invoking the virtues of the "American national character," virtues solidly rooted in the middle class, which is claimed to be the "real pillar upholding modern societies" (Poulantzas 1973:34).[5] In sum, native cultural categories, while not of themselves basic social structures, can, as Levi-Strauss maintained, "furnish an important contribution to an understanding of the structures" (1963:282).   This is true, for instance, of the ideological (Warnerian) category of "middle class."

The middle class, in fact, has posed the most vexing problem for Marxists. This is because it is undeniable that in modern capitalist societies the existence of an "intermediary strata" makes a dichotomy of capitalist and worker difficult. Marx recognized the existence of a middle class, which he called the "middle bourgeoisie," but he believed that it was doomed to extinction, as society would become more and more polarized between capitalist and proletariat. However, this has not happened, of course, and most Marxists now accept the reality of such a class (if not always so labeled). Moreover, it is generally agreed that it is composed for the most part of "technocrats," managers, semiautonomous employees, and small businessmen (Wright 1976; Poulantzas 1973).

The position of the middle class vis-à-vis the working class and the bourgeoisie is even more controversial. In the popular mind, of course (as well as among many non-Marxist scholars), the middle class is simply a group of people whose income, occupation, education, and other social indicators situate them between the "lower" class and the "upper" class in the hierarchy of status-prestige positions that mark the class continuum that Warner and Lunt claim to have discovered. Among Marxists the most cogent argument comes from Eric Olin Wright, who convincingly demonstrates the *structural* contradictions that certain occupations possess in their relation to the means of production: They share characteristics with both capitalist and proletariat.

Thus, Wright observes that the middle class, such as it is, "occupies its intermediate position not because it is outside the process of increasing capital, but because, as part of this process, it takes its characteristics from *both* sides" (1976:29). I should point out that Wright is extremely reluctant to use the term "middle class." He prefers instead to refer to the ensemble of occupations that others sometimes designate as "middle class" by the phrase "contradictory class locations." Wright's contradictory class locations are *not* congruent with Warner's middle class. The former arrives at his model by analyzing the relationship of these locations to the productive process. The contradictory nature of these locations lies in the fact that they enjoy a "petty share of the prerogatives and rewards of capital, but they also bear the mark of the proletarian condition" (1976:33).

But it is in its ideology that the middle class serves its most critical function in capitalist society. On the one hand, it can be argued that many of the positions in the middle class (or "contradictory class locations," to use Wright's terminology) are structurally located within the proletariat (e.g., low-level managers), but that as a result of ideological status distinctions, often based on mental vs. manual labor, these often break ranks with other proletarian workers. The net result of this is to inhibit the emergence of "class consciousness."[6] On the other hand, it is clear that the middle class serves as a dedicated purveyor of the "American creed" generally and the ideology of "classless inequality" specifically.[7] Lastly, the middle class serves as a formidable buttress between the capitalist and the proletariat. By often allying itself to the former, it further ensures the hegemony of bourgeois ideology.

One final word on classes in general: The question of the existence and function of a middle class, or an ensemble of contradictory class locations—however we may wish to categorize this ideological bloc—has been earnestly debated among both Marxist and non-Marxist scholars (see Ossowski 1963). Its resolution may be neither feasible nor necessary. Once we accept that technocrats, engineers, teachers, and any number of "mental" workers occupy structurally contradictory positions in the overall class configuration, the important task is to address ourselves, as Miliband and Gramsci have done, to the phenomena of politicocultural hegemony. It is through hegemony that a complex array of sociocultural institutions, from consumerism to Lawrence Welk, are marshaled in the legitimation of the dominant bourgeois class's "way of life."

When all is argued and written, bourgeois institutions play a normative role in keeping the workers in their proper place by encouraging individual competitiveness, thereby stifling any collective efforts that might successfully challenge "the American creed." Despite this, the historical study of Texas-Mexican conjunto music, like that of early white country and black musics, should serve to remind us, as Abercrombie, Hill, and Turner have contended (1980), that the "dominant ideology" is not monolithic enough to strip the working class totally of its own cultural resources. As I hope this study shows, the case of conjunto music is one example of how the tejano working class, at least, has utilized this one aspect of folk music to legitimize its culture while at the same time preserving some semblance of integrity in the midst of often harsh and uncompromising conditions.

Notes

1. "Acculturation" is the term anthropologists generally prefer. However, I agree with Gordon, who notes that in using this term "nothing is said about the social relationships of the two groups [in contact], the degree or nature of 'structural' intermingling, if any . . . (1064:62). I have thus opted for the expression "cultural/structural assimilation."

2. The phrase is Inkeles's (1979). In an unabashedly patriotic account, Inkeles lists the ten or so fundamental qualities that are claimed to describe "the American national character" and that, for Inkeles, are at the root of America's greatness.

3. The development of ideology in socialist orders—especially hegemonic ideology—is an open question. As used here, ideology requires a richly elaborated body of ideas, one that, despite serious disjunction with social reality, enjoys wide dissemination, if not total consensus, among both dominant and subordinate classes. For example, the unshakable belief in class-blind opportunity based on individual initiative and the equally unchallengeable reality of class inequality in capitalist societies can only be reconciled by a strong ideology. In Soviet-style orders, on the contrary, the clumsy efforts at legitimizing inequality apparently fool no one. And the inevitable resort to naked oppression in crushing dissent should be a reminder of the Soviet system's failure to create consensus. A thriving, hegemonic ideology of the bourgeois type so brilliantly analyzed by Barthes (1972) can hardly be expected to flourish in such an oppressive environment.

4. In a work in progress I explore the shifting relationship between conjunto and orquesta after the mid-1960s, and the class and cultural realignment of tejano society the new relationship signified.

5. A recent editorial from the *Clovis* (California) *Independent* aptly illustrates Poulantzas's point. Extolling the President's "tax victory" as a "victory for all Americans," the editorial goes on to state that "America is strong because it has a large and strong middle class of working people" (August 5, 1981).

6. Objectively speaking, a group of people might meet the criteria of a Marxist class in terms of its relation to the means of production and the life chances such a relation offers. But something more is required to mobilize it into a "class for itself"—i.e., into a group fully conscious of its position in the productive process and its interests vis-à-vis those of another class. This "something" involves a complex set of attitudinal changes (Lopreato and Hazelrigg 1972:115ff.) that gives rise to an ideology consonant with a class's productive interests. Other kinds of group consciousness are possible, of course—for example, ethnic consciousness, which in the case of Texas-Mexicans had much to do with the maintenance of a separate culture. However, consciousness of one condition does not necessarily lead to or coincide with consciousness of the other. And the ideology of cultural assimilation can nullify the other two.

7. Gunnar Myrdal attempted the monumental task of analyzing what he called this "paradoxical" creed. Myrdal writes:
" . . . there is evidently a strong unity in this nation and a basic homogeneity and stability in its valuations. Americans of all national origins, classes, regions, creeds, and colors, have something in common: a social *ethos*, a political creed. It is difficult to avoid the judgment that this 'American Creed' is the cement in the structure of this great and disparate nation" (1962:3).

Abbreviations used:	acc.	accordion
	b.s.	bajo sexto
	tam.	tambora de rancho
	tol.	tololoche
	l.h.	left hand
	r.h.	right hand
	e.b.	electric bass
	gui.	guitar
	sn.	snare drum
	b.d.	bass drum
	mar.	maracas
	bon.	bongo drums
	voi.	voice(s)
	h.h.	high hat

Appendix B
Musical Transcriptions

No. 1. *Los Siete Pasos* (schottische) recorded ca. 1935 by Bruno Villar-real

No. 2 *La Petacona* (polka) recorded 1937 by José Rodríguez

No. 3. *Las Perlas* (polka) recorded 1937 by Narciso Martínez

No. 4. *Dispensa el Arrempujón* (polka) recorded 1937 by Santiago Jiménes

No. 5. *Quiero Verte* (polka) recorded ca. 1948 by Pedro Ayala

No. 6. *A la Orilla del Mar* (bolero) recorded ca. 1955   by Valerio Longoria

No. 7. *Atotonilco* (polka) recorded ca. 1956 by Tony de la Rosa

No. 8. *Ingrata Mujer* (vals ranchero) recorded ca. 1958 by El Conjunto Bernal

No. 9. *La Capirucha* (polka) recorded ca. 1960 by El Conjunto Bernal

No. 10. *Rara Despedida* (canción corrida) recorded ca. 1964 by El Conjunto Bernal

que tra - te   re - te-ner ___ te   sin   a - lar -

glide

de

+8va -

References

Primary Sources: Personal Interviews

Ayala, Pedro. September 5, 1978; November 11, 1978; December 1, 1978.
Bernal, Paulino. May 8, 1980; May 9, 1980.
De la Rosa, Tony. December 6, 1979; January 30, 1980.
Escobedo, Gibby. February 19, 1980.
Galván, Eddie. February 29, 1980.
González, Carlos. May 8, 1980.
Guerrero, Tony. March 28, 1980.
Jiménez, Santiago. April 5, 1979; May 31, 1979.
Jordán, Esteban. June 22, 1980.
Lawson, Oscar. February 19, 1980.
Longoria, Valerio. April 16, 1981; April 26, 1981.
Marroquín, Armando. January 31, 1980.
Martínez, Freddie. March 13, 1980.
Martínez, Narciso. August 3, 1978; August 7, 1978; November 4, 1978; February 2, 1979.
Pineda, Moy and Delia (Gutiérrez). July 9, 1979.
Pulido, Roberto. April 2, 1980.
Ramírez, Arnaldo. March 27, 1980.
Rosales, Martín. March 8, 1980.
Saragoza, Johnny. March 5, 1980.
Treviño, Reymundo. March 14, 1980.
Vela, Rubén. May 9, 1980.

Primary Source: Letter

Spottswood, Richard. November 10, 1980.

Secondary Sources: Newspapers

Clovis Independent. August 5, 1981.
Excelsior. March 6, 1930.

San Antonio Express. April 19, 1874; June 18, 1881; August 20, 1881; September 15, 1882; September 16, 1886; April 4, 1890; April 7, 1890.

Other Secondary Sources

Abercrombie, Nichols, Stephen Hill, and Bryan S. Turner. *The Dominant Ideology Thesis.* London: George Allen & Unwin, 1980.

Abrahams, Roger D. "Introductory Remarks to a Rhetorical Theory of Folklore." *Journal of American Folklore* 81 (1968): 143-158.

———. "The Complex Relations of Simple Forms." In *Folklore Genres,* Dan Ben Amos, ed. Pp. 193-214. Austin: University of Texas Press, 1976.

Achor, Shirley. *Mexican Americans in a Dallas Barrio.* Tucson: University of Arizona Press, 1978.

Ackerman, James S. "A Theory of Style." *Journal of Aesthetics and Art Criticism* 20 (1962): 227-237.

Adamson, Walter L. *Hegemony and Revolution: A Study of Antonio Gramsci's Political and Cultural Theory.* Berkeley: University of California Press, 1980.

Aguirre Beltrán, Gonzalo. *El Proceso de aculturación y el cambio social en México.* México, D. F.: Editorial Comunidad, 1970.

Althusser, Louis. "Marx's Immense Theoretical Revolution." In *The Structuralists From Marx to Levi-Strauss,* Richard and Fernande DeGeorge, eds. Pp. 239-254. Garden City: Doubleday and Company, 1972.

Baqueiro Foster, Gerónimo. *La música en el periodo independiente.* México, D. F.: Instituto Nacional de Bellas Artes, 1964.

Baron, Robert. "Syncretism and Ideology: Latin New York Salsa Musicians." *Western Folklore* 36 (1977): 209-225.

Barrera, Mario. "Class Segmentation and the Political Economy of the Chicano, 1900-1930." In *New Directions in Chicano Scholarship,* Ricardo Romo and Raymund Paredes, eds. Pp. 167-181. La Jolla: University of California at San Diego, 1978.

———. *Race and Class in the Southwest.* Notre Dame: University of Notre Dame Press, 1979.

Barth, Frederik. "Introduction." In *Ethnic Groups and Boundaries,* Frederik Barth, ed. Pp. 9-38. Boston: Little, Brown, and Company, 1969.

Barthes, Roland. *Mythologies.* New York: Hill and Wang, 1972.

Bateson, Gregory. "Culture Contact and Schismogenesis." In *Steps to an Ecology of Mind.* Pp. 61-72. San Francisco: Chandler Publishing Company, 1972.

Bauman, Richard. "Differential Identity and the Social Base of Folklore." In *Toward New Perspectives in Folklore,* Américo Paredes and Richard Bauman, eds. Pp. 31-41. Austin: University of Texas Press, 1972.

Beals, Ralph L. "Problems of Mexican Indian Folklore." *Journal of American Folklore* 56 (1943): 8-16.

Beals, Ralph L., and Harry Hoijer. *An Introduction to Anthropology.* New York: McMillan Company, 1965.

Becker, Howard S. *Outsiders: Studies in the Sociology of Deviance.* New York: Free Press, 1963.

Béhague, Gerard. "Bossa and Bossas: Recent Changes in Brazilian Urban Popular Music." *Ethnomusicology* 17 (1973): 209-233.

_____. *Music in Latin America: An Introduction.* Englewood Cliffs: Prentice-Hall, 1979.

Benavides, Norma S., et al. *Cancionero-Songbook.* Laredo: Webb County Historical Commission, 1977.

Blacking, John. *Venda Children's Songs: A Study in Ethnomusicological Analysis.* Johannesburg: Witwatersrand University Press, 1967.

_____. *How Musical is Man?* Seattle: University of Washington Press, 1973.

_____. "Ethnomusicology as a Key Subject in the Social Sciences." In *Memorian, Antonio Jorge Dias.* Pp. 71-93. Lisboa: Instituto de Alta Cultura, 1974.

Blauner, Robert. *Racial Oppression in America.* New York: Harper & Row, 1972.

Blom, Jan-Peter, and John H. Gumperz. "Social Meaning in Linguistic Structures: Code-Switching in Norway." In *Directions in Sociolinguistics,* John J. Gumperz and Dell Hymes, eds. Pp. 407-434. New York: Holt, Rinehart and Winston, 1972.

Briggs, Vernon M., Walter Fogel, and Fred H. Schmidt. *The Chicano Worker.* Austin: University of Texas Press, 1977.

Burke, Kenneth. *A Rhetoric of Motives.* Berkeley: University of California Press, 1969.

Cárdenas, Gilbert. "Mexican Labor: A View to Conceptualizing the Effects of Migration, Immigration and the Chicano Population in the United States." In *Cuantos Somos: A Demographic Study of the Mexican-American Population,* Charles H. Teller et al., eds. Pp. 159-181. Austin: Center for Mexican American Studies, 1977.

Casanova, Carlos González. *The Fallacy of Social Science Research: A Critical Examination and New Qualitative Model.* New York: Pergamon Press, 1981.

Dahrendorf, Ralf. *Class and Class Conflict in Industrial Society.* Stanford: Stanford University Press, 1959.

De León, Arnoldo. *Las Fiestas Patrias.* San Antonio: Caravel Press, 1978.

Dinger, Adeline. *Folk Life and Folklore of the Mexican Border.* Edinburg, Texas: Hidalgo County Historical Museum, 1972.

Dolgin, Janet, et al. "As People Express Their Lives, So They Are . . . " In *Symbolic Anthropology,* Janet Dolgin et al., eds. Pp. 3-44. New York: Columbia University Press, 1977.

Echánove Trujillo, Carlos. *Sociología mexicana.* México, D. F.: Editorial Porrua, S. A., 1973.

Eco, Umberto. *A Theory of Semiotics.* Bloomington: University of Indiana Press, 1976.

Eidheim, Harald. "When Ethnic Identity is a Social Stigma." In *Ethnic Groups and Boundaries,* Frederik Barth, ed. Pp. 39-57. Boston: Little, Brown, and Company, 1969.

Fanon, Frantz. *A Dying Colonialism.* New York: Grove Press, 1965.

Fogel, Walter. *Mexican Americans in Southwest Labor Markets.* Los Angeles: University of California, 1967.

Foley, Douglas. *From Peones to Politicos: Ethnic Relations in a South Texas Town, 1900-1977.* Austin: Center for Mexican American Studies, 1977.

Foster, George M. *Culture and Conquest.* Chicago: Quadrangle Books, 1960.

Franco, Jean. *The Modern Culture of Latin America*. Baltimore: Penguin Books, 1970.

Galindo, Miguel. *Nociones de historia de la música mejicana*. Colima, Mex.: El Dragón, 1933.

Gamio, Manuel. *The Life Story of a Mexican Immigrant*. Chicago: University of Chicago Press, 1931.

———. *Mexican Immigration to the United States*. Chicago: University of Chicago Press, 1971.

García, Mario T. *Desert Immigrants: The Mexicans of El Paso, 1880-1920*. New Haven: Yale University Press, 1981.

García, Richard. "Class, Consciousness, and Ideology—The Mexican Community of San Antonio, Texas: 1930." *Aztlan* 9 (1978): 23-69.

Garrido, Juan S. *Historia de la música popular en México*. México: Editorial Contemporáneos, 1974.

Geertz, Clifford. *The Interpretation of Cultures*. New York: Basic Books, 1973.

Geijerstam, Claes af. *Popular Music in Mexico*. Albuquerque: University of New Mexico Press, 1976.

Godelier, Maurice. *Perspectives in Marxist Anthropology*. Cambridge: Cambridge University Press, 1977.

González, Alicia María. "Guess How Doughnuts are Made: Verbal and Nonverbal Aspects of the *Panadero* and His Stereotype." In *"And Other Neighborly Names": Social Process and Cultural Image in Texas Folklore*, Richard Bauman and Roger Abrahams, eds. Pp. 104-122. Austin: University of Texas Press, 1981.

Gordon, Milton. *Assimilation in American Life*. New York: Oxford University Press, 1964.

Gramsci, Antonio. *Selections From the Prison Notebooks*, Quintin Hoare and Geoffrey Newell Smith, eds. and trans. New York: International Publishers, 1971.

Grebler, Leo, et al. *The Mexican-American People: The Nation's Second Largest Minority*. New York: Free Press, 1970.

Gutiérrez, Felix F., and Jorge R. Schement. *Spanish-Language Radio in the Southwestern United States*. Austin: Center for Mexican American Studies, 1979.

Hart, C. W. M., and Arnold R. Pilling. *The Tiwi of North Australia*. New York: Holt, Rinehart and Winston, 1960.

Herskovits, Melville. *Man and His Works*. New York: Alfred Knopf, 1948.

Hollingshead, August B. "Selected Characteristics of Classes in a Middle Western Community." In *Class, Status and Power*, Reinhard Bendix and Seymour M. Lipset, eds. Pp. 213-224. Glencoe, Ill.: Free Press, 1953.

Hood, Mantle. *The Ethnomusicologist*. New York: McGraw-Hill, 1971.

Hymes, Dell. "Editorial Introduction." *Language in Society* 1 (1972): 1-14.

Inkeles, Alex. "Continuity and Change in the American National Character." In *The Third Century: America as a Post-Industrial Society*, Seymour Martin Lipset, ed. Pp. 290-416. Chicago: University of Chicago Press, 1979.

Keil, Charles. *Urban Blues*. Chicago: University of Chicago Press, 1966.

Lafaye, Jacques. *Quetzalcoatl and Guadalupe: The Formation of Mexican National Consciousness, 1531-1813.* Chicago: University of Chicago Press, 1976.

Landolt, Robert G. *The Mexican-American Workers of San Antonio, Texas.* New York: Arno Press, 1976.

Lefebvre, Henri. "Ideology and the Sociology of Knowledge." In *Symbolic Anthropology*, Janet Dolgin et al., eds. Pp. 254-269. New York: Columbia University Press, 1977.

Levi-Strauss, Claude. *Structural Anthropology.* New York: Basic Books, 1963.

———. *The Savage Mind.* Chicago: University of Chicago Press, 1966.

Limón, José. "El Primer Congreso Mexicanista de 1911: A Precursor to Contemporary Chicanismo." *Aztlan* 5 (1974): 85-106.

———. "Texas-Mexican Popular Music and Dancing: A Symbological Interpretation." Unpublished manuscript, 1977.

———. "*Agringado* Joking in Texas-Mexican Society: Folklore and Differential Identity." In *New Directions in Chicano Scholarship*, Ricardo Romo and Raymund Paredes, eds. Pp. 33-50. La Jolla: University of California at San Diego, 1978.

———. "The Folk Performance of 'Chicano' and the Cultural Limits of Political Ideology." In *"And Other Neighborly Names": Social Process and Cultural Image in Texas Folklore*, Richard Bauman and Roger Abrahams, eds. Pp. 197-225. Austin: University of Texas Press, 1981.

Lomax, John. *Folk Song Style and Culture.* Washington: American Association for the Advancement of Science, 1968.

Lopreato, Joseph, and Lawrence E. Hazelrigg. *Class, Conflict, and Mobility.* San Francisco: Chandler Publishing Company, 1972.

Lukacz, Georg. *History and Class Consciousness.* Rodney Livingstone, trans. Cambridge: MIT Press, 1968.

Madsen, William. *The Mexican-Americans of South Texas.* New York: Holt, Rinehart and Winston, 1964.

Manning, Frank E. *Black Clubs in Bermuda: Ethnography of a Play World.* Ithaca: Cornell University Press, 1973.

Marks, Morton. "Uncovering Ritual Structures in Afro-American Music." In *Religious Movements in Contemporary America*, Irving Zaretsky and Mark Leone, eds. Pp. 60-134. Princeton: Princeton University Press, 1974.

Marx, Karl. *Capital.* 3 vols. New York: Vintage Books, 1977.

Mayer-Serra, Otto. *Panorama de la música mexicana.* México: Fondo de Cultura Económica, 1941.

McDowell, John H. "The Corrido of Greater Mexico as Discourse, Music, and Event." In *"And Other Neighborly Names": Social Process and Cultural Image in Texas Folklore*, Richard Bauman and Roger Abrahams, eds. Pp. 44-75. Austin: University of Texas Press, 1981.

McLemore, S. Dale. *Racial and Ethnic Relations in America.* Boston: Allyn and Bacon, 1980.

McWilliams, Carey. *North From Mexico.* New York: Greenwood Press, 1968.

Meier, Matt S., and Feliciano Rivera. *The Chicanos: A History of Mexican Americans.* New York: Hill and Wang, 1972.

Memmi, Albert. *The Colonizer and the Colonized.* Boston: Beacon Press, 1967.

Mendoza, Vicente T. *La música tradicional española en México.* México, D. F.: Nuestra Música, 1953.

———. *Panorama de la música tradicional de México.* México: UNAM, 1956.

Miliband, Ralph. *The State in Capitalist Society.* New York: Basic Books, 1969.

Montejano, David. "Frustrated Apartheid: Race, Repression and Capitalist Agriculture in South Texas." In *The World System of Capitalism: Past and Present,* Walter L. Goldfrank, ed. Pp. 131-168. Beverly Hills: Sage Publications, 1979.

Montoya, Jose. "El Louie." In *Aztlan: An Anthology of Mexican American Literature,* Luis Valdez and Stan Steiner, eds. Pp. 333-337. New York: Vintage Books, 1972.

Moore, Joan. *Mexican Americans.* Englewood Cliffs: Prentice-Hall, 1970.

Murguía, Edward. *Assimilation, Colonialism and the Mexican American People.* Austin: Center for Mexican American Studies, 1975.

Myrdal, Gunnar. *An American Dilemma: The Negro Problem and Modern Democracy.* New York: Harper and Row, 1962.

Nelson-Cisneros, Victor. "La Clase Trabajadora en Tejas." *Aztlan* 6 (1975): 239-266.

Ortner, Sherry B. "On Key Symbols." *American Anthropologist* 75 (1973): 1338-1346.

Ossowski, Stanislaw. *Class Structure in the Social Consciousness.* New York: Free Press of Glencoe, 1963.

Page, Charles H. "Social Class and American Sociology." In *Class, Status and Power,* Reinhard Bendix and Seymour Martin Lipset, eds. Pp.45-48. Glencoe, Ill.: Free Press, 1953.

Paredes, Américo. *With His Pistol in His Hand.* Austin: University of Texas Press, 1958.

———. "Folk Medicine and the Intercultural Jest." In *Spanish Speaking People in the United States,* June Helm, ed. Pp. 104-119. Seattle: University of Washington Press, 1968.

———. *A Texas-Mexican Cancionero.* Urbana: University of Illinois Press, 1976.

———. "The Ancestry of Mexico's Corridos: A Matter of Definition." In *Journal of American Folklore* 76 (1963): 231-235.

Patterson, Tim. "Notes on the Historical Application of Marxist Cultural Theory." *Science and Society* 34 (1975): 257-291.

Paz, Octavio. *The Labyrinth of Solitude,* Lysander Kemp, trans. New York: Grove Press, 1961.

Pelto, Pertti J. *Anthropological Research: The Structure of Inquiry.* New York: Harper and Row, 1970.

Peña, Manuel. "Ritual Structure in a Chicano Dance." *Latin American Music Review* 1 (1980): 47-73.

———. "The Emergence of Conjunto Music, 1935-1955." In *"And Other Neighborly Names": Social Process and Cultural Image In Texas Folklore,* Richard Bauman and Roger Abrahams, eds. Pp.280-299. Austin: University of Texas Press, 1981.

———. Folksong and Social Change." *Aztlan* 13 (1982): 14-42.

Plascencia, Luis F. B. "Lowriding in the Southwest: Cultural Symbols in the Mexican Community." In *History, Culture and Society: Chicano Studies in the 1980s*, Mario T. García et al., eds. Pp. 141-151. Ypsilauti, Mich.: Bilingual Review Press, 1983.

Poulantzas, Nicos. "On Social Classes." *New Left Review* 78 (1973): 27-54.

Ramos, Samuel. *Profile of Man and Culture in Mexico*, Peter G. Earle, trans. Austin: University of Texas Press, 1962.

Redfield, Robert. "The Folk Society." *The American Journal of Sociology* 52 (1947): 293-308.

Reisler, Mark. *By the Sweat of Their Brow: Mexican Immigrant Labor in the United States, 1900-1940*. Westport, Conn.: Greenwood Press, 1976.

Roemer, John. *A General Theory of Exploitation and Class*. Cambridge: Harvard University Press, 1982.

Romo, Ricardo. "The Urbanization of Southwestern Chicanos in the Early 20th Century." In *New Directions in Chicano Scholarship*, Ricardo Romo and Raymund Paredes, eds. Pp. 183-207. La Jolla: University of California at San Diego, 1978.

Romo, Ricardo, and Raymundo Paredes. *New Directions in Chicano Scholarship*. La Jolla: University of California at San Diego, 1978.

Rubel, Arthur J. *Across the Tracks: Mexican Americans in a Texas City*. Austin: University of Texas Press, 1966.

Sapir, Edward. "Culture, Genuine and Spurious." In *Selected Writings of Edward Sapir*, David G. Mandelbaum, ed. Pp. 308-331. Berkeley: University of California Press, 1949.

Saragoza, Alex. "The Formation of a Mexican Elite: The Industrialization of Monterrey, Nuevo Leon, 1880-1920." Ph.D. Dissertation, University of California at San Diego, 1978.

_____. *Fresno's Hispanic Heritage*. Fresno: San Diego Federal Savings and Loan Association, 1980.

_____. "Behind the Scenes: Media Ownership, Politics, and Popular Culture in Mexico." In *Papers of the Conference of United States and Mexican Historians*, 1983a (Unpublished manuscript).

_____. "Mexican Cinema in Cold War America: 1940-1952." In *Proceedings of National Association for Chicano Studies*, 1983b (Forthcoming).

Schapiro, Meyer. "Style." In *Anthropology Today*, A. L. Kroeber, ed. Pp. 287-312. Chicago: University of Chicago Press, 1953.

Schermerhorn, R. A. "Ethnicity in the Perspective of the Sociology of Knowledge." *Ethnicity* 1 (1974): 1-14.

Schneider, David M. "Notes Toward a Theory of Culture." In *Meaning in Anthropology*, Keith H. Basso and Henry Selby, eds. Pp. 197-220. Albuquerque: University of New Mexico Press, 1976.

Seeger, Charles. "On Proletarian Music." *Modern Music* 11 (1934): 121-127. (1934): 121-127.

Singer, Milton. "The Concept of Culture." In *International Encyclopedia of the Social Sciences*, David Sills, ed. Pp. 527-543. New York: Free Press, 1968.

Siverts, Henning. "Ethnic Stability and Boundary Dynamics in Southern Mexico." In *Ethnic Groups and Boundaries*, Frederik Barth, ed. Pp.101-116. Boston: Little, Brown and Company, 1969.

Stevenson, Robert. *Music in Mexico*. New York: Thomas Y. Crowell Company, 1971.

Strachwitz, Chris, with Philip Sonnichsen. *Texas-Mexican Border Music, Vols. 2 and 3: Corridos Parts 1 and 2*. Berkeley: Arhoolie Records, 1975a.

Strachwitz, Chris. Jacket notes in *Texas-Mexican Border Music*, vol. 4. Berkeley: Arhoolie Records, 1975b.

———. Jackets notes in *Texas-Mexican Border Music*, vol. 13. Berkeley: Arhoolie Records, 1978.

Taylor, Paul S. *An American-Mexican Frontier*. Chapel Hill: University of North Carolina Press, 1934.

———. *Mexican Labor in the United States: Migration Statistics*. New York: Johnson Reprint Corporation, 1968.

Titon, Jeff. "Thematic Pattern in Downhome Blues Lyrics." *Journal of American Folklore* 90 (1977): 316-330.

Turner, Victor. *Dramas, Fields, and Metaphors*. Ithaca: Cornell University Press, 1974.

U. S. Bureau of the Census. "Nativity and Parentage of the White Population: Country of Origin of the Foreign Stock." *U. S. Census of the Population: 1940*. Washington, D. C.: U. S. Government Printing Office, 1943.

Valdez, Luis. "Introduction: 'La Plebe.'" In *Aztlan: An Anthology of Mexican American Literature*, Luis Valdez and Stan Steiner, eds. Pp. xiii-xxxiv. New York: Vintage Books, 1972.

Van den Berghe, Pierre L. *The Ethnic Phenomenon*. New York: Elsevier, 1981.

Vega, Carlos. *Panorama de la música popular Argentina*. Buenos Aires: Editorial Losada, 1944.

Vizcaya Canales, Isidro. *Los orígines de la industrialización de Monterrey*. Monterrey: Librería Tecnológico, 1971.

Warner, W. Lloyd, and Paul S. Lunt. *The Social Life of a Modern Community*. New Haven: Yale University Press, 1941.

Wasson, R. Gordon, et al. *Maria Sabina and Her Mazatec Mushroom Velada*. New York: Harcourt Brace Jovanovich, 1974.

Weber, Max. *From Max Weber*, H. H. Gerth and C. Wright Milles, eds. and trans. New York: Oxford University Press, 1958.

Weinberg, Meyer. *A Chance to Learn: A History of Race and Education in the United States*. Cambridge: Cambridge University Press, 1977.

Selected Discography

Balde Gonzáles
   "Si no te amara tanto"/"No te preocupes por mi" (78 rpm). Ideal 695.
   "Qué me puede ya importar"/"Oye corazón (78 rpm). Melco 3950.

Beto Villa y su orquesta
   Beto Villa. Falcón FLP 108.
   Saludamos a Texas. Ideal 104

Beto Villa y su orquesta con Narciso Martinez
   "Salvador Vals"/"San Antonio Rose" (78 rpm). Ideal 357.

El Conjunto Bernal
   Mi Unico Camino. Ideal ILP 103.
   El Baile Grande. Bego 1006.
   Una Noche en la Villita. Bego 1015

Los Relampagos del Norte
   Con la Tinta de mi Sangre. Bego (Royalco-Falcon) BG-1061

Polkas, con sus Mejores Interpretes: Tony de la Rosa, Los Guadalupanos, Gilberto Lopez, El Conjunto Bernal. Ideal ILP 127.

Roberto Pulido y Los Clasicos
   Seguire mi Camino. ARV (Falcon) ARVLP-1051.

Texas-Mexican Border Music, Chris Strachwitz, gen. ed. 16 vols.
   Arhoolie 9003-9007;9011-9013; 9016-9021; 9023-9024.

Tony de la Rosa
   Polkas y Rancheras. Ideal ILP 101.
   Atotonilco. Ideal ILP 116.

Valerio Longoria
   "Seca Tu Llanto"/"El Rosalito" (78 rpm). Ideal 1032.
   "Amor de Verdad"/"Al Arrullo del Mar" (78 rpm). Ideal 1664.

*A companion LP that documents the development of conjunto music has been edited by Manuel Peña. It is available from Arhoolie Records, 10341 San Pablo Avenue, El Cerrito, California 94530

Index

Afro Hispanic Music, 15

Agringado, 9, 147

Aires nacionales, 7

Alabado, 21

Alegres de Terán, 36, 80, 98

Almeida, Santiago, 54

American national character, 167 176, 178

Anglo-*tejano* relations, 4, 61-62, 114-115
  and tejano education, 55, 61-61
  and cultural assimilation, 117-118 137-138

Arcaraz, Luis, 10

Arrancherado, 12

Assimilation
  cultural, 8, 13, 164-166
  structural, 5, 164-165
  as ideology, 11, 135, 165
  See also Anglo-tejano relations;
  Texas-Mexican society

Ayala, Pedro, 30, 36-39, 78, 155, 261

Ayala, Ramón (y los Bravos del Norte), 106, 108

Azcárraga, Emilio, 71

Baile decente, 47-49

Baile de negocio, 48-50, 58, 62

Baile de regalos, 37-38

Bajo sexto, 3, 32, 37, 43, 53-54, 67, 84 96, 99

Ballroom dance, 79, 99

Bel canto, 22, 34, 35, 43

Bernal, Eloy, 90, 92

Bernal, Paulino, 79, 143-144, 153, 161

Bolero, 83-84. See also *Canción romántica*

Bourgeois ideology, 171, 172

Bravos del Norte. See Ramón Ayala

Bricoleurs, tejano musicians as, 33, 37

Brown, Les, 13

Brownsville, 32, 41, 49

Caballero, Lorenzo, 81

Cadetes de Linares, 107

Canción, 22
  corrida, 74, 83, 95, 97, 152
  ranchera, 7, 73-74, 90, 97-98, 100-104, 150
  romántica, 34, 83-84, 99
  valseada, 83
  and *gesunkenes kulturgut*, 84

Carmen y Laura, 72

Carpas de maromas, 81, 87

Carr, Vikki, 97

Casiano, Jesús, 53, 78

Catholic Church, 21, 45

Cavazos, Lolo, 46, 78

Chicano Movement, 159

Chicho y Margarita, 7

Ciego Melquiades, 51

Class
  concept of, 119-121, 163, 173-178
  in Texas-Mexican society, 5, 8, 117-119, 122-131, 131-132, 173-174
  Warnerian, 174, 176

See also Texas-Mexican society
Class consciousness, 177, 179
  in Texas-Mexican society, 8-9, 64,
  147-153
Colonias, 114
Conflict
  interethnic. See Anglo-tejano
  relations
  intraethnic, class, 3, 8, 122-123, 136
  138, 148, 153, 155-156
Conjunto Bernal, 2, 80, 89-94
  and limits of conjunto, 100, 102-105
  decline of, 105, 157
Conjunto music
  and *baile decente*, 47-49
  and *baile de negocio*, 48-50
  and commercialization, 51
  Anglo attitudes toward, 50, 110
  as a counter-ideological expression,
  110, 147-153
  as a folk expression, 46, 64, 101
  as a working-class expression, 1, 4, 8,
  19, 51, 75, 77, 101, 134, 136, 143, 178
  as an ethnic expression, 63, 136
  emergence as a musical style, 2, 3,
  64-65, 67, 74-75, 84, 86-88, 90-92,
  94-97, 140
  tejano middle class attitude toward,
  50, 137, 140-145
Conjunto musicians
  as organic intellectuals. See Organic
  intellectuals
  education of, 55, 61-62
  socioeconomic status of, 46, 55, 60
  64, 82, 86, 93
Conjunto-*norteño* competition,
  105-107
Conjunto-orquesta relationship, 4, 12
  67-68, 109, 144-145, 161
Contradictory class locations, 120-121,
  177
  in Texas-Mexican society, 124
Convite, 87
Corridos, 14, 114, 149
Costeños, los, 7
Costumbrismo, 31
Cuadrille, 21
Cuarteto Carta Blanca, 40

Cugat, Xavier, 15
Culture
  concept of, 163, 169, 175
  and ideology, 167-172, 175
Cumbia, 107
Customs inspections, 44

Dance promoters, 79
Danza habanera, 21
Danzón, 9
De la Rosa, Tony, 79, 85-88, 157
Díaz, Porfirio, 20

Ecological competition/adaptation,
  166-167
El Paso, 32, 33, 45, 115,
Ethnicity, concept of, 163-165
  and assimilation, 164-165
Ethnic boundaries, 13, 114, 118,
Ethnic discrimination, 55, 61-62, 125.
  See also Anglo-tejano relations

Falcon Records, 67, 109
False consciousness, 168, 175
Fats Domino, 12
Fender, Freddie, 97
Fiestas patrias (16 *de septiembre*),
  38, 161
Flores, José (Peregrino), 32
Folk music
  Black, 39, 178
  white country, 146, 178
Folksong style, 6, 24
Folk traditions, Texas-Mexican, 136
Función, 36, 37

Gaytán y Cantú, 6, 35, 57, 73
Gente de roce social (*gente decente*),
  9, 174
Gente raspa, 9, 176
German immigrants, 35
González, Balde, 9, 12, 143
Guanajuato, 39
Guerrero, Tony, 15
Guízar, Tito, 71

Gutiérrez, Eugenio, 67, 161
Grupos tropicales, 107, 160

Haley, Bill, 12
Hermanas Padilla, 6
Hermanos Bañuelos, 40
Hernández, Oscar, 102, 104, 105
Huapango, 7, 43

Ideal Records, 71-78. See also
   Marroquín, Armando
Ideology. See Culture in
   socialists orders, 178
Iglesias, Julio, 108
Immigration
   of Mexicans to the U.S., 26, 79
   of Mexican musicians, 29
Infante, Pedro, 71
Italian opera, 21, 34

Jaitón(a), 117, 139, 156, 174
Jiménez, Flaco, 108
Jiménez, Santiago, 41-42, 46, 59-63,
   78, 152
Jordán, Esteban, 100, 107

La Plebe, 138
Laredo, 24, 33
Lerdo de Tejada, Miguel, 99
Little Joe (and the Latinaires), 15, 102
Longoria, Valerio, 79, 81-85, 157
López, Isidro, 13, 103

"Maistros" de música, 28
Marroquín, Armando, 71-78
Martínez, Narciso, 2, 4, 42, 56, 49,
   51-59, 72, 78, 161
Matamoros, 23, 25, 28, 32
Maximilian, 20
Mendoza, Lydia, 7, 42
Mexicanismo, 11
Migration of tejanos, 79, 98, 159
Miller, Glenn, 12, 13
Minuet, 21
Monterrey

and cultural link with Mexican Texas
   19, 24, 25, 26, 42-43
as industrial capital, 19, 20, 22, 23
as musical center, 25, 29, 50
as *sultana del norte*, 22, 23, 25, 28
Mujeres de la calle, 49
Musical style, 1, 2, 6
   and early *tejano* ensembles, 19, 30, 33
   34, 43
   as *gesunkenes kulturgut*, 29
Música moderna, 108, 158
Música ranchera, 10
Música tejana, 77
Músicos de ayer, 46
Músicos modernos, 78

Naranjo, Rubén, 108
Negrete, Jorge, 71
Norteño, 26
   culture, 26
   music, 2, 69, 98, 99, 105-107
Nueva generación, 70, 85, 97, 157

Organic intellectuals, 146-147, 157,
   172
   conjunto musicians as, 147-157
   curanderos as, 133, 151
   country musicians as, 146-147
Orquesta
   and cultural assimilation, 12, 139
   and *gesunkenes kulturgut*, 31
   as "high class" music, 68, 75, 139
   as middle-class expression, 9, 14, 139
   143, 145
   as *ranchero* music, 75, 103
   as a working-class expression, 32
   tejana, 4, 10, 43, 74-75, 103, 145
   típica, 7, 14, 30-32, 43
Orquesta Fronteriza, 32, 40, 51
Orquesta Típica Mexicana, 31
Ozuna, Sunny, 15
   and the Sunglows, 103

Pachucos, 140-142, 153, 161, 162
Panadero, 49
Peralta, Angela, 33
Polca tamaulipeca, 136

Polka, 21
  and *el tacuachito*, 80, 95
  and the *corrida*, 74
Praxis, 169
Pulido, Roberto (y los Clásicos), 109,
  153-154

Radio, Spanish-language, 41, 51, 69,
  108, 150
Ramírez, Arnaldo, 66, 71, 143. See
  also Falcon Records
ranchero, lo, 10, 11
  and conjunto music, 11, 63
Record companies
  American, 7, 15, 39-42, 70-71, 97
  Texas-Mexican, 71-72, 75-78
  role in commercialization, 39-40, 51
  75-78
  See also Falcon Records; Ideal
  Records
Redowa, 21, 25, 38, 57, 97
Regiomontano, 23, 25, 43. See also
  Monterrey
Relámpagos del Norte, 106
Reyna, Cornelio, 106
Rio Grande Valley, 28, 80, 107, 115
Rocha (Pedro) y Martínez (Lupe), 6,
  35, 40
Rodríguez, José, 46, 52-53
Romance, 21
Romanticism, 21
Romantic nationalism, 10
Root metaphor, 11. See also Sum-
  marizing symbol
Rosales, Martín, 71, 152
Russell, Andy, 97

Salon music, 21, 22, 57
  diffusion of, 30
  See also Minuet; Redowa; Schot-
  tische; Waltz
San Antonio, 23, 40, 62, 115
San Joaquín Valley, 160
Schottische, 21, 25, 38, 57, 97
Summarizing symbol, 11. See also
  Root metaphor

Tacuachito, el, 80, 87, 140, 153
Tambora de rancho, 34, 36-39, 43
  53, 161
Texas-Mexican society
  and class differentiation, 5, 8, 117-119
  122-131, 131-132
  and cultural isolation, 114-115
  and upward mobility, 3, 5, 8, 9, 118,
  127-129
  and urbanization, 3, 5, 8, 116, 117
  as rural, folk society, 114-115
  as colonized, 119, 125
  effects of cultural assimilation on, 3,
  117-118
tololoche, 3, 60, 67, 84, 96, 99
Tremendos Gavilanes, 106
Tres Reyes (de Daniel Garcés), 80,
  88-89
Tropical music, 108

Urbanization, 3. See also Texas-
  Mexican society

Valdez, Luis, 161
Valens, Richie, 97
Vals bajito. See Redowa
Vargas, Pedro, 71
Vela, Rubén, 79, 89
Villa, Beto, 9, 10, 67, 74-75, 161
Villancico, 20, 21
Villarreal, Bruno, 40, 43, 46, 52-53,
  58, 78
Vocal duets, 47. *See also* Carmen y
  Laura; Chicho y Margarita; Gaytan y
  Cantú; Hermanas Padilla; Rocha y
  Martínez

Waltz, 21, 57
Women
  and the *baile de negocio*, 47-49
  in the labor force, 128-130
  singers, 7
World War II as threshold, 5, 116

Zúñiga, Agapito, 80, 88